Hidden Hands

Hidden Hands: International Perspectives on Children's Work and Labour focuses on one specific and neglected area of contemporary child welfare: that of children's paid work and labour in industrialised countries. There is growing acknowledgement that children are routinely involved in various forms of productive activity outside school, ranging from paid employment through to domestic labour and caring responsibilities.

Drawing on original research conducted in the industrialised societies of North America, Western Europe and Russia, this book constitutes a distinctive and original contribution to debates in this important area of childhood. While providing the first cross-cultural examination of children's various productive roles and their relationship to children's broader social lives, this book also considers the implications for their education, welfare and well-being.

This valuable new book will be of interest to students studying in these areas, as well as practitioners in the social, child and youth services and Non-Governmental Organisations who focus on children.

Phillip Mizen is a Lecturer in Sociology in the Department of Sociology at the University of Warwick. **Christopher Pole** is a Senior Lecturer in Sociology at the University of Leicester. **Angela Bolton** is a Principal Research Officer at Barnardo's.

Future of Childhood Series

Series editor: Alan Prout

Hidden Hands

International perspectives on
children's work and labour

**Edited by Phillip Mizen,
Christopher Pole and
Angela Bolton**

First published 2001 by RoutledgeFalmer
11 New Fetter Lane, London EC4P 4EE

Simultaneously published in the USA and Canada
by RoutledgeFalmer
29 West 35th Street, New York, NY 10001

RoutledgeFalmer is an imprint of the Taylor & Francis Group

© 2001 Phillip Mizen, Christopher Pole and Angela Bolton, selection
and editorial matter; individual chapters, the contributors

Typeset in Bembo by
Curran Publishing Services Ltd, Norwich
Printed and bound in Great Britain by
MPG Books Ltd, Bodmin

British Library Cataloguing in Publication Data
A catalogue record for this book is available from the British Library

Library of Congress Cataloging in Publication Data
A catalog record for this book has been requested

ISBN 0–415–24243–6 (hbk)
ISBN 0–415–24244–4 (pbk)

This book is dedicated to Charlotte, Lizzie, Billy and Eliot.

Contents

PART II
**International perspectives on children's work and
labour in the industrialised world**   89

Figures

Tables

Contributors

Jo Aldridge is a Senior Research Associate in the Young Carers Research Group, Department of Social Sciences at Loughborough University, United Kingdom. She has published widely on young carers' issues, focusing particularly on promoting a rights based agenda for young carers and their families.

Saul Becker is the Director of the Young Carers Research Group and a Senior Lecturer in social policy at the Department of Social Sciences, Loughborough University, United Kingdom.

Angela Bolton is a Principal Officer, Research and Development, at Barnardo's, the United Kingdom's largest children's charity. Formerly, she was Research Fellow on the Work, Labour and Economic Life in Late Childhood Project conducted at the University of Warwick. Her main research interests are research with children, children's participation and penal policy for women.

Chris Dearden is a Research Fellow in the Young Carers Research Group, Department of Social Sciences at Loughborough University, United Kingdom. She has been investigating young carers' issues since 1993 and has had numerous articles and research reports published.

David M. Hansen is a doctoral candidate at the University of Illinois, Department of Human and Community Development. His recent article, 'Adolescent Employment and Psychosocial Outcomes: A Comparison of Two Employment Contexts', concerned variations in adolescent experiences depending on the job setting.

Sandy Hobbs is a Reader in Psychology at the University of Paisley, United Kingdom. He has a long-standing interest in the issue of child employment. He has co-authored *Child Employment in Britain* and *Child Labour: A World History Companion*.

Heinz Ingenhorst is Chair in Sociology at the Westphalian Wilhelms-University in Münster, Germany. He has contributed to various research projects, including those undertaken in the Institute for Sociology and Education, the Institute for Sociology and the Institute for Business Studies and the Social Sciences, all at the Westphalian Wilhelms-University. His main research interests are child labour in Germany, immigration and community work.

Helga Krüger is Professor of Sociology, University of Bremen, Germany and co-chair of the Bremen Life Course Research Centre. Her main areas of research and publications are in the area of: the transition from school to work, socialisation in education and the labour market, equal opportunities and gendered life course patterns.

Julia Loumidis is a Researcher in the Centre for Social Policy Research, University of Loughborough, United Kingdom. Her current research interests include an evaluation of the New Deal for disabled people, children's knowledge of financial issues and the lifestyle and living standards of children.

Jim McKechnie is a Senior Lecturer in Psychology at the University of Paisley, United Kingdom. He has published extensively on child employment and was the joint editor of the final report of the International Working Group on Child Labour and co-author of *Child Employment in Britain*.

Valery Mansurov is Deputy Director of the Institute of Sociology of the Russian Academy of Science, Moscow, and President of the Russian Society of Sociologists. As well as researching and publishing on child labour in Russia, he has published in the area of power and the intelligensia.

Sue Middleton is Co-Director of the Centre for Research into Social Policy, University of Loughborough, United Kingdom. Her research interests centre on poverty and social exclusion among children and young people and their transitions to adulthood, areas in which she has published widely.

Phillip Mizen is Lecturer in Sociology at the University of Warwick, United Kingdom. His many publications on children, young people and work include *Young People, Training and the State: In and Against the Training State*.

Jeylan T. Mortimer is Professor of Sociology, Director of the Life Course Center, and Principal Investigator of the Youth Development Study at the University of Minnesota. Her most recent book, *Adolescents, Work, and Family* (co-edited with M. Finch), examines socialisation to work in employment and family settings.

Christopher Pole is a Senior Lecturer at the University of Leicester, United Kingdom where he teaches courses in sociology of education and qualitative research methods. His research interests are in the fields of the sociology of childhood and sociology of education, areas in which he has published widely.

Alan Prout, series editor, is Professor of Sociology at Stirling University, United Kingdom and Director of the Economic and Social Research Council's Children 5–16 Research Programme.

Jens Qvortrup is Professor and Director at the Norwegian Centre for Child Research, Trondheim. He was also Director of the international study 'Childhood as a Social Phenomenon' (1987–92); and founding president (1988–98) of the Research Committee on the Sociology of Childhood (International Sociological Association). His main interests are structural, historical and generational perspectives on childhood.

Anne Solberg is a Senior Researcher at the Norwegian Institute for Urban and Regional Research in Oslo. Her research interests are twofold: the theme of children's work and everyday life; and the analysis of how such knowledge is generated through the research process.

Miri Song is a Lecturer in Sociology at the University of Kent at Canterbury, United Kingdom. She is the author of *Helping Out: Children's Labor in Ethnic Businesses* (Temple University Press 1999) and *Choosing Ethnic Identity* (Polity 2001 forthcoming), and is co-editor (with David Parker) of *Rethinking 'Mixed Race'* (Pluto 2001 forthcoming).

Acknowledgements

We would like to thank the following for their help with this volume. Thanks to the Economic and Social Research Council for providing the funding for the seminar from which the idea for this book arose. Thanks also to the anonymous referees at RoutledgeFalmer, who encouraged us to expand our interest in children's work and labour into a more international one, and to Anna Clarkson and Alan Prout for their support and encouragement in the production of the manuscript. Special thanks to Paul Russell for the speed and skill of his translation and to Yaw Ofosu-Kusi for the preparation of the bibliography.

Preface

No serious discussion of the future of childhood can afford to omit a critical examination of the relationship between children and work. The separation of children from paid work is one of the defining features of modern discourses about what childhood is and should be. That paid work has never actually been absent from children's lives, and is probably a majority experience even for children in advanced industrial economies, has only recently begun to loosen the discursive grip of this idea. However inaccurate it might be as a description of social reality, the notion that childhood should not contain work has exercised, and continues to exercise, a powerful effect on thinking about what children should properly be and do. Indeed, so normatively powerful did this become that it affects not just what children are supposed to do but also the ability of observers to notice what they actually do. As several contributors to this collection imply, it takes a definite act of will to notice children's work. In various ways it is routinely rendered invisible and deleted from the social account.

Nevertheless, clear-eyed accounts show that children's work (in fields, factories, offices, households and so on) is of enormous significance, especially when viewed in its global context. Many of the consumption goods that form part of the taken-for-granted fabric of contemporary society pass through the hands of child workers. Children are networked into the global economy as workers as well as producers. That this is so often, and rightly, occasions moral concern and political protest. These, however, are increasingly moving away from a simple demand for the abolition of child work. Abolition can be seen as problematic for various reasons: it does not adequately differentiate forms of children's labour; it does not take into account the importance of children's work for family survival; experience has shown that expelling children from work can lead to worse, not better, life conditions; and children themselves tend to argue for improving their working conditions and combining work with education.

Although mainly focused on the 'developing countries', the abolition debate highlights the need to rethink the general relationship between childhood and work, including how it is manifest in the industrialised societies discussed in this volume. Such reconsideration is beginning to recognise that the relationship is more complex than sentimentalised accounts of childhood allow. Close description and analysis of children's work therefore tends to disturb comfortable or complacent views about childhood. For example, if children are seen also to be workers, how do models of childhood need to be modified to take account of this? If we are to see children as social actors in the context of their work, what is the relationship between structural determinants and children's agency for different children? How are the consequences of work for children to be understood? How are the benefits and costs, present and future, to be weighed? What counts as work? What are the consequences for concepts of work when we take into account, for instance, how children's activities at school contribute to social reproduction? In revealing children's 'hidden hands' and grappling with their meaning and significance, this collection raises important questions about what childhood is, what it should be, and how the relationship between work and childhood might be re-thought for the future.

Alan Prout
Series Editor for the Future of Childhood

1 'Hidden hands'

International perspectives on children's work and labour

Christopher Pole, Phillip Mizen and Angela Bolton

Several of the chapters in this volume started out as papers presented at a one–day conference on children's work and labour held at the University of Warwick, in the United Kingdom, in May 1999. The idea for the conference itself emerged from a study of children's work and labour, 'Work, Labour and Economic Life in Late Childhood', based at the universities of Warwick and Leicester (Mizen, Pole and Bolton 1999) and funded by the Economic and Social Research Council as part of the wider research initiative 'Children 5–16: Growing into the Twenty-First Century'. The aims of the conference, and indeed of our own individual research project within the programme, were to place under the spotlight children's work and labour in contemporary Britain, while also providing a platform from which to promote the wider discussion of what now amounts to a considerable body of research. These aims remain those which essentially underpin this volume.

However, while both the original research project and conference focused only on Britain, this volume widens the scope considerably by looking at the work and labour of children in a range of different countries spanning North America, western Europe and Russia. In this respect we feel our book makes a distinctive contribution to recent and on–going debate. Not only do the various contributions extend across several different national contexts, they are united by their specific interest in the phenomenon of children's work and labour in the 'developed' or 'industrialised' world. In one sense it may seem surprising that the issue of children's work and labour should still be considered a legitimate source of research and enquiry in what are generally speaking very wealthy countries, where the labour of children is usually regarded as a past evil or somebody else's 'problem'. But the very fact that we have been able to include contributions from researchers that range from the large and prosperous economies of the United States of America and Germany, through to economies like Russia 'in transition' to a free market, is testimony to the fact that in many countries throughout the 'developed' world, the act of labouring among children still constitutes a 'normal' aspect of their everyday lives.

Most of the chapters in this volume begin from the premise that employment for children in the countries this volume covers is a majority experience, or at least one not confined to a small minority. This simple statement itself may well come as a revelation to many readers and if this is the case then we have accomplished one of our objectives in putting this book together. Read on a country by country basis, the chapters included here should allow the reader to obtain a good idea of the extent and nature of work and labour among children in a number of key countries in the industrialised world. But our intention is also to do more than this by highlighting the different approaches that have been utilised when considering the phenomenon of children's work and labour in the 'developed' world. Traditionally, studies of children's labour in countries such as those covered here have emphasised the significance of work as a source of socialisation and preparation for what was regarded as the serious or 'proper' work to be undertaken after the end of formal full-time education. Here too, a number of the chapters approach the issue in their respective countries by treating children's work and labour as significant primarily in terms of its developmental implications. The task for analysis is therefore to come to a measured opinion about the appropriate role for work in promoting healthy psycho-social development. Other chapters included here advocate a different emphasis, however. In these chapters, attention is shifted away from what work signifies for children's future lives to what children say about their work in the present. This in turn is part of a more general shift in emphasis towards a more child-centred approach to the study of children's work and labour. Here the starting point is children's own experiences of work and the fact that the decision to enter work constitutes a rational response to the immediate experiences of childhood, whatever these may be. Consequently, a number of the chapters included here endorse the general view that work must be seen as integral to understanding what childhood *is* and what children *are*, rather than merely as a means of speculating on what childhood experience may lead to and what children may become as a result.

In inviting researchers to contribute to this volume a further intention has been not just to portray the different kinds of work in which children engage, but also to consider the consequences of their participation in paid employment for different aspects of their lives. These include their motivations for working, the significance of money to their lives, the impact of child employment on their families and the relationship between school and work. As editors of the volume, it seemed to us that although – as with adult workers – children engage in work primarily because it provides them with an income, it is their reasons for doing so and the use to which this income is put that can extend our understanding of child employment beyond a simple cash nexus, to include the consequences, responsibilities and possibilities which access to money brings to working children. Accordingly, contributors to the volume have considered child workers not just as peripheral wage labourers incidental to the businesses in which they are involved, but also more centrally as producers. They also consider their roles as consumers and the relationship between this and aspects of youth culture and their capacity for participation therein. In short, the volume attempts to unpack the complexities of child employment not merely from the perspective of the work place and in relation to the wage worker (the child), but also in relation to wider social and economic issues which shape the reasons for work, the experience and some of the consequences of it.

In the main, this volume is concerned with children's paid work. This should not be taken as indicating either a lack of awareness on our part of other forms of children's labour, nor a relegation of the importance of these below that of remunerated work. Indeed, the chapter by Saul Becker and his colleagues is testament to the sometimes considerable involvement of children in the care of a relative. Furthermore, Jens Qvortrup's chapter argues forcefully for the need to treat children's school work as a form of socially necessary labour, since it is through schooling that children add value to future processes of wealth creation. The one notable omission, however, is a dedicated chapter examining children's relationship to and involvement in domestic labour. Aspects of this relationship are addressed in Anne Solberg's chapter on children's work and labour in Norway, where she argues forcefully for the need to view children as a productive element, and not simply a cost, in a clearly established domestic division of labour. Nevertheless, our decision not to include a whole chapter on children's domestic labour is simply a pragmatic one. The research in this area that we are most aware of has already been well discussed elsewhere (Morrow 1996).

Collectively the chapters have established that work is a key aspect in the lives of many children throughout Europe, North America and Russia, and that in many cases it has great economic and social significance to the lives of the children and their families, and indeed to their employers. The authors have shown that work is not an activity which is incidental to the definition and experience of childhood. Moreover, the fact that this point has been made by different authors in the context of different and contrasting national economies and work cultures serves to emphasise the point. Any attempt to understand contemporary childhood and the forms it takes in industrialised countries, therefore, must surely incorporate and recognise the significance of children's work and labour.

This volume consists of eleven chapters authored by some of the leading researchers in the field of children's work and employment in their respective countries and in some cases beyond. Chapters 2 to 6 deal with issues relating to children and work in the United Kingdom while chapters 7 to 11 are provided by authors from Denmark, Germany, Norway, Russia and the USA. While points of comparison and similarity between the different countries are not always made explicit in the text, these become very clear as the chapters are read in relation to one another.

The contents

The chapter by Jim McKechnie and Sandy Hobbs that opens Part I in many respects sets the scene for the volume by outlining the extent and nature of children's work in Britain. In doing this, the chapter provides a useful overview of much of the literature on children and work relating, in particular, to the UK and the USA. The chapter also introduces important questions about the relationship between work and schooling, and discusses the complexity of the relationship between children's participation in paid work and the experience of poverty. These issues are picked up in the following chapter by Sue Middleton and Julia Loumidis, who highlight the recent government initiatives aimed at reducing poverty in the UK, under the aegis of the New Deal. While the emphasis here is firmly on getting adults back to work as a means of alleviating poverty, Middleton and Loumidis point out that the situation is much more ambiguous in relation to children's work. Here, the policy emphasis is upon keeping as many children and young people in full-time education as possible, at least up to the age of 18. The chapter examines these contradictions and the experience of children's work more generally in the context of a nationally representative survey of life styles and living standards of 11–16 year olds in the UK. Data from the survey give rise to a discussion of the economics of part-time work, how experiences differ between young people in varying socio-economic circumstances and the implications for the future lives of the young people.

In Chapter 4 Phillip Mizen, Christopher Pole and Angela Bolton pick up some of the themes introduced in the previous chapter but from a different methodological position. Based on detailed qualitative research of just seventy children, this chapter examines children's work experiences in terms of the types of jobs that they do, their motivations for work, the uses to which they put their wages and the significance of work to their lives and to their families. The chapter engages with issues of poverty, independence for the young worker, social life and spending patterns. While the research takes as its starting point some of the insights from the 'new sociology of childhood', the authors argue that an emphasis on children's agency on its own is not sufficient to explain their participation in the labour market. They stress the need to take account of structural forces which govern children's social lives and, in the context of work, position them as a powerless social group.

In the chapter by Miri Song, the labour of children in Chinese take-away restaurants in the United Kingdom is the focus. Through her qualitative study, Song argues that the dominant western notion of children as dependent upon their parents is to some extent brought into doubt as far as the experience of these children and their families is concerned, since it is the former's labour that is crucial to both the welfare of their parents and the viability of family businesses. Such a distinctive relationship, she argues, is further underlined by the experience of being part of an immigrant community. The resulting isolation and subjection to racist practices further intensify the moral and material pressures on children to direct their ability to labour towards the family interest.

In Chapter 6 the emphasis shifts slightly in terms of the definition of work as Saul Becker, Chris Dearden and Jo Aldridge examine the role of children as carers. Indeed part of the chapter is a discussion of whether caring should be considered as a form of work. Having established fairly unequivocally that it should, the chapter then draws on the authors' research to outline the possible implications of children's caring duties for their own physical and emotional health, their schooling and general well-being. The chapter is important in raising questions about the concept of childhood as a protected phase in the life course.

Chapter 7 by Jens Qvortrup provides a useful link between the chapters that focus on Britain and those on other countries. The chapter raises issues relevant to all modern economies by picking up the theme of education and children's work in the context of the contribution which the family makes to post-industrial society. Qvortrup argues that the concept of children's waged work is in some senses anachronistic, as this no longer fosters the kinds of skills which are central to wealth creation. What is more important in this respect is children's school work. Qvortrup sees this as making a major input to what he calls 'the modern social fabric'. Although this is unpaid labour and, in this sense, there are parallels with the chapter by Becker *et al.*, its importance lies in its capacity to foster exchange values which now dominate modern economies, rather than use values characteristic of manual activities and workmanship. Its importance is further demonstrated, according to Qvortrup, by the expansion of the time children now spend in full-time schooling relative to their time spent in waged work.

The chapter by David Hansen, Jeylan Mortimer and Heidi Krüger offers a comparison of children's work in the USA and Germany. The authors point to many similarities in the experience of work in the two countries as they focus on the consequences of employment, the contexts of work and alternative pathways open to adolescents. The existence of high and low quality jobs is seen as significant in the relationship between school and work. High quality jobs are seen to offer students an opportunity to gain confidence and to develop positive occupational skills while those of low quality may provide less positive opportunities.

Like many of the children discussed in the chapter by Hansen *et al.*, those on whom Anne Solberg reports in Chapter 9 conduct their work alongside adults. However, in this chapter the concern is more with ways of 'seeing' children's work and labour, and the analytical implications that follow from this, than it is with classification and description. By adopting a self-reflexive approach rooted in her own experience of researching children's work in Norway over the past two decades, Solberg outlines the changing ways in which she has come to view the work and labour of children. Her central argument is that traditional modes of seeing children's work, ones rooted in a concern with what work means for their future, constitute a barrier to recognising how children are centrally involved in various types of productive activity that are constitutive of the communities in which they live. From the fishing communities of northern Norway, through to the suburbs of Oslo and the institution of the Norwegian family itself, Solberg insists on the need to look carefully and in detail at what children actually do, rather than what they are destined to become.

The final two chapters offer an insight into children's employment in contrasting economies, those of Germany and Russia. In both countries, despite their different histories and their relative economic strengths and weaknesses, child labour is common. The chapter by Heinz Ingenhorst offers a largely descriptive account of the extent of children's work and labour in modern Germany. Demonstrating parallels with the chapter by Mizen *et al.*, it discusses the reasons why children work and the significance of their wages to the family budget, to patterns of consumption and to their social lives. The chapter also considers some of the negative aspects of earning money. These are seen as a loss of free time and exposure to pressure and dangers while at work.

In Chapter 11 Valery Mansurov sets the growth of child labour in Russia against the backdrop of social and economic change since *perestroika*. He outlines children's growing motivation to work in response to, on the one hand, increasing family poverty and uncertainty as parents may wait months to be paid for their own labour; and, on the other, the perception that market reforms make early labour experience a more relevant grounding for the future than their participation in the troubled system of state education. Amid the simultaneous decline in official programmes of job placement and summer camps, children are increasingly to be found in the informal job market of street trade, car washes and newspaper vending, and in the dangerous and growing criminal gangs who are all too willing to recruit children.

Part I

Children, work and labour in modern Britain

2 Work and education

Are they compatible for children and adolescents?

Jim McKechnie and Sandy Hobbs

In debates about the work undertaken by children and adolescents, employment and education are often referred to as if they are mutually exclusive activities. This is most clearly seen at the international level, where many propose that a compulsory education system is one of the key weapons in a country's battle against 'child labour' (Fyfe 1989; Weiner 1991). The International Labour Organisation has claimed that 'Compulsory education has historically been one of the most effective instruments in eliminating child labour in practice' (ILO 1996). Others, while broadly endorsing such a view, have argued that in any analysis the quality, relevance and cost of education must be taken into account. Bequele and Myers (1995) have suggested that although education may solve some problems of child labour, in certain circumstances it may be a part of the problem itself.

Although this chapter will not pursue the global debates on child labour and education, it is worth stressing the international context in which discussions of child employment in contemporary Britain take place. Countries such as Britain are sometimes treated as if they represent a model for the treatment of children to which economically underdeveloped economies should aspire. This is based partly on the assumption that Britain long ago 'solved' its child labour problem. As Lavalette (1998) notes, it is sometimes claimed that the reduction of child labour in Britain was due to the introduction of compulsory education. An alternative interpretation is that, rather than force children and adolescents out of employment, compulsory education changed the *nature* of that employment. It has moved the main forms of employment from full-time to part-time and changed the status of such employment. This in turn led to a change of focus for debates about children working. The concern for many became one of how to regulate the relationship between part-time work and education so that education was not harmed.

Let us briefly sketch out three alternative positions on this question. First, some propose that employment may in fact be a positive experience for the individual. Such a view implies that we have produced a false dichotomy between employment and education. They are not mutually exclusive, and gaining work experience alongside schooling is a crucial part of preparation for adult roles. Cunningham (1999) demonstrates that this view was particularly prominent in Britain in the middle of the twentieth century. Whether this employment is a part of the formal education system is of minor importance. The important issue is to ensure that experience of work is gained, since it makes a positive contribution to the individual's development. Such views are reflected in the pronouncements of many official bodies in the United States, such as the President's Science Advisory Committee Panel on Youth in 1974 and the National Commission on Youth in 1980. In line with this thinking, in the early 1980s the US Labor Department sought to relax the legislation on child employment to increase the job opportunities for teenagers (Greenberger 1983). That work can serve this 'educational' role can be supported by research showing that working can lead to skill development and to conceptual development (Rogoff and Lave 1984; Saxe 1988; Boyden 1994; McKechnie and Hobbs 1998a).

A second identifiable position might be termed the 'benign view' of employment. It is a view to which policy makers are drawn. Historically we know that employment often took extremely exploitative forms. However, such cases no longer exist because legislation and education have combined to stop this happening. Laws are in place to 'protect' children. This legislation defines the nature of acceptable employment for young people and specifies when, and under what circumstances, it can be undertaken. Implicit in this view is that, at the very least, legally restricted employment will have little chance of harming children. Education can take its proper place as the true 'work' of children. Such a view has a major problem to face in that researchers have clearly shown that the legislation is ineffective (Hobbs and McKechnie 1997). A second problem is that the legislation lacks a sound rationale, being based largely on common sense assumptions.

The third view can be found in what Marsh (1991) refers to as the zero sum model. At the heart of this model lies the view that education is the central task for children. Given the limited time available in terms of the child's activities, commitment to employment will draw the individual away from education and this will in turn have a negative effect on education. In effect, work is viewed as incompatible with education.

The aim of this chapter is to evaluate the research evidence to see if it supports one view or another in Britain. However, while concern over the impact of work on education may be the central issue, the level of that concern will be partly influenced by the number of children who work. Therefore, before we focus on the work–education evidence, it is necessary to establish the extent of employment in Britain.

The extent and nature of child employment in Britain

The 1990s saw a growth in research on child employment in Britain – only a few studies can be found in the 1970s and 1980s – and we shall focus on the research from the 1990s. Readers wishing a fuller review of the material from the 1970s onward are referred to Hobbs and McKechnie (1997, 1998) and Leonard (1999a). Why did the 1990s witness a growth in this area of research? Two factors are important. First, there were the political debates about legislation and policy relating to child employment in Britain. These were driven in part by local authorities, trade unions and non-governmental organisations claiming that legislation has been ineffective in this area. The opportunity to broadcast these views arose from the proposal for a European Union Directive on the Protection of Young People at Work which was eventually passed in 1994 despite some hostility from the then British government (Cornwell *et al.* 1999). Second, the increasingly high profile of children's rights issues, stimulated by the Convention on the Rights of the Child, has led a number of non-governmental organisations to argue that there is a need to 'listen to children's voices'. Child employment has been one arena in which this issue has been pursued by some researchers (Pettitt 1998; Leonard 1999b).

Not surprisingly these different forces have resulted in an array of varying insights into child employment in Britain. For want of better terminology, the policy-driven agenda has resulted in a quantitative data base, while qualitative data has emerged from the 'children's voices' perspective. The quantitative and qualitative data complement each other. We shall draw on both types of material.

The most obvious questions to address are: how many children work, what do they do and for how long? The quantitative data accumulated allows us to answer these question with a fairly high degree of accuracy. However, there is a need to clarify what is meant by 'child' and 'employment'. Child employment research in Britain has been dominated by studies focusing on children under 16 years of age. This in part stems from the fact that legislation on employment applies to children aged 13 to 16 years. Researchers have not paid as much attendance to post-16 year old school students' employment in Britain (see Lucas and Lamont 1998; McKechnie *et al.* 1998). We will follow the conventions in this literature and use the term 'child' while acknowledging that in fact 'young person' or 'adolescent' may be more appropriate.

The term 'employment' presents a different set of problems. Many activities and forms of relationships may be termed 'employment'. The work may be paid or unpaid. The employer may be a family or non-family member. What activities are to count as work? Researchers have varied in the way that they have approached these issues, making comparisons problematic (Hobbs *et al.* 1996; Hobbs and McKechnie 1997). The fact that researchers have adopted a range of approaches when defining employment implicitly testifies to the diversity of economic activities that children participate in.

In our own research, we have included baby-sitting as a form of employment. One reason was that many females reported this activity as their employment (Lindsay 1997). To exclude it would underestimate the extent of female work. Other studies have excluded this form of employment on the grounds that it is not covered by the relevant legislation (Pond and Searle 1991). Both arguments have some validity.

Our inclusion of baby–sitting was in line with our operational definition of work, 'paid employment outside of the family' (Hobbs and McKechnie 1997). We acknowledge that children are involved in a wide range of employment relations, including domestic work within the family, but argue that different research methods are required to investigate such activities.

A detailed comparison of various studies and the various methods employed is outwith the scope of this present chapter. We will instead summarise the main conclusions that can be justified. The first issue relates to the number of children who work. One of the earliest estimates suggested that 1.75–2 million children were employed in Britain (Pond and Searle 1991). This estimate was challenged by the government of the day, suggesting that the results were unrepresentative of the country as a whole. However, reviews of research show considerable consistency of results between different investigations. Hobbs *et al.* (1996) estimated the number of children working in Britain as 1.1–1.7 million, a figure not very different from that proposed by Pond and Searle. The publication of a government-sponsored representative sample study (Hibbett and Beatson 1995) estimated that one million 13–15 year olds work. When compensating calculations are made to include workers under the age of 13 years, a group ignored by Hibbett and Beatson, this estimate rises to 1.4 million. There seems little justification for further debate on the amount of work undertaken by children of school age.

Note that these figures refer to children working at the time of the study or in the recent past. In our own research we have shown that there is a sizeable group of what may be termed 'former workers', who have worked but are not working at the time of the study. Children move in and out of jobs and any true estimate of the numbers working needs to include this group as well. On the basis of this argument we would propose that the number who will have experienced paid employment outside the family by the time they reach 16 years of age lies between 2.2 and 2.6 million. There is a danger of being obsessed with precise calculations. The important conclusion is that it is the norm for children to work; it is part of the normal experience of childhood in contemporary Britain.

What is this work that children undertake? Lavalette (1998) argues that legislation in the early part of the twentieth century created a framework where certain forms of work were viewed as suitable for children. In effect specific tasks were viewed as being within the ability of children, could be combined with education and provided 'pocket money' for those employed. The archetypal 'children's job' is the newspaper round. We have argued elsewhere that the notion of 'children's jobs' is a myth (Lavalette *et al.* 1995). The reality is that children have been and still are employed across a range of settings. Two recent studies demonstrate this point. O'Donnell and White (1998) found children employed in shops, hotels, restaurants, offices, factories and at home. They also report children employed in cleaning, door-to-door sales, on farms and in amusement arcades. A similarly diverse range of jobs has been found by other recent studies (McKechnie *et al.* 1999). In many cases children are employed in sectors that we are more likely to associate with adult employment (McKechnie *et al.* 1997). However, some degree of caution is required. While children may be working in adult jobs, such as shop work, we cannot assume that they are carrying out the same tasks as adults in these settings. More detailed research is required to address such issues.

The nature of such employment may reflect the demands of the local economy. Regional differences in the types and dominant forms of employment have been found (McKechnie *et al.* 1993). Research evidence also indicates that factors such as gender and age play a role in the form of employment experienced (Lindsay 1997; O'Donnell and White 1998; McKechnie *et al.* 1998). Lindsay argues that age and gender interact in influencing when children work and the form of employment they enter.

Research that has been driven by an interest in the policy and legislation of child employment has found that the majority of employment is illegal and that monitoring processes are ineffective (Hobbs and McKechnie 1997). Within this context researchers have considered the amount of time children spend in employment. A number of studies in Britain have collected information on the number of hours worked. Hibbett and Beatson (1995) reported that 51 per cent of 13 to 15 year olds worked up to five hours per week, 33 per cent worked between six and twelve hours and 16 per cent committed over twelve hours per week to their jobs. Our own research has produced similar results with an average of eight hours per week. However, it should be noted that approximately 20 per cent of school students were devoting in excess of ten hours per week to work. Mizen (1992) found the average time committed to work in his study was seven hours, though 29 per cent worked in excess of eight hours per week. O'Donnell and White (1998) report the average working week was 7.75 hours. Lavalette (1994) reported around a quarter of his sample worked more that ten hours per week. The degree of consistency between these studies on the number of hours worked is apparent. It is also clear that in every study a large enough percentage of employees work in excess of ten hours per week to warrant attention. The reader should bear in mind that the typical school week accounts for twenty-eight hours.

As we have already noted family employment and unpaid work are usually excluded from such studies. In these circumstances the research outlined above underestimates children's economic role in the workplace. The fact that this research has been driven by a policy–legislation agenda also imposes some limitations. To some extent it could be argued that the employees' views of work have been ignored. However, there is a small but growing literature that has considered children's perceptions of their work. This qualitative strand of research arises in part from concerns over children's rights, in particular the view that children's views and perceptions should be given a place in the policy arena (Pettitt 1998; Leonard 1999b).

Most quantitative data on the nature of children's work derives from questionnaires and interviews. Information on children's views comes from a wider a range of techniques. These have included interviews, focus groups and essay writing (Murray 1991; McKechnie *et al.* 1995; Morrow 1994; Save the Children 1998; Leonard 1998, 1999b). An interesting new addition to this has been the use of children's photographic records (Pole *et al.* 1999). It is more difficult to draw conclusions across a number of qualitative studies. However, some central points are worth noting. In considering the reasons for working, such studies indicate that children work to combat boredom, gain experience and establish independence. The key reason for working is usually given as money.

The disposal of the income earned has also been explored. Child employees spend their income on a range of goods such as sweets, cigarettes, alcohol, clothes, music and magazines. Earned income is also used to finance the individual's social life, allowing them to go out with friends and participate in social occasions (Murray 1991; Leonard 1998, 1999b). In some case children reported contributing directly to the family budget (Save the Children 1998).

These studies also provide information on this group of employees' views on the workplace. What is apparent is that, like adults, child employees evaluate the workplace, recognising the good and bad aspects of their jobs (McKechnie *et al.* 1996; Leonard 1999b). Children also have strong views on the role of legislation and their right to work (McKechnie *et al.* 1995; Leonard 1999b). It is worth noting that, although children have specific and relevant views on this issue, the 1998 government review on child employment legislation failed to take any soundings from the very group targeted by the legislation. Despite the growth of research in this area, there are still significant gaps in our knowledge, which we have outlined elsewhere (McKechnie and Hobbs 2000).

Work and education

Is it possible to decide whether work has a positive or negative effect on education, or indeed if it has any substantial impact at all? Research on this is limited, but it does provide some clues to an answer to this question. The most obvious issue is the relationship between employment and school performance, which is usually assessed in terms of grades achieved during assessment. However, it is also possible to think of employment affecting education in a number of other ways. For example gaining employment may affect students attitudes toward school, either reinforcing the need for qualifications and school success or providing an alternative source of reward for the student. The impact of employment may also be assessed by considering the length of time that the student commits to education. Is it the case that early employment experiences result in students leaving school sooner than their classmates? Alternatively the employment experience may be related to post-school education paths. One might also hypothesise that early job experience combined with education may be advantageous in helping the student make the school-to-work transition more effectively. Could it be the case that those who work are more likely to gain employment, better pay and employment potential?

One of the most cited studies on the impact of work on educational performance in Britain is that of Emrys Davies (1972a). This work was carried out for the then Department of Health and Social Security. Surprisingly, most writers citing it in support of the claim that part-time work is detrimental to schooling do so on the basis of a short four-page summary (Davies 1972b). This has been the only readily available information on Davies' work. The full report has been unavailable for a number of years. Having recently been able to gain access to the full report we can provide some elaboration of his views.[1]

The stimulus for commissioning Davies to carry out his research was a study in Tyneside which reported high levels of child employment. This employment, much of it illegal, was linked to students' poor commitment to school (Cunningham 1999). It appears that Davies' remit was to consider the extent of employment and its effect on education. The study in England and Wales was based on a representative sample of 13 to 15 year old school students. The final sample was less representative than planned but was deemed by Davies to cover a sufficiently wide range of schools, catchment areas and socio-economic status of pupils' families.

Davies adopted a broad definition of work in an attempt to reflect formal and informal, paid and unpaid employment. Two categories of employment were used: Category A and B. The former included work which was covered by the legislation. Category B work fell outside the legislation framework but included forms of employment that Davies considered important. For example paper delivery falls into Category A, while baby-sitting is Category B. The former involves work for profit within a trade or occupation, the latter is a personal service without financial gain for the employer.

When operationalising the impact on education Davies focused on a number of 'components in education'. These include ability, industry, behaviour, attendance, truancy, punctuality and attitude to the school-leaving age. Information on these various 'components' was obtained from school records. No exam grades or standard test results were used to indicate academic performance. Students' ability was defined by teaching staff.

Through a series of ANOVAs Davies found that the greater the number of hours worked, the more likely students were to be less able, less industrious, less well behaved, play truant more often, be less punctual and wish to leave school at an earlier age. Some variations in these general patterns were found (see Table 2.1).

The pattern of relationships differs somewhat for males and females, Category A and B jobs, and paid and unpaid employment. Thus the education–work relationship seems to be mediated by the form of work and types of employment carried out by students. This in turn could vary for males and females.

For Davies, his research highlights the costs of employment to education.

Table 2.1 Summary of Davies' results: relationship between 'components in education' and hours worked in different job categories for males and females

| Variable | Hours per week Cat. A | | Cat. B | | Paid jobs | | All jobs | |
	M	F	M	F	M	F	M	F
Ability	−	ns	ns	−	−	−	−	ns
Industry	−	ns	−	−	−	−	−	−
Behaviour	−	−	−	−	−	−	−	−
Attendance	ns	−	ns	−	ns	−	−	−
Truancy	ns	ns	+	ns	+	+	+	ns
Punctuality	−	−	ns	−	−	−	−	−
SLA*	−	−	−	−	−	−	−	−

Key: '−' indicates significant negative relationship; '+' indicates significant positive relationship; 'ns' indicates no significant relationship; SLA stands for attitude to school leaving age

However, although costs increase with the hours worked, it is worth noting that the majority of students who were working committed less than twelve hours per week to their jobs.

The fact that Davies did not use any standardised test performance or formal assessment grades may be considered a limitation of his work. A later study using data that is broadly contemporaneous with Davies did make use of examination results. Dustman *et al.* (1996) investigated the work–education relationship by using information derived from the National Child Development Survey (NCDS) cohort data in 1974. The NCDS follows the paths of a cohort of individuals born in 1958. Dustman and his colleagues make use of the third wave of data from this survey when the participants were 16 years old in 1974, two years after Davies' report was published. The NCDS focused upon jobs held by students during term time and was concerned with paid employment.

Dustman and his colleagues initially compared workers and non-workers. This analysis shows that there is a significant relationship between work status and the number of O levels and CSE grades attained. Those students at age 16 years who were not working while attending school had 'on average a 25 per cent better performance in terms of the number of passes' (Dustman *et al.* 1996: 96). In addition, workers were more likely to fail to attain any pass grades than non-workers. These researchers then considered the hours worked (the average fell between six and nine hours per week). They found a significant relationship between hours worked and passes obtained. The negative effect of work on academic performance increases with the number of hours worked. It is worth noting that Dustman *et al.* found no significant effect from working a small number of hours per week. Students in this situation fare as well as non-workers. However, the impact of employment on education became apparent for those working six to nine hours per week and increased from this point.

Dustman *et al.*'s results may be regarded as independent corroboration of

Davies' views about the negative effect of employment on education in the early 1970s, based on data that is contemporary with Davies' own work. Caution requires that we have some doubts about the applicability of these findings to the present day. Education has undergone a number of changes over the last few decades. In a number of studies throughout the 1990s we have endeavoured to develop some understanding of the present relationship between school students' jobs and their education. In the most detailed study we considered the effects of 'paid employment outside the family' under-taken by S4 school students. Academic performance was assessed by Scottish Standard Grade exam performance. Commitment to schooling was assessed by considering self-reported truanting, intention to return to school beyond compulsory age, career intentions and further education, school-based atten-dance records and progression to year S5 (post compulsory education) (Hobbs and McKechnie 1997).

In looking at employment status, we categorised students in terms of those currently working, former workers and those who had never worked. In addi-tion current workers were categorised in terms of low (up to five hours), medium (over five, up to ten hours) and high levels of employment (over ten hours per week). The majority of students worked less than ten hours per week with approximately 20 per cent of workers committing over ten hours a week to work, a large enough percentage to warrant attention. Table 2.2 provides a summary of the main findings.

The pattern of results on all three variables – attendance, return to S5 and academic performance – is the same. Those in the current-employment/high-hours category were significantly more likely to have poorer attendance, were less likely to return to school and had poorer exam performance. The results from this work thus reinforce the general findings from the data sourced in the 1970s.

However, there is a second finding in our work that warrants attention. The results suggest that we should not think of work hours and their impact simply in terms of a linear relationship. Current workers who commit a small number of hours to employment – up to five hours – had better attendance, were more likely to return to S5 and had better exam performance than

Table 2.2 The relationship between academic indicators, work status and hours worked

Employment	Attendance	Return	Performance
Current: low hours	94.5	85.6	40.9
Current: moderate hours	91.8	75.6	35.6
Current: high hours	91.2	66.0	33.4
Former workers	92.1	75.6	35.6
Never worked	93.0	79.8	37.9

Key: Attendance – attendance as percentage of total attendance possible
    Return – percentage of students returning to S5
    Performance – numerical indicator of number of exams sat and grades (see Hobbs and McKechnie 1997)

those students who had never worked. This non-linear model may imply that some work experience is beneficial in terms of its impact on schooling. Results from Dustman *et al.*'s research indicate some support for this in that no difference emerges between performance of students working a small number of hours and those who do not work. Bachman and Schulenberg (1993) warn about assuming that no work is necessarily better than one to five hours work per week.

What is not clear is why benefits may emerge for this group. It could be suggested that students working a low number of hours per week gain potential benefits from employment which influence their performance in the education arena, for example the practical application of knowledge learned in school and vice versa. Alternatively, the experience of employment could act as a salutary reminder of the importance of doing well in school in order to develop a successful career. Further research is needed before any conclusions can be reached.

All of the above research has focused on students up to and including 16 years of age. One study has looked at the relationship between work and education in students who return beyond the compulsory education period. Tymms and Fitz-Gibbon (1992) showed that working had a negative effect on A-level grades, and that working over nine hours per week increased the effect. However, the impact of employment in this study was not great and the authors conclude that working a few hours – under nine per week – is not incompatible with success in education. Thus, Tymms and Fitz-Gibbon's results appear to be in line with the general pattern of results from the research on younger students. However, some caution is required in drawing a simple parallel, since the relationship between work and education may be different for pre- and post-compulsory education students. In the post-16 population we are considering a group of students who, at least notionally, have opted to continue in education. They may have different attitudes to part-time work and education, having crossed that particular Rubicon.

All of the research described, including our own, has focused on the overall length of time devoted to work. Other aspects of the pattern of employment may also be important. For example, there is some evidence that suggests employment in the morning before going to school is associated with truant-ing and work-related absences from school (Davies 1972a; Hobbs and McKechnie 1997). Other factors might also be shown to have an impact. To allow for the emergence of other data, we have proposed a 'balance model' of employment (Hobbs and McKechnie 1997; McKechnie and Hobbs 1998b). This model acknowledges that the impact of employment may be good or bad and that the task is to identify what factors influence this balance. Factors that should be considered include the number of hours worked, when they are worked, the type of job being done and the experience of employment. While there are a number of ways in which such information could be gathered, it is worth noting that the qualitative studies that we mentioned previously have tended to ignore this issue.

The context will play a role in defining the factors within the balance model and the interrelationship between them (Hobbs and McKechnie 1997). For example, the nature and form of a particular education system may allow students to carry out more or less part-time work before negative effects on academic performance emerge. Alternatively, certain types of employment may overlap with certain goals within a given education system, while others may conflict with these goals. However, the central argument is that it is naive to think of part-time work as good or bad. Such a simple dichotomy fails to address the complex interrelationships that probably exist.

A few studies attempt to investigate the views of employees about the work–education relationship. One feature stressed has been the problems involved in combining work and school (Save the Children 1998). Such issues are important but we would argue that some insight into the evaluation of work and school from the employees' perspective would be informative. One study in the United States has suggested that students exert a strong degree of control over their work (Green 1990). In this study it was suggested that students control the time committed to employment if they perceive it conflicting with other aspects of their lives. Others have suggested that opportunities for young employees to control their commitment at the workplace are limited (McKechnie *et al.* 1996). Perhaps the use of qualitative approaches could develop our understanding of this further.

In the United States, research on the work–education relationship is more extensive than that currently existing in Britain. Researchers have looked at a range of work–education relations including post-education employment (see Steinberg and Cauffman 1995 and Frone 1999 for reviews). We shall focus on the relationship between employment and academic performance and attitudes to education, since this most clearly parallels British research.

Frone (1999) argues that there is evidence to link the number of hours worked with US students' attitudes to education. Typically, North American studies contrast those who work in excess of twenty hours per week with those working below that level. Cross-sectional and longitudinal studies link long working hours with negative outcomes such as poorer attendance, lower academic aspirations and lower motivation. There is also some evidence that working less than twenty hours per week is significantly associated with continuing in education for longer periods (Mortimer and Johnston 1998a). This has led some to argue that learning to maintain a balance between limited hours of work and education may not impair education. It may in fact help the student to adjust to the typical pattern of life in post-school education where learning and employment coexist (National Research Council/Institute of Medicine 1998).

US research findings on the relationship between the quantity of hours worked and academic performance are not consistent. Frone (1999) notes twelve cross-sectional studies, five of which found no association between hours worked and grades, while seven did find a significant negative relationship. Longitudinal studies have also produced contradictory findings. Marsh (1991) and Mortimer and Finch (1986) found that the quantity of work is negatively associated with academic grades. Other studies have found no consistent relationship between work intensity and academic performance (Mortimer and Johnston 1998a). These inconsistencies may in part reflect variations in sampling but other explanations are possible as well. First, researchers in the US have adopted a specific definition of high and low intensity of work, contrasting those working more and less than twenty hours per week (National Research Council/Institute of Medicine 1998). It is possible that a finer categorisation of hours would clarify the interpretation of the work–grades relationship. Second, it is possible that some students are aware of the potential impact work may have on their performance and adopt strategies to combat it. Steinberg and Cauffman (1995) have suggested that students choose less demanding courses in order to maintain grade point averages. These researchers also suggest that teachers may reduce the demands on students because they know about their work schedules.

While debates in the US literature on the role of the quantity of employment continue (Mortimer and Johnston 1998b; Steinberg and Avenevoli 1998), there is also an awareness of the need to attend to the experience of employment, sometimes referred to as the quality variable (Mortimer and Finch 1996; Markel and Frone 1998). Barling *et al.* (1995) have argued that the quality of the employment experience must be considered if we are to truly understand the impact of employment.

There are several reasons for caution in assuming that findings from these studies can be applied to Britain. First, the education systems in these two countries are different. Second, since most children in British studies are found to work less than ten hours per week, the use of twenty hours as the watershed in the majority of American research makes extrapolation to Britain dangerous. Third, research in the US has focused on adolescent populations ranging from 14 to 19 years of age, whereas in Britain, as we have seen, the focus has been on 14 to 16 year olds. This raises questions of comparability. We would also argue that age may act as an important variable mediating employment and the experience of employment (McKechnie *et al.* 1998).

Issues

When we first started looking at child employment we were informed by many that all we were doing was looking at an indicator of poverty. The assumption was that children from lower socio-economic groups were more likely to work. Following this line of reasoning, any relationship between work and education will be a by-product of social class influences on education.

In our research in different parts of Britain, we have collected from participating schools information on their levels of free school meals and of clothing grants. Treating these as simple indicators of poverty in the students' families, our data provides no support for the view that schools with higher levels of poverty indicators are more likely to have higher numbers working. In so far as there are differences, schools with higher poverty indicators tend to have lower proportions of working children (Hobbs and McKechnie 1997). However, we have found some evidence that children in poorer areas who work tend to do so for longer hours (Hobbs *et al.* 1993). Davies (1972a) also found that economic status was related to the number of hours worked.

Dustman *et al.* (1996) in their study also considered the link between poverty and employment. Relying on data from the Family Expenditure Survey (FES) covering 1968–91 and the NCDS data referred to earlier, they concluded that the effect of household income on part-time employment was insignificant. Children from poor households are no more likely to work than those from higher income households. They go on to argue that parental unemployment is unlikely to result in children being employed. If anything they suggest children with unemployed parents are at a disadvantage in that they are less likely to have part-time work. One possible reason for this is that unemployed parents may not have the connections to the part-time labour market and fail to introduce their children to work opportunities.

How are we to interpret such findings? We would suggest that a simple 'poverty causes child employment' position is built upon outdated views. It has been argued that in post-war Britain child employment lost the stigma that it had had for a century and a half. Instead, employment for children was seen as having the potential of providing positive experiences. This opened the door for what had been a working-class experience to become an acceptable part of the middle-class child's experience (Lavalette 1998; Cunningham 1999). However, that is not to say that in some cases poverty does not play a role. Children's earned income sometimes makes an important contribution to the household (Save the Children 1998; Leonard 1999b) but this explains only a minority of cases of child employment in Britain.

If it cannot be claimed that child employment and poor educational performance are related simply because they share poverty as a common cause, can we instead treat working hours as the 'cause' and poor performance at school as the 'effect'? The short answer is 'no', but behind this lies a more complex picture. Two possible interpretations of the British data exist.

First, individuals who gain employment and commit more time to it find that school becomes less important to them. Commitment to education then drops, as do attendance and grades. A second, alternative, interpretation is that, if students perceive that they are not doing well in school, they become disenchanted with the demands of education. They then seek employment as a way of gaining some alternative rewards.

Both of these processes could explain the pattern of results that have been found in Britain. There is also some evidence from US research that both processes co-exist and account for the pattern of relationships with education

(Steinberg *et al.* 1993). More recent US research has focused on the selection hypothesis. This proposes that links between education and employment can be explained by students opting to work, and to work for different intensities (Schoenhalls, Tienda and Schneider 1998). In Britain, Tymms and Fitz-Gibbon (1992) have suggested that study of post-16 year old school students offers some support for the self-selection model.

Both interpretations highlight important issues. If work is a causal factor there is a need to understand the circumstances in which it impacts on education. Alternatively, if the selection hypothesis is correct it suggests that students make decisions about the value of school and opt into employment as an alternative. Such a proposal should raise questions about the extent to which education is perceived as relevant by some students, and education systems may need to consider how to accommodate them. For example some pilot projects allow students in the final year of compulsory education to combine work and school (Revell 2000).

Conclusion

We started this chapter by outlining a number of alternative views of the relationship between work and education. We would suggest that the research evidence suggests that work and education are not incompatible. This supports the 'balance model' which views work as potentially good or bad. Its impact on education will depend on the circumstances of the employment and the nature of the education system.

We also need to accept the reality facing the majority of children in Britain. That reality involves combining education with employment. The education system sends out mixed messages about the value of work. On the one hand formal 'work experience' is highlighted as a valuable part of education. On the other children's real employment experiences are to all intents and purposes ignored by educators as being of little if any 'educational value'.

By acknowledging that children in Britain work, the education system may be able to respond in a constructive manner. Young employees need to become aware of their rights as workers. Classes in citizenship should take account of the fact that many of those present are already contributing to the economy. Moreover, at a time when the government is piloting schemes to pay school students to stay on at school (Elliot 2000), the self selection hypothesis needs to be thoroughly explored to provide more insight into children's motivation to seek employment and to move away from education.

Research interest in child employment in Britain has at best been inter-mittent. In the 1990s some momentum has been gained in opening up this issue once again. In doing so, researchers are becoming aware of the extent of the phenomenon. It is also apparent that there are a number of significant gaps in our knowledge (McKechnie and Hobbs 2000). To investigate these issues a number of research projects are required. These will have to include longitudinal studies if we are truly to untangle the causal relationship between work and school performance. Similarly, quantitative and qualitative methods will need to be adopted to address the range of issues in this area. Now that the issue has been 'rediscovered', it should be acknowledged that it offers us an insight into children's experience in modern Britain and the forces that shape that experience.

Note

1 We would like to thank Robin Feline of the Department of Health for his help in locating Emrys Davies' report.

3 Young people, poverty and part-time work

Sue Middleton and Julia Loumidis

Reducing poverty among both children and adults has figured large in the statements of the present Labour government in the United Kingdom. Alastair Darling, Secretary of State for Social Security, announced in early 1999: 'We're moving the fight against poverty back to the centre stage of British Politics, right across government we are tackling *poor job prospects*, poor housing, poor education and poor health' (Darling 1999b, emphasis added). The decision to place the attack on 'poor job prospects' at the start of this list was unlikely to have been accidental. Government has repeatedly emphasised that it believes that the solution to poverty lies in paid work, hence the raft of policies that have been introduced under the global heading of 'New Deal'. Work is now seen as the main policy solution to poverty, not just for long-term unemployed people, but for lone parents and disabled people too.

> We want to assist people who want to work. Employment Zones, the Single Work Focused Gateway, and the New Deal for partners of the unemployed improve the skills and employability of unemployed people. By giving them support tailored to their individual needs the unemployed will find a gateway into independence and dignity, through work, and will not be forced into a life on benefit.
>
> (Darling 1999a)

For parents work is said to be desirable, not only in providing the means by which living standards can be raised, but also in providing children with good role models. 'We all know too well the effect that years of unemployment or illness have on individuals. It demoralises. People come to expect nothing different. And, in turn, their children expect no better for themselves' (Darling 1999b). The government's current economic project assumes, therefore, that paid work for adults is an unquestionably positive experience and will provide a good role model for children.

Government attitudes to children and young people in the labour market are less clear and seem to depend on overt assumptions about the age at which paid work is appropriate. Minimum wage legislation, for example, does not apply to under-18 year olds at all, although whether this is because young people are not thought to merit such protection or whether it is assumed that they should not be in the labour market at all is unclear. From 18 to 21 years a lower minimum wage rate applies. However, the provisions of New Deal, with their emphasis on the duty to participate in the labour market, apply to young people from the age of 18 years.

For young people under the age of 18 years, the main thrust of policy is to encourage as many as possible to remain in full-time education. More young people are already staying on in education than ever before. Participation rates in full-time education among 16 year olds rose from 52 per cent in 1989 to 71 per cent in 1998; for 17 year olds the rates increased from 36 per cent to 58 per cent over the same period; while for 18 year olds they increased from 19 per cent to 37 per cent (DfEE 1999). In order to increase further post-16 participation a new means-tested allowance, the Education Maintenance Allowance (EMA) is currently being piloted. From September 2000 in most urban areas, young people in families with incomes of less than £13,000 per annum will be eligible to receive a weekly allowance during term time of at least £30 per week if they stay on in full-time education. The assumption behind this policy initiative is that money plays a crucial part in young people's decisions to leave education at the minimum school leaving age of 16 years.

It is also anticipated that the EMA will limit young people's participation in paid part-time work. The underlying assumption here is that there is a negative association between part-time work and educational achievement, although there has been little evidence to support or contradict this in Britain to date. McKechnie and Hobbs suggest (Chapter 2 in this volume) that the relationship between education and work is far more complex and less clear cut. Yet the importance of young people's work to the economy cannot be disputed. A recent report used Labour Force Survey Data to show that the student population (those aged 16 to 24 and in full-time education) rose by 72 per cent between 1984 and 1998 (Income Data Services 1999).

Evidence about the role of part-time work in the lives of young people *below* school leaving age is hard to find. Research has tended to focus on the experiences of young people in specific schools or regions, rather than on the national picture (see for example Pond and Searle 1991; McKechnie *et al.* 1993; Lavalette 1994). This chapter attempts to begin to fill this gap by summarising findings about the part-time working experiences of young people aged 11 to 16 years drawn from a nationally representative survey of the lifestyles and living standards of British children undertaken in 1995. The analysis does not comment on the educational or health and safety implications of labour market participation for under-16 year olds. Rather our focus is on the economics of part-time work, how experiences differ between young people in varying socio-economic circumstances and the possible implications of such differences for young people's futures.

In the next section the source of evidence for this analysis is described. This is followed by an examination of young people's experiences of working part-time: who works, what they do, the hours they work, rates of pay and how much they earn. How young people use their earnings in contributing to family living standards is then explored and, finally, the extent to which the experience of part-time work can be said to be setting a good precedent for young people's future lives and living standards. The focus throughout is on differences between the experiences of young people in lone parent and two parent families, and between those in families on Income Support and those in families with at least one adult in paid work.[1] These dichotomies are used as proxies for poverty and affluence which seems a reasonable assumption given that:

*   In lone parent families, 71 per cent of children were estimated to be poor in 1994–5 according to the definition of having after housing cost household incomes below 50 per cent of the average (DfEE 1997).
*   In households receiving Income Support, 78 per cent of individuals were in the bottom 30 per cent of the income distribution after housing costs in 1994–5 (DfEE 1997).

The evidence

Much of the evidence in this chapter is drawn from previously published and some new analysis of the Small Fortunes survey of the lifestyles and living standards of British children (Middleton *et al.* 1997; Middleton and Shropshire 1998; Shropshire and Middleton 1999). This survey, funded by the Joseph Rowntree Foundation, was undertaken in 1995 with a pre-stratified random sample of 1,239 individual children aged from birth to 17 years, and their parents. Among the wealth of information collected, permission was sought from all children over the age of 5 years and from their parents for the child to complete a face-to-face interview. A total of 435 such interviews were completed, a response rate of 80 per cent. Much of the analysis in this paper is of the responses of the 229 young people over the age of 11 years who were questioned about their experience of part-time work and their career aspirations.

In addition, the parent having the main day-to-day responsibility for the care of the selected child (almost invariably the mother) completed a range of documentation. Of most relevance for this analysis is a diary of all expenditure on the child during one week, and a self-completion questionnaire to collect information about spending on other items and activities occurring less frequently than weekly. Data in the survey were subsequently weighted to correct for sampling and non-response errors, and to represent all children in Great Britain. All data presented in this paper have been weighted. A profile of the unweighted sample is shown in Table 3.1. Numbers in some sub-groups are quite small and findings related to these should be treated with caution.

Table 3.1 Young people in the study

Sex:	
Girls	107
Boys	122
Age:	
11–12 years	66
13 years	38
14 years	51
15 years	49
16 years	25
Family type:	
Lone parent	98
Two parent	131
Benefit status:	
On Income Support	52
Not on Income Support	177
All	229

Young people's experiences of the labour market

As Figure 3.1 shows, almost two-fifths of young people over the age of 11 years (39 per cent) had a paid job of some type outside the home. This is similar to the findings of earlier research (Pond and Searle 1991). Participation in part-time work increased with age, peaking among 15 year olds – more than two-thirds of whom worked part-time – and then declining. This also confirms earlier research that suggests that some young

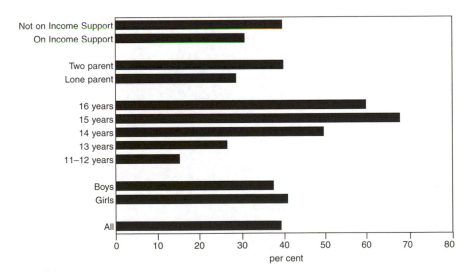

Figure 3.1 Which young people work

people stop working during their final year of compulsory schooling as examinations approach (McKechnie *et al.* 1993). However, far more young people aged 14 and 15 years were working in this sample than has been suggested by other studies. McKechnie *et al.* (1996) suggested that between one-third and one-half of 14 and 15 year olds in twenty schools had part-time jobs. These data suggest national figures of between one-half and two-thirds. It also seems that some young people are starting their working lives at a very early age; more than one-fifth of 11 and 12 year olds already had a part-time job. Young people from lone parent families and those in families on Income Support were *less* likely than other young people to have a part-time job.

In Table 3.2, logistic regression analysis disentangles the role of each of the range of characteristics shown in Figure 3.1 in predicting the probability of a young person having a part-time job. In other words, it shows the likelihood that a young person with a particular characteristic, such as being in a lone parent family, will have a job when all the other characteristics in the model are taken into account. Age is by far the most important factor in predicting part-time work, with a 15 year old almost twenty-eight times more likely to have a part-time job than an 11 year old. Birth order is also important, with first-born children being significantly less likely than only children to work and later-born children significantly more likely. While there is no significant difference in the likelihood of children in Income Support and non-Income Support families having a part-time job, children in two parent families were

Table 3.2 Predicting part-time work (The reference child is male, 11 years old and has no brothers or sisters. He lives in a lone parent family on Income Support)

	Odds of young person working
Gender	
Girls	1.00
Age	
12 years	3.58*
13 years	4.61*
14 years	11.98*
15 years	27.79*
16 years	21.59*
Birth order	
First born	0.75*
Later born	1.28*
Family type	
Two parent family	2.15*
Income Support receipt	
Not on Income Support	0.93

* significant p<0.05

over twice as likely to work as children from one parent families, irrespective of age and birth order.

The reasons why young people in lone parent families are less likely to have paid work are unclear. It may be that lone parents are more likely to live in neighbourhoods where there are fewer opportunities for part-time jobs. For example, the availability of newspaper delivery rounds which, as we will see, are a popular form of employment, depends on large numbers of people having their newspapers delivered and may therefore be less common in deprived areas. A second possible explanation is that young people in lone parent families might have to take more responsibility for younger siblings. Third, since they are less likely to be in the labour market themselves, lone parents will be less able to give their children access to the word-of-mouth contacts who might provide part-time work.

However, when the labour market experiences of those young people from lone parent and Income Support families who *do* work is examined, a worrying picture emerges (Figure 3.2). Part-time jobs were classified into 'formal' employment by a business or company, and 'informal' employment working for neighbours, baby-sitting and so on (Table 3.3). Young people working in formal employment settings might be expected to have at least some protection from exploitation and dangerous environments under health and safety legislation compared with those working informally. While just over half (57 per cent) of young people with part-time jobs had formal work, this declined to only one-third of young workers from one parent families and just over two-fifths (43 per cent) for those in families on Income Support. In contrast, around three-fifths of young people from two parent families or families not on Income Support had formal employment.

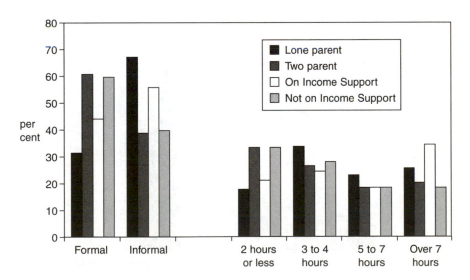

Figure 3.2 Job type and hours worked

Table 3.3 Formal and informal employment

'Formal' jobs	'Informal' jobs
Shop work	Baby-sitting
Restaurant work	Gardening
Glass collecting	Wash neighbour's car
Washing up	Cleaning
Farm hand	Help neighbours
Paper round	Play in band

Young workers in lone parent or Income Support families were also more likely to work more hours in an average week than other children (Figure 3.2). One-third of working young people on Income Support were employed for more than seven hours per week, compared with less than one-fifth of young people from families not claiming Income Support. Overall young people with part-time jobs were paid an average of only £2.22 an hour. Young people from lone parent families fared particularly badly. The average hourly wage rate for a working young person in a lone parent family was 28 per cent less (£1.65 per hour) than for a young person from a two parent family (£2.30 per hour) (Figure 3.3).

This combination of working for longer hours with lower average rates of pay resulted in young people in lone parent and Income Support families having higher average weekly earnings than other young people (Figure 3.3). Average weekly earnings for a young worker in a lone parent family were 37 per cent higher than for those in two parent families; earnings for young people on Income Support were 64 per cent higher than for those not on Income Support.

In summary, therefore, the early labour market experiences of young people

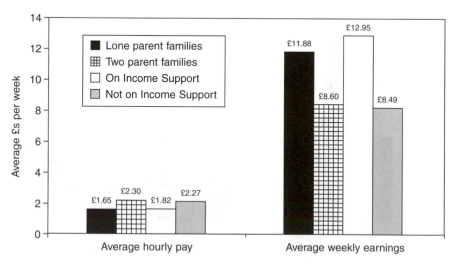

Figure 3.3 Rates of pay and earnings

from lone parent families and families on Income Support were different and not as positive as for other young people. While less likely to have part-time jobs, when they *did* work they were more likely to:

- work in informal rather than formal settings
- work longer hours
- receive lower rates of pay, but
- have higher earnings, although these were solely as a result of the longer hours worked.

They may already be replicating the labour market experiences of their parents. The working lives of lone parents who do work are known to be characterised by part-time, low paid and insecure employment (Bryson *et al.* 1997).

Young people's earnings and spending

Theoretically young people's earnings could be seen as a part of total family income. In this sense, young people's earnings might be used to assist in improving family living standards. In practice, of course, young people will use their earnings in a number of ways. They might decide to spend some or all of their wages on themselves, to save some or all of their income from work, or to contribute some or all to the family income. It is thus worth exploring the contribution that young people's earnings could make to total family income if they chose to use them in this way.

Young people's earnings formed a small but important part of the total income of families, particularly those on Income Support and in lone parent families. The average earnings of young people in lone parent families or on Income Support were three times larger as a share of family income (6 per cent) than those of young people in two parent families or families not on Income Support (2 per cent). This is inevitable given that young people from one parent families or families on Income Support earned more on average than other young people, while the average income of these families was lower. However, further analysis revealed that young people's earnings reduced the income gap between richer and poorer families. Before young people's earnings were included, average income in a lone parent family with a working young person was 47 per cent lower than that of a two parent family with a working young person. Once young people's earnings were taken into account this difference decreased to 45 per cent.

These differences are small in percentage terms but could be of great importance to the living standards of poorer families. Qualitative studies have repeatedly reported that relatively small increases in incomes, of around £15 per week, would make a significant difference to the lives of families on Income Support (Kempson 1996). We have seen that working young people in families on Income Support earned an average of almost £13 per week. This could make a major difference to their families' living standards. The desirability of young people who are still in compulsory education contributing to their families' incomes in this way is, of course, another matter.

Young people's earnings may also improve family living standards if they use a proportion of their earnings to provide for their own needs, freeing resources which parents would otherwise have to spend on them. Although the Small Fortunes survey did not ask young people directly about what they did with their earnings, there is evidence of the amounts that young people spent on themselves. Figure 3.4 compares the spending patterns of working and non-working young people and shows that working young people in all family types spent more on themselves than non-working young people in similar families. However, the differences for lone parent and Income Support young people were particularly large. For example, working young people in families on Income Support spent 87 per cent more on themselves than non-working young people. It seems, therefore, that working young people, particularly from poorer families, were contributing to their own budgets rather than saving their earnings.

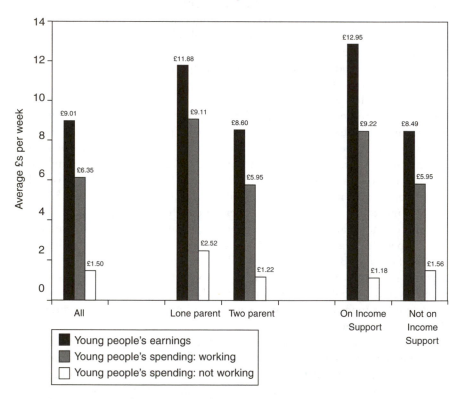

Figure 3.4 Young people's earnings and spending

This would only result in an overall improvement in the families' living standards, however, if young people's contributions were substituting for, rather than adding to, parents' spending. As Figure 3.5 shows, working young people received significantly lower spending from their parents than non-working young people. Overall this difference was 8 per cent, but was very much greater between working and non-working young people in lone parent families. It seems that, particularly for working young people in lone parent families, the money that they earned resulted in only marginal improvements in their personal living standards. Rather, their earnings were used indirectly to improve the living standards of the family as a whole.

The conclusion must be that many working young people are making a significant contribution to their families' living standards. This will need to be taken into account in any government intervention designed to reduce young people's participation in the labour market, particularly those from less affluent families.

Work as a role model

Finally, we turn our attention to evidence about paid work as a 'good role model' for young people. Government pronouncements on this subject have been clear in that they believe there to be a direct and negative association between parents who are not in paid employment and the outcomes for

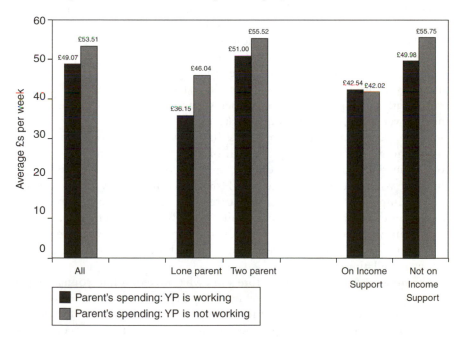

Figure 3.5 Young people's work and parents' spending

young people. As we have already suggested, there are complex relationships between the experience in childhood of poverty and the paid work of one's parents and the effect of these on labour market outcomes in later life. If work is a good role model for young people, then it might be expected that more young people in working families than non-working families would have a part-time job. We have already provided some evidence that in the families most likely to include full-time workers (two parent families or those not on Income Support), young people were more likely to have part-time jobs than other young people. Further analysis showed that 41 per cent of young people with one or more parents in full-time work had a part-time job compared with only 32 per cent of young people with neither parent in full-time work. However, in the light of the evidence presented above about the relatively negative labour market experiences of young people from poorer households, it could be argued that the decision to stay out of the labour market is a sound one.

Another potentially favourable effect of work might be to encourage young people who work to have higher career aspirations. There is some evidence from qualitative research that this is so. In a report of a study of 122 school students from low income families in Belfast, Leonard (1998) suggests that involvement in part-time paid work characterised by boring, monotonous and routine tasks can encourage young people to have higher career aspirations and to stay on at school. Evidence from the young people in our study, however, suggests the opposite (Figure 3.6). Young people were asked what they wanted to do when they left school and their responses were classified into socio-economic groups according to the lowest point of entry into that job or profession (Standard Occupational Classification 1995). Broadly speaking, jobs such as teaching, medicine and the law that have labour market entry points into socio-economic group 4 or 5 are those that require higher education and/or professional qualifications. Jobs such as clerical work, sales and the building trades, with entry points into lower socio-economic groups 6 to 16, require much lower, if any, educational qualifications.

Young people with part-time jobs have lower career aspirations than those who do not work. Only one-half of those with part-time jobs aspired to jobs in the higher socio-economic groups compared with almost two-thirds of young people with no job. However, other family characteristics are also important in young people's career aspirations. Young people from lone parent and Income Support families clearly have lower career aspirations than other young people. Furthermore, young people with no parent in full-time work have lower aspirations than those who have at least one parent in full-time work.

The message for policy is therefore somewhat mixed. While young people in jobless families are less likely to have a part-time job and tend to have lower career aspirations than other young people, paid work for young people below school leaving age does not necessarily improve career aspirations. While numbers are too small for firm conclusions to be reached,

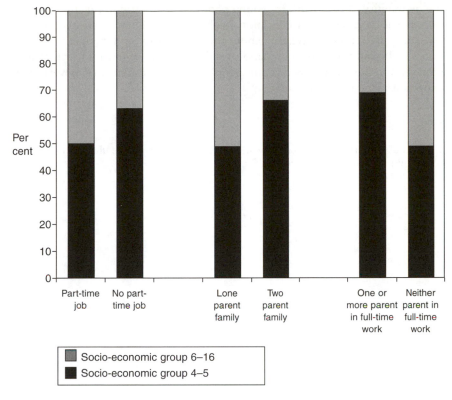

Figure 3.6 Young people's career aspirations

further analysis has suggested that having a part-time job is associated with lower career aspirations, even when family type and the work status of parents are taken into account.

Conclusion

Paid part-time work for young people from deprived families has very little to recommend it when viewed purely from the young person's perspective. Fewer young people in such families have part-time paid jobs and this behaviour seems sensible since, when they do work, they do so for longer hours and for lower rates of pay than their more affluent peers. Poorer young people earn more as a result of their longer hours, but most of these earnings go indirectly towards improving their families' living standards rather than their own. Paid work also seems to have a negative effect on young people's long-term career aspirations. Nevertheless, the significant contribution that working young people's earnings make to their families' incomes cannot be ignored.

There are, of course, many other factors to be taken into account in judging the desirability of paid work for young people who are still in full-time education, not least its effect on educational achievement. There is an urgent need for nationally representative data about the impact of young people's working hours and conditions on examination results. Nevertheless it is clear that paid work is not the panacea for young people in poor families that government expects it to be for their parents.

Note

1 Income Support is the principal form of state support for people unable to work and ineligible for social insurance benefits.

4 Why be a school age worker?

Phillip Mizen, Christopher Pole and
Angela Bolton

If the paid employment of children in Britain today is indisputable, its purpose is far less clear. While survey after survey has consistently produced 'overwhelming evidence that *employment is a majority experience* for children' (Hobbs *et al.* 1996: 16, original emphasis), less certainty exists over why it is exactly that children become school age workers. One reason for this omission has been the necessity of producing credible base-line data on rates and types of employment, particularly given sustained hostility from successive governments to the idea that children's work amounts to anything more than a few hours for easy pocket money. A further reason has been the assumption that children's work is significant primarily in terms of its developmental implications. The considerable interest in the United States in what is termed 'adolescent working', for instance (see Hansen *et al.* in this volume for an excellent review), tends to view school age employment as an index of psychological adjustment and/or a role-rehearsal in children's socialisation into normative patterns of working. Thus questions of work's significance to the immediate are marginalised in favour of an assessment of the costs and benefits of working to children's transitions into the well-adjusted workers of tomorrow.

This chapter is more interested in what children have to say about their work than in what work has to say about these children. It takes as its starting point the importance of paid employment as a 'majority experience' among British secondary-school age children but its purpose is to consider what motivates these children to seek out and take up opportunities for work. To this end, this chapter begins from the experiences of children themselves. As Prout and James (1997) suggest, one alternative to viewing children's actions as developmentally significant is to stress their capacity for meaningful activity that makes sense in its own terms. Thus, by starting from a position in which children's involvement in paid work owes as much to their agency as it does to their psychological or sociological conditioning, the object of attention is shifted away from an interest in what children are destined to become to what they actually are (i.e. paid workers) and why they are that way (i.e. their motivations for working). This is not to lose sight of the material forces this agency expresses. As we have argued elsewhere, in the enthusiasm to acknowledge the capacity for rational action in the present, there is a danger that the emphasis on agency can slip into an uncritical acceptance of children's ability to choose (Mizen *et al.* 1999). It is the argument of this chapter that listening to children's accounts of their lives at work has as much to tell us about the constraints that organise their childhood as it does about their ability to choose.

The research

Placing children at the centre of research involves not just a set of theoretical issues but methodological ones as well. The research this chapter draws upon was designed to explore the interior of children's working worlds and to listen to children talk about and reflect upon their lives at work. It involved working closely with a group of seventy working children, all of whom agreed to participate with the research for a twelve-month period of their lives. Across this period, a number of complementary and linked qualitative methods were used to gather data: semi-structured interviews at the beginning and end of the twelve-month period; small group discussions; bi-monthly thematic 'work diaries'; individual discussions of diary entries; and children's own photographic accounts of their work using one-use disposable cameras, together with an additional written account. This chapter draws mainly on the interviews and diary discussions. A fuller assessment of the project methodology can be found in Pole *et al.* (1999b).

In asking the children to participate, one key objective was to generate a sample of children working in jobs that are broadly *illustrative* of the types of employment that school age workers are known to do (Hibbett and Beatson 1995). For many, their employment at the time the research commenced was not their first job; some were holding two or more jobs simultaneously and through the course of the year we spent talking to them a pattern of job changing emerged. Thus many of the children had the opportunity to reflect upon a number of different experiences of work. A further objective was to ensure the children came from different socio-economic backgrounds and to achieve this the children were drawn from six secondary schools in contrasting areas of England and Wales, with contrasting socio-economic characteristics. These included: a large inner city school in one of the most deprived areas of the Midlands of England; a large school in a respectable working-class area of a large Midlands city; a medium-sized school in a small town on the East Anglian coast; a medium-sized school in a large East Anglian town whose pupils came from both rural and urban areas; a medium-sized school in a Welsh valley community that had experienced extensive de-industrialisation; and a large former grammar school whose pupils mostly came from a middle-class suburb of a large Welsh town. The sample was also comprised of equal numbers of boys and girls, and included children from different minority ethnic groups. It covered the school years 8 to 10 (but mostly years 9 and 10) and, when the research began, included students between 11 and 16 years old.

A deficit of quality

Questions of motivation for working are especially important when we consider what it is precisely that children are employed to do. Interestingly, while survey research has provided a clearer categorisation of the types of children's employment, there is little known about the detail of working, its character, the types of workplaces involved, tasks undertaken, its quality and the nature of the work relations that structure children's time at work. One central objective of the research, therefore, was to obtain a clearer picture of children's experiences 'on the job'. From the beginning it was evident that opportunities for skilled work, or at least a job involving some element of skill, were rare. Only occasionally would a job allow, for example, the chance to acquire some specific skills: basic book-keeping or accounting, knowledge of administrative practices, specific techniques in animal husbandry or other specialist farming practices. Opportunities for creativity were similarly absent and largely limited to those few children who had managed to harness a particular musical or artistic talent to a commercial opportunity: performing a song and dance routine for a parent's cabaret act or painting murals for family or local businesses:

Greg[1]   Yeah I do murals for people. They just, um, I just ask them if they wanted anything done, and I have to go down there and like, um, paint whatever they want on the walls [. . .] The one I've just done was about, err, 10 foot high by about 9 foot across, I got £60 for it [. . .] It was a desert scene for the, err, sun-bed room.

(14, East Anglia coastal)

These types of jobs were the exception, however, and employment was far more likely to mean unskilled work around the edges of the formal labour market. The most vivid examples of this were jobs performing simple and repetitive manual tasks at high volume: packing clothes, chocolates or confectionery in small workshops and factory units; picking fruit and vegetables on farms and market gardens; and working from home packing greetings cards or undertaking light assembly work 'put out' from local suppliers:

Jayda   Well, I do outwork for a factory. I do vent plugs for car batteries [. . .] you've got this little, like, pop thing, you've got this thing that you've got to hold and there's a hole in it; you put the pip in it and push it down and then there's another thing which clips into it and then there's like a little rubber ring which goes round it [. . .] Well, we get five boxes of it every week.

Int.   What . . . does it pay all right?

Jayda   It's not that bad, it's probably about £14 a box.

Int.   And how many are in the box? Is it a lot?

Jayda   2,000.

(14, Midlands inner city)

Most opportunities for work came from the service sector, particularly in catering, retail and distribution and 'personal services'. Youth labour has become an increasingly important element in the expansion of the service sector where, in the United Kingdom, the fast food industry now provides the biggest single source of employment for school leavers (OECD 1996). Few large organisations would appear to employ children below the minimum school leaving age, however, with most of the chains of public houses and hotels, big supermarkets and grocery retailers, franchised restaurants and fast-food outlets preferring to recruit their part-time workers from the growing number of further and higher education students looking for work (Lucas 1997). This is not to say that the employment of children by large service sector organisations is unknown. Among the children who participated in our research, one boy worked for a large chain store of electrical retailers and two girls and a boy (in different locations) for the same national chain of fast food restaurants.

Service sector employment therefore usually meant small employers, partic-ularly the smaller catering establishments that have proliferated alongside the consolidation of the large fast food and chain restaurants. The restaurants, cafés, sandwich shops, fish and chip shops, mobile burger bars and hot dog stands, coffee and tea shops that make up this independent sector compete directly with the large national and multinational catering organisations, frequently selling similar products to the same customers. 'In these smaller catering estab-lishments labour emerges with crystal clarity as the indispensable ingredient for profits and indeed for economic survival' (Gabriel 1988: 150). Many are family businesses, levels of self-employment are high and the use of part-time and casual labour is extensive. For these types of organisations children can offer a ready source of cheap and flexible labour, one that is available at short notice, tolerates irregular hours and has low expectations of work.

Much of this work is dirty, hot and arduous. As kitchen 'hands' in restaurants, hotels and cafés, the children worked fetching equipment and utensils, carry-ing provisions, disposing or recycling waste, working their way through sinks of washing up, loading and unloading heavy dishwasher baskets, preparing piles of vegetables or trying to keep some semblance of cleanliness in the turmoil of meal-time activity:

Int.   Right. So you're washing up plates and pans and things are you?
Peter   Yes. Cook's stuff.
Int.   They don't have a dishwasher?
Peter   Yes they have a dishwasher, well a steriliser and, but I just scrape the plates like when they have a lasagne.
Int.   Yes?
Peter   Like once people have left it for quite a long time it goes all hard on the plates and you have to get if off and put it in the dishwasher to sterilise it.

(14, East Anglia coastal)

Apart from kitchens, the children had also found employment in public houses and social clubs, replenishing stocks of bottled beers, soft drinks and bar snacks, or pushing their way through crowded saloon-bars to empty ashtrays and collect spent glasses. Others had worked in take-away restaurants and pizza parlours, relaying orders to the kitchen, answering the telephone and handling payments; or washing up, cleaning floors and walls, clearing tables, serving food and working cash registers in restaurants and cafés:

Int.   Right, OK, right. So tell me a bit about what you are doing at The Thai Restaurant.

Suzanne   Er not a lot, just mainly taking the cash cards and sorting that out, running up and down stairs to the bar to get the drinks, er I order the food for them what they want, I take the orders but I won't actually give them their food because I don't know what it is, because I don't know Thai food . . . I just come up . . .

Int.   Fair enough.

Suzanne   Um and that's basically it, clearing the tables, general stuff.

                                     (15, East Anglia town)

This pattern of low-quality catering work was repeated in retail and distribution, the other major source of employment for the children. One or two had found work with bigger retailers such as department stores or local supermarket chains:

Ian   I go down, get designated a checkout and sit down and for four hours put things through the till. The only vigorous part of it is learning all the different numbers for the weighing machine.

                                       (15, East Anglia town)

But in the main, retail employment also meant working for smaller employers. Some of the children had been employed in the stock rooms of corner shops and off-licences, on the checkouts of small supermarkets or grocery stores, or serving customers in hardware, electrical, clothes and shoe shops. Others still had found work stacking shelves, pricing goods or cleaning the corner shops, newsagents and convenience stores that populated their communities:

Surinder   Work behind the till, um stack the shelves, price goods and unload the vans, and mop the floor, sweep up as well, that's about it.

                                       (16, Midlands inner city)

Many of the children had at some time or another held a newspaper round before or after school. These could involve delivering as few as twenty or thirty newspapers, six or seven days a week, perhaps taking no longer than thirty to forty-five minutes. Bigger rounds were also common, perhaps taking an hour and a half each day and involving anywhere between 50 and 150 deliveries:

Calvin   Yeah, the evening took longer an hour and a quarter. On Saturday it could take me anything up to two hours because there's two bags the same size as there would be for one day and it takes much longer.

Int.   Right, oh right, did you just carry them or did you use a bike or anything?

Calvin   On week days I used to carry and on the weekends I used to still carry them, but I used to put a bag somewhere else so I could do the first bag and then I could get the other bag, so it's convenient to just walk round and get it and then just come back.

Int.   Yes, right um what you put it in a garden or something?

Calvin   Yeah I would put it on a lamp post.

(13, South Wales suburban)

Beyond newspaper deliveries, the children had also worked undertaking home deliveries for take-away restaurants, delivering leaflets or collecting money door-to-door for family businesses. For some of the boys, opportunities for employment were to be found delivering milk to door steps well before the school day had even started:

Luke   Well I get up at, start at 5 o'clock, finish at 8.00, that's on a school week, and in the holidays I start at 5 and work until 10.00 or 11.00 [am].

(14, Midlands city)

Finally, others had worked in various capacities as cleaners. For two of the boys this involved periodic employment for a large agency supplying contract cleaners to national sporting and cultural events. For the girls, cleaning jobs were more likely to mean employment during the tourist season as 'housekeepers' in holiday parks, cleaning caravans and chalets; or providing cleaning services to offices and shops; or cleaning the homes of neighbours and family friends:

Sarah   I clean for one of my mum's friends, she needs a cleaner so I do that [. . .] Well just like I have to hoover everywhere and that, load the dishwasher, and just clean up.

(14, East Anglia town).

Choosing to work

When considered against the background of such low quality job opportunities, questions of motivation for working become of central importance. Once it is acknowledged that the 'labour market' for school children is comprised principally of employment in poor quality service sector jobs, questions of why these children choose to seek out and enter paid employment are brought to the fore.

'I like socialising with other people'

When considering the children's motivations for working, three themes emerged as especially important. The first of these involved the social dimension to working, and the simple fact that working inevitably brought the children into contact with significant numbers of other people – whether employers, other workers or customers – proved an alluring factor:

Int.   Is that important in a job, that it is sociable?
Hannah   Yeah, yeah. I mean if a job paid really, really well but I didn't like anyone there, I'd probably do it you know as long as it paid really, really well, um, but this job pays well and the people there are really, it's, you know, a nice place to work as well.

(15, South Wales suburban)

Only the children employed to deliver newspapers worked primarily alone, since even with smaller employers work almost always involved contact and interaction with other people. The social element to working was certainly not without its problems – irritable or capricious employers, disgruntled or unsatisfied colleagues, ill-mannered and unpleasant customers – but by and large, these day-to-day annoyances could be tempered by work's value as an opportunity to meet new individuals and groups not usually encountered in the normal routines of school, family and play: shoppers, drinkers, diners, revellers, customers or work colleagues. It was in this way that work allowed the fostering of new friendships or the strengthening of existing ones, while working with others meant the chance to chat, deliberate over shared concerns and the chance to be valued:

Suzanne   You've got all these people around you that you can talk to and that. You're meeting all these people. You're thinking about things and that, just keeps you well motivated [. . .] They're [i.e. the other workers] like a big family because I'm with them most of the time anyway, and there's only us until we get a new girl and they join the family. And there's no people around you apart from the customers, so we get on. We all work together and help each other out as well.

(15, East Anglia town)

This social dimension to work also meant the opportunity for fun. Working with others invariably precipitated opportunities for 'a laugh', the chance to share jokes, swap humorous anecdotes, act out caricatures of employers, colleagues or notorious customers, or engage in gentle teasing:

William   Oh definitely, yes, um recently he has took on some more younger barmaids, I mean they are all barmaids, I am the only bloke there which is pretty funny because I . . . for example now every, at the end of the night I have got to mop the bar and they all mock me for that saying, 'I, you are the only bloke who I know with a mop in his hand or cleaning', etc., like that and, like, they all gang together but its just in a light-hearted way.

(15, Midlands city)

This social element was also an antidote to boredom, since work added another social dimension to those of school, family and home. Being at work with others helped occupy time that would otherwise be surrendered to a diet of the same old television shows and computer games. It could provide a welcome alternative to the otherwise precarious reliance on parental hospitality and the chance to get 'off the streets':

Louise   I do enjoy it though, it helps me to meet people, and I've got nothing to do on a Saturday afternoon anyway, so, it's helping me really as I'm helping her.

(15, South Wales valley)

'I think I have gained my independence'

A further motivation for working was independence. One clear aspect of this was independence *vis-à-vis* school, although the motivation for working was only rarely one of simple disaffection with schooling. Nevertheless, some children felt work did provide a status not normally extended to them through their education. Whereas schooling might mean a curriculum of uncertain or irregular value, the denial of choice and subjection to the arbitrary authority of teachers, work was perceived as offering the chance to be appreciated and meant scope for equal treatment:

Cerys   Like in school they tell you what to do. But when you are working I don't know, it's different to school, you think if I do this right you know, they trust us at work because we know what to do and we do everything right. But like in school it's different isn't it? Perhaps they don't trust you to do something and like because you are working they treat you differently to school because . . . err I don't know.

(13, South Wales valley)

Work was also associated with perceptible changes in family relations. With work came a loosening, or at the very least a softening, of the bonds of parental authority that for some of the older children in particular were threatening to become constricting. Entry into work brought with it a discernible shift in relations with parents and family, one whose practical impact was felt in terms of more freedom of movement, less direct supervision and a discernible increase in the control they exercised over decision making:

Jessica   I think I have gained my independence 'cos like, my parents have let me go a bit more, 'cos whereas before they were really strict, you know, but now they are just, you know, they don't just let me do what I want, but they let me have my freedom, you know, to do, well not what I want, but . . . you know.

(16, Midlands city)

Greater independence also came with earning money. This was not simply a consequence of having more money, although the greater spending power that always came with working certainly underlined the children's growing auton-omy. Money from work also brought with it a further degree of separation from the bonds of parental authority. Earnings from work did not suffer the same obligations as those attached to pocket money, for example, leaving the children greater autonomy to spend money on items their parents would disapprove of: cigarettes, alcohol, make-up and 'going out':

Int.   Did it make you feel more self reliant at all or more confident?
Stacy   Yes, I felt more independent because I have my own money and I didn't have to go to my parents for money, but now I do and it's a big step down.
Int.   Is it?
Stacy   Yes, from me independence.

(13, Midlands city)

Money to 'get things' and 'do things'

The importance of money as a motivation for working cannot be over-stated. Both the children's desires for access to new forms of sociability and the abil-ity of work to further cement their developing independence may have been important motivations behind the decision to seek out and take up paid employment. But it was the prospect of money from work that dominated:

Int.   I guess what we're not sure about so much is why you work?
Dick   To get money.
Int.   That's it?
Dick   That's it, yes.

(15, East Anglia town)

This instrumental attitude was one that many of the children shared:

Amy   I'm in it for the money. I am not . . . I thought I would be in it just to meet new people and it would be exciting a new job, I thought that at first, for the first few weeks, but now it's just all about money.

(15, Midlands inner city)

This in turn begs the question of why money takes on such an importance for these children. White, for example, talks of 'a new kind of child labour' (1996: 830) performed by certain groups of children no longer shackled by the yoke of necessity. For these children, entry into work is no longer an expression of need but more the outcome of their consumer aspirations and the desire to construct particular styles of life dictated by a globalised culture of youth. In their commanding review, Boyden *et al.* too assert that 'research from rich countries of Northern Europe and North America suggests that the income earned by children and adolescents goes primarily for the purchase of fashionable clothing and other luxuries' (1998: 120). In both the US and UK, a growing orthodoxy now proclaims the importance of work as a middle class suburban experience (see James *et al.* 1998).

For the children here the decision to work was certainly their own and in no cases were they involuntary workers. Accordingly, their earnings from work were their own and none experienced anything more than a loose or indirect supervision of its disposal. Although it was common for the children to talk of 'needing' the money from work, none claimed to do so in the strictest sense of the term. Indeed, in many ways it was the *lack* of necessity, the very absence of the constraints imposed by rent, mortgage, utility bills, groceries and the need to support dependants, that made the money these jobs could offer attractive:

Int.   You don't have to work?
Jenny   I don't have to.
Int.   No?
Jenny   No, because I haven't got any bills to pay, I just like money and I can do whatever I want with it. And that's why I work, I think, because I can do whatever I want with it, I don't have no bills, nobody trying to take the money away from me.

(15, East Anglia town)

This sense of relative freedom nevertheless often sat uneasily alongside the appreciation of a deeper set of constraints that structured their decisions to work. Entering employment was not a matter of simple choice but simultaneously constituted an acknowledgement among the children that money was the principal means through which participation in the 'normal' routines of childhood could be effected. Without money the ability to gain some purchase on the places, games, sports, amusements and entertainments that structure the use of 'free' time was severely restricted. Without money from work these children faced the possibility of real exclusion:

Ian   It's not, like, to hoard it and be the wealthiest, or whatever, it's so that I can do things like go to the cinema and go out with my mates. I want to go to places that I wouldn't be able to otherwise, that's the reason for having money. Not just to save it or hoard it or anything.

(15, East Anglia town)

Money was also necessary for travel to and from their leisure pursuits, as well as a requirement for admission to the leisure facilities that dominated their localities: leisure centres, swimming pools, bowling alleys, multi-screen cinemas, public houses, clubs and discos:

Amy   Well, I like going to clubs, night-clubs, pictures, go-karting, ice-skating, everything, really.

(15, Midlands inner city)

Just going to town to meet friends, 'hang about' town and city centres, window shop or shop for real, all required access to cash:

Cerys   Well, before I started the job, all my friends used to do things like baby-sitting and things like that and they all used to go to [the city centre] every Saturday, when they had their pay . . . and get things. And I used to be the only one left out so I thought if I do something I will be able to go with them and things like that.
Int.   What sort of things were you missing out on?
Cerys   They all used to go out for days to [the city centre] and they all used to buy things and then they all used to come home and say, 'look what I've got'.

(13, Wales valley)

The same was apparent if the children were to 'get things'. In order to share in the same forms of concrete social exchange as peers, money to buy things was essential. Through money from work the children could gain access to the same sorts of music as their friends, wear the same clothes, access the same cultural forms, pursue the same interests, follow the same hobbies, participate in the same sports and experience similar levels of gratification. It was not just the symbolic value of these everyday items that the children aspired to but their practical value as the basis of social participation. Thus money mostly went towards the 'things' that have become the staple of children's social worlds: the odd piece of cheap jewellery, make-up, toiletries, magazines, games, CDs, videos, confectionery and fast food:

Int.   So what sorts of things do . . . would you spend your money on?
Sarah   Make-up, nail varnish, clothes, girls' things.
Int.   Do you spend all you the money you earn each week, would you save it or . . .?
Sarah   I spend it all. I've got about £5 in my bank.

(14, East Anglia town)

For most of these children at least, suggestions of a culture of conspicuous consumption are therefore misplaced. What these children would regard as luxuries were clearly beyond the means of most. A computer, bicycle, foreign holiday or 'designer label' clothes were scarce, and more likely the consequence of a prodigious saving regime or of having to rely on parental largesse than the relative affluence brought about by working. One of the children did work to pay for the telephone bills she generated while surfing the internet and a second to fund her riding lessons. But in the main, money from work was usually directed towards accessing the 'ordinary'; a second pair of shoes or trainers, new underwear, a haircut, a non-school pair of trousers or a new skirt for going out with friends:

Jayda   'Cos, I just wanted to buy my own things, I wanted to buy clothes and just stuff like that [. . .] Yeah, things that my parents won't buy me, 'cos they think they are not worth it [. . .] Clothes, hair stuff, just things that I wanted, you know, I like to buy jewellery quite a lot, my mum classes it as junk.

(14, Midlands inner city)

'It takes a bit of stress off your mom'

For a number of these children, the importance attached to money as a source of participation expressed a further set of constraints. Historically the association between children's work and material deprivation has been a strong one, but more recently this has been subject to revision, particularly where children working in the developed capitalist economies are concerned. In Britain poverty has been largely excluded from the contemporary literature as a *general* explanatory factor and it is now generally accepted that 'many children work without obvious economic need' (Hobbs and McKechnie 1997: 92). Boyden *et al.* also comment on how 'poverty is associated with high incidence of child work in developing regions; in rich countries the relationship is reversed' (1998: 129). Morrow (1994) too argues that the traditional relationship between deprivation and children's work needs to be inverted when applied to modern Britain.

> These 'enterprising' children contradict the stereotypical view of children who work as 'exploited victims' and 'child slaves', and they may be advantaged over their less well off peers, not only by their relative affluence, but also by their informal experience of work when it comes to competing for jobs later on.
>
> (Morrow 1994: 141)

The relationship between children's work and their material circumstances is indeed a complex one. In Britain, where the issue has been addressed, the assumption has been that child poverty is an absolute condition, one marked by the absence of those fundamentals necessary to family life. Added to this, there is little systematic data upon which to explore the impact of material deprivation on children's employment, the one exception being the chapter in this volume by Middleton and Loumidis. What is surprising, though, is that the absence of any sustained consideration of the relationship between children's employment and poverty has unfolded alongside some of the most profound changes to the distribution of income and wealth this century. For children the consequences of these have been truly catastrophic. From estimates of one in ten children in poverty some twenty-five years ago, the figure is now around one in three (UNICEF 2000; Treasury 1999; Hills 1995).

Not only do these figures provide further context for the determination of the children who took part in our research to access a real degree of social inclusion. They also underline the continuing importance of constraint, hardship and necessity as factors motivating children to work. Most of the children possessed some general sense of their family's financial circumstances, although only a few had any knowledge of the detail of family budgets. In the context of financial difficulties, the children were often clearly reluctant to place further burdens on parents already struggling to get by. Requesting money in these circumstances could produce feelings of guilt or disloyalty, while also risking the probability of refusal. In these cases, work provided an alternative source of income, with requests for money to parents a last resort:

Sally   Yes and I hate asking my mum for money. A lot of people could go up to their parents and say, 'give us this, give us that', I don't like doing that. I only ask my mum for stuff if I really need it.

(15, East Anglia town)

Thus entry into work could be motivated by the desire to shift at least some of the responsibility for meeting children's costs away from hard-pressed parents:

Mark   It's the first source of money, instead of scraping and saving. It's like my cousin, my cousin's been doing a paper round for years on end and he said, 'you should just do it because it just brings a little bit of money for your pocket or it takes a bit of stress off your mom', so anything you can find you gotta' do.

(15, Midlands inner city)

Of course, this meant using money from work to take up some of the pressure resulting from their changing leisure and recreational activities in the ways outlined above. Work could also allow the children to assume a progressively greater responsibility for funding at least some of their everyday needs:

Ronan   It was my mum that keeps urging me to get some, like some money, because she is always paying for my subs and everything because I play hockey and football and tennis [. . .] I play everything and she goes, 'oh you need to get a job to help me a bit sometimes', when she is a bit stuck for money.

(15, Midlands city)

Money from work could be put towards all or part of the costs of every day items such as a winter coat, an item of school uniform, money for school meals or their alternatives like 'junk food' or a visit to the local 'chippy', bus fares to and from school, or the purchase of new shoes:

Lorraine   I actually, it sounds really weird, but I actually bought myself a new school sweatshirt, I needed one so, I thought because I kind of wrecked my last one.

Int.   Yeah.

Lorraine   And mum said she wasn't going to buy me a new one so I thought right, I'll buy myself one then. Aha, be flash I'll buy myself a new one.

Int.   Nice, yeah.

Lorraine   And um, then I bought myself some new school shoes which have kind of got a bit tatty now.

(14, East Anglia town)

More immediately, some of the children would make direct contributions to the family economy. These contributions were never regular nor expected by parents, sometimes they were even unknown, yet some of the children nevertheless had taken it upon themselves to use their wages to buy such things as groceries. These purchases were generally unsolicited and would involve the purchase of smaller items for the evening meal, perhaps dropping into a local shop on the way home from school or work, or ensuring there was milk, tea or bread for breakfast the following morning:

Louise   Look, because when she was, my father was at work look, but he couldn't cope there and he had a nervous breakdown, and his friend got him a job and he got back to normal work, but he's on monthly pay, look, so he gets about £700 but they got to pay the rent and everything, so it's no good asking for £10 for a deodorant and all that, so I got my own [. . .] and my mother, every week we'd always have £3 each and there's four of us lot, she couldn't afford it, so I said, 'Oh, I'll get my own stuff now'; like I say I prefer that because it's made me respect more and be independent. But I will buy things for the others as well; I won't be selfish and keep it to myself, it's like if my mum needs bread or if any of my sisters need anything. I will share though.

(15, Wales valley)

In more exceptional circumstances, like the separation or divorce of family members, the children would assume a greater degree of responsibility:

Teddy   Yes but my mum and dad are divorced you see so we go there every other week and she don't get no money off him you see, so all the money that she gets from when she does odd work, because she's on social security and that, she has got to buy like my brother and sister's stuff.

Int. So your work helps out with the family?

Teddy Yes, I sometimes give mum some money but I don't usually, but I just buy my own stuff and that; it helps out.

Int. What about food, do you buy your own food?

Teddy Sometimes I do . . . get what I like [laughter].

(14, East Anglia coastal)

Purchasing groceries could also be a way of circumventing opposition from parents clearly uncomfortable at the prospect of receiving financial help from their school age children. Even in the context of considerable hardship, parents could refuse outright the offer of cash or find alternative means of ensuring its return. In these circumstances, cash transfers to parents could be justified in different ways: a few pounds for parents to go out for a drink, socialise with friends or to indulge themselves in some minor way:

Gillian I'd like say if my dad was going to the pub I would say, 'here you are have a drink on me' or something like that, or buy him a pack of fags like every weekend or something like that. So I was like getting him something, but I wasn't like giving them the money you know what I mean. They'd rather me get them something than give them money [. . .] They don't really like taking money off me. So I like say, what I'll do is, say if I know they're short of bread or milk today and they haven't been out, I'll go and buy some bread and milk and put it in the fridge. . . . I'll buy my mum some fags or I'll buy my dad something, you know what I mean. . . . I don't give them money because they tend, they won't, I'll give it and then she's [mum] put it in my bank account or something.

(13, East Anglia coastal)

Even so, cash transfers were successfully accomplished in particularly pressing circumstances. Money from work could go to parents as 'loans' without the expectation of repayment or as a contribution towards an unexpectedly large utility bill, a minor emergency or as temporary relief until the next wage packet or benefit payment:

Int. How do you help your mum out?

Kaitlin If she's stuck for money sometimes I do lend her some or just give it to her because I don't mind, like 'cos she's brought me up all these years and clothed me and fed me and that, so I, if she's stuck for some money I do give it to her because I don't mind helping her, you know [. . .] I buy most of my CDs and I buy some clothes for myself and school pens and stuff, I do buy all that myself, so my mother won't have to concentrate on me she can, won't have to worry for me, she can buy for the other two [children], 'cos I've always got my own.

(15, South Wales valley)

And again, cash transfers to parents could provide a degree of relief in a family crisis precipitated by unemployment, separation or divorce:

Surjit   Yeah, I thought about giving the money to my mum because my mum dropped out of work as well because she didn't feel very well, she used to have a migraine and my mum used to always like be short of money, sometimes like when my father was out of work and I felt that I should give my mum my money as well, and my mum really appreciated it. Well, she didn't want the money but I gave it her because I wanted her to have it.

(15, Midlands inner city)

Conclusion

The starting point of this chapter was the significance of paid employment as a 'normative' feature of contemporary British childhood. While in recent years there has been no shortage of research material to confirm its scale, the simple question of why it is exactly that children seek work in such large numbers has received significantly less attention. The importance of understanding what motivates children to become school age workers is underlined when we consider the work that they do. As the research demonstrates, much of children's employment is more reminiscent of part-time adult work than it is of the employment of secondary-school age children. It is in this respect that it is inappropriate to talk about children's employment in a narrow sense as if there were specific 'children's jobs' or a particular 'market' for children's labour. Children can be found at work in a range of jobs that stretch along a continuum beginning with baby-sitting and delivery work, through home working and light assembly work and on to employment in retail and catering. This should not obscure the fact that the quality of this work is generally low, with few opportunities to exercise particular talents or acquire specific sets of skills. In the main, children's work requires little more than the capacity for unskilled manual labour.

Rather than seeing this involvement in paid employment as something developmentally significant, this chapter has been concerned with the relevance of work to the immediate. In this respect, insights from the so-called 'new sociology of childhood' (James *et al.* 1998) do offer a useful point of critique to the orthodox position. The insistence on childhood as something socially constructed, rather than as externally fixed or 'natural', not only reinstates the need to consider how children's lives are organised in relation to broader social developments, but also requires us to consider the assertion that children's social relations are worth studying in their own right. It takes as its point of diversion the refusal to see children's actions as an expression of preordained forces important in terms of what these children are destined to become rather than what they actually are. In this respect, therefore, as researchers we are forced to take seriously the fact that work holds some meaning for children themselves, that its significance may lie in the immediate, and that what children have to say about their work is worthy of close attention.

The argument presented here, however, also suggests that the stress on children's agency alone is misplaced. Qvortrup (1997), among others, reminds us that childhood is at least as much a matter of structural forces as it is about children's (obvious) abilities to make rational decisions. Children are an especially powerless social group whose capacity to influence the changing economic, educational, familial and technological conditions that structure their childhood is strictly limited. It seems to us that without such a qualification, this new found emphasis on agency, on what children do and say and the values they hold, amounts to little more than an uncritical acceptance that what is at issue is how children exercise choice.

The argument developed in this chapter is that for children in Britain today, as for everyone else, the motivations for working express a relationship between choice and constraint, freedom and necessity. In considering children's motivations for working, choice unquestionably appears an appropriate term to describe their decision to seek out and take up opportunities for paid employment. This is clearly apparent in the value attached to work as a further validation of their growing independence and autonomy from both school and family; as well as its importance as a new source of social networks. Choice is also clearly apparent in the fact that none of the children who took part in our research were involuntary workers, at least in the strictest sense of the term. In fact, it was the very absence of the sorts of constraints imposed by the impending responsibilities of adulthood that made working in these poor quality jobs such an attractive option to the children. It is in this way that the children's motivations to work represented the active decision to generate additional disposable income in their quest for further leisure.

However, the very imperative attached to money from work is also an expression of constraint. At its most acute, this was graphically evident in the importance attached to paid employment as one 'solution' to the very real family poverty that some of the children had to contend with. For all the children, however, there was a clear realisation that money was a necessary precondition of play and that leisure time is seldom 'free' time. The colonisation of children's leisure time by commercial organisations, together with the commercialisation of civic responsibility by local authorities, means that the socially inclusive provision of the past has been replaced by the more (socially) exclusive standards of the market. As these children clearly appreciated, money from work was a requirement for going out with friends, essential for mobility and the key to accessing sport and leisure. Conversely, without money, these children also recognised that they faced the very real prospect of exclusion. This was not simply exclusion in symbolic forms, such as exclusion from the styles and tastes that have come to delineate the changing boundaries of contemporary youth culture. It was more than this: a recognition that access to money was essential for the concrete forms of social interaction that now constitute an important, if not defining, element of the contemporary social relations of childhood.

Notes

The authors would like to express their thanks to the Economic and Social Research Council, who funded the project 'Work, Labour and Economic Life in Late Childhood' (Award No. L129251035) as part of their programme of research: 'Children 5–16: Growing into the Twenty First Century'.

1 The children were asked to provide their own pseudonym and these are used throughout the chapter. All quotations are verbatim. The information in parenthesis at the end of each quotation provides the age of the child when the research commenced and their geographical location.

5 Chinese children's work roles in immigrant adaptation

Miri Song

Studies of child labour in developing nations have pointed to the importance of children's labour for family survival strategies, especially in poor households (see Ennew 1982; Cain 1977; Lai 1982). While children's labour in Third World countries has received some attention in Western societies, there has also been growing interest and concern about children's work in Western, developed countries. In the late 1980s, the United Nations Children's Fund pointed to how changes in the labour market, family structure and environmental conditions, among other factors, were impacting upon child poverty and deprivation more generally in industrialised Western societies (Bradshaw 1990). There has been growing interest in recent years in the rights of children and young people in Western societies such as Britain (James and Prout 1990; Pond and Searle 1991; Roche 1996; Jenks 1996; Morrow 1992; Chisholm *et al.* 1990), as evidenced by the International Year of the Child in 1979 and the passage of the 1989 Children Act in Britain.

In contrast with depictions of children in developing societies, children in most studies of Western family economies (with parents in waged labour) are usually seen as dependants who require economic resources, rather than as active producers for the family economy (see Cheal 1983; Rossi and Rossi 1990). The most commonly recognised way that children assist their parents in Western societies is in their contributions to household chores (see White and Brinkerhoff 1981; Brannen 1995) or when, as *adults*, they assist their parents in old age. The Western idealisation of childhood, as a stage which should be relatively carefree and concerned with social and creative development, is now a normative expectation, if not an unwritten 'right', of children in contemporary Western societies (Ariès 1972; James and Prout 1990).

This chapter examines the various work roles that children play in Chinese take-away food businesses in England, including their experiences of working with and for their families, and the ways in which their labour is negotiated. Chinese take-away food businesses constitute one kind of 'ethnic business'.

Children's roles in immigrant family adaptation

The recent sociological literature on ethnic businesses has stressed their competitiveness in comparison with the small business sector as a whole (Light

1972; Watson 1977; Ward and Jenkins 1984; Waldinger, Aldrich, and Ward 1990).
As an important means of immigrant adaptation, ethnic businesses include many
kinds of enterprises, such as Indian newsagents, Pakistani market traders, and
Korean greengrocers. Because many immigrant groups are relatively disadvantaged in the labour market, due to limited human capital, language difficulties,
and the various forms of racism and discrimination they encounter, small business
ownership has traditionally been a means of achieving economic and social
mobility. Immigrant groups have traditionally tended to enter into businesses
which are characterised by low entry-barriers, such as shopkeeping, clothing
manufacturing, restaurants, and taxi driving (Zhou 1992). For instance, in the
USA, Korean shopkeepers have opened greengrocers, fish stores, and liquor stores
in predominantly poor African-American and Latino neighbourhoods in large
cities such as Los Angeles and New York (Light and Bonacich 1988; Min 1996).
In Britain, Asian shopkeepers have dominated some inner urban areas of London
not served by large grocery chains (Ward 1985).

The ethnic enterprise has been described as a *family mode of production*
(Waldinger, Aldrich, and Ward 1990: 144). As families mature, the labour both
of wives and of children becomes available (Werbner 1987: 224). Ethnic businesses are said to use similar strategies and resources in the ways they resolve
various business problems, such as access to capital, information, and cheap and
reliable labour, often that of family members, who will work for less than
market wages and who are reliable employees. Thus, the family is said to
embody a form of social capital in immigrant self-employment (Sanders and
Nee 1996; Waldinger *et al.* 1990). However, in spite of numerous passing
references to the importance of family labour as a key resource in many ethnic
businesses, family labour and families' relations of production have rarely been
examined or elaborated upon.[1] In particular, children's labour in ethnic businesses has tended to be 'invisible' in such research.

The dearth of research on children's labour in ethnic businesses may be due
to the assumption that children are simply not economically 'productive'
members in most contemporary Western family economies. However, another
possibility is that various forms of children's labour (particularly performed in
the family context) are simply overlooked. A few studies have suggested why
children may not figure centrally in immigrant groups running various types
of enterprises. In the case of Soviet Jews in the USA, Gold (1992: 184) found
several cases of parents who limited their children's connections with their
stores, in the hope that their children would enter into higher education
instead. In the case of Korean business owners in the USA, there is no clear
documentation of, or consensus about, the degree to which business owners
rely upon their children's labour. For instance, Min (1996) suggests that Korean
business owners are more likely to rely upon co-ethnic or Latino employees
than on their children, presumably, for similar reasons to those of the Soviet
Jews. However, Kye Young Park argues,

They also see other Korean immigrants use their children's labour as a

simple and cost-free way to save wage expenses in businesses. A few immigrants adopt an orphan or other people's children for the specific purposes
of using their labour in small business.

(Park 1997: 83)

Despite the fact that dominant Western norms (and laws) frown upon both
the idea and practice of children being active and productive contributors to
their household economies, for many immigrant families in the USA or
Western Europe it is becoming clear that children may play key roles in the
successful social and economic adaptation of their families. For instance, children in these families may not only provide labour in ethnic businesses, but
they may also act as language mediators on behalf of their parents, as was
recently reported in *The New York Times* (Alvarez 1995).

Chinese take-away businesses in England

It is not uncommon to see family members such as children taking orders or
packaging food in Chinese take-away businesses. They are visible to the
public eye as workers in these enterprises. However, as discussed above, very
little is known about how children in immigrant families may contribute to
the running of ethnic businesses. Moreover, the existing literature on children's work in Britain has tended to have a very general and quantitative
focus (e.g. Pond and Searle 1991). By comparison, this chapter highlights
Chinese children's own perspectives and experiences of their family labour
participation.

A recent national survey of ethnic minorities in Britain revealed that rates of
self-employment were relatively high, but that the Chinese in Britain have the
highest rate of self-employment: 30 per cent of Chinese men and 26 per cent
of Chinese women in paid employment were self-employed (most of them in
catering) (Modood *et al.* 1997). The Chinese in Britain provide an interesting
case study of children's labour in ethnic businesses because the Chinese are still
a relatively under-studied ethnic minority group in Britain (for recent studies,
see Parker 1995; Song 1999; Chung 1990; Pang 1993). Furthermore, Chinese
take-away businesses are small, labour-intensive enterprises which are
conducive to the participation of children, especially since these families' home
and work lives are largely intertwined.

Children's labour within a family business has traditionally been regarded as
more benign than industrial employment (Maclennan *et al.*1985). However,
most depictions of family-run *ethnic* businesses in Britain have been largely
disapproving. One reason why children's work in such businesses may be negatively singled out in Britain, as in other Western societies, is that children's work
in ethnic businesses (such as Chinese take-aways) is performed in a racialised
work niche. The work performed in them is associated with derogatory and
shady images and stereotypes concerning 'foreign' immigrant livelihoods. Work
in a Chinese take-away business, as colourfully depicted in Timothy Mo's

novel, *Sour Sweet*, does not evoke the wholesome images of children on an early morning paper route or helping out on the family farm.

In one of the early studies of Chinese children from the 1970s, Jackson and Garvey (1974, 1975) argued that the educational needs of Chinese children were not being met in the British school system, due to their English language difficulties, and that their school performance was damaged by their work in their parents' take-away businesses. The authors also reported that Chinese children were often not registered in schools (see also Simpson 1987). Chinese families and children in Britain have typically been depicted by social workers and other practitioners in terms of family pathologies brought about by the social isolation and alienation stemming from the long work hours and confinement associated with running take-away businesses (see Fewster 1990; Pistrang 1990). The overall image conveyed of Chinese families, and presumably of other immigrant families engaged in ethnic businesses, has been that Chinese parents are rather ruthless and hard-hearted in their manipulation of children's labour and that Chinese children's lives are thus miserable. Various sociological studies of ethnic enterprise and ethnic economy have also tended to characterise such businesses as oppressive and exploitative for the families who run them (see Light and Bonacich 1988; Baxter 1988).

It is undeniable that working in a Chinese take-away business is anything but glamorous, given the very long and arduous hours required by such enterprises. However, such a dire assessment of Chinese families running these businesses in Britain discounts the potentially complex and contradictory experiences of Chinese children working in their family take-aways. Without disputing the claim that Chinese people's concentration in the catering trade reflects, to a certain extent, their economic and social marginalisation in Britain, I would argue that such wholly negative depictions of these families' lives are too simplistic, particularly with respect to the experiences of children in these families (see also Pang 1993).

This chapter is drawn from research based upon a small sample of twenty-five Chinese families running take-away businesses in the Southeast of England (Song 1999). According to the 1991 Census, there were estimated to be about 157,000 Chinese in Britain, with 77,700 males and 79,300 females (Owen 1993). The majority of Chinese immigrants in Britain are British subjects who were born in the (then) commonwealth of Hong Kong, with approximately 75–80 per cent of the present Chinese population originating from the rural New Territories of Hong Kong (Watson 1977: 183). They are primarily Cantonese and Hakka speakers with relatively little formal education (Parliament 1985: 5). It is this group of Chinese, from the New Territories, which constitutes the focus of this study.

Within this study, I interviewed Chinese young people about their childhood experiences of working with and for their families. Although I use the terms 'young people' and 'children' interchangeably throughout the chapter, I use the term 'children' to refer to a family relationship, *vis-à-vis* parents, rather than to individuals of a particular age. The forty-two young people in this study, comprised of twenty-seven female and fifteen male respondents, were at least 17 years old or older. Most of these respondents were in their early to mid-20s. I arrived at forty-two young people from twenty-five families by interviewing two siblings in seventeen of the twenty-five families. I also interviewed the mothers in five of the families, as well as some other Chinese people who were associated with the catering sector. Chinese community workers in the Southeast provided the initial contact with families, and called families that might be interested in participating in my research. Given my difficulties in gaining access to families, word-of-mouth snowballing was crucial to this study.

The gradual incorporation of children's labour

The issue of children working in ethnic businesses, such as Chinese take-away businesses in Britain, raises questions about the interpretation and assessment of children's labour in a context in which parents' waged work and children's dependency is the norm. In order to gain a fuller understanding of these children's work roles, we must remember that ethnic businesses not only provide a livelihood but they actually constitute an entire way of life for immigrant families. A number of questions arise in reference to children's labour in ethnic businesses. First, in what ways do children contribute their labour in ethnic businesses, and how should this labour be conceptualised? Second, how do children experience their labour, in the context of family life, and how is their labour elicited and maintained over time?

There tended to be a very common employment trajectory for these Chinese families, beginning with waged work in Chinese restaurants and take-aways, developing to restaurant and take-away partnerships, and culminating in sole shop ownership.

Children in most of the sample families (twenty of twenty-five) were gradually 'incorporated' (Finch 1983) into their take-away businesses when they were relatively young (often at the age of 7 or 8), either at business start-up, or in the early years of the shop. The young people in a minority (five) of families reported undergoing a marked transition from non-involvement to working in their businesses; this typically occurred when they were in their early teens. However, for children in twenty families, incorporation into the business gradually evolved as an important part of family life:

M.S. Can you tell me how you started working in the shop, how you got involved?

Foon I don't know. They've never asked us. It's almost as though it's just expected. We just watched and learned when we were young. There was no training course or anything. . . . When we came back from school, we came back to the shop and hung around. That's where the TV was, at the counter, in the shop. We didn't have a TV upstairs [their living quarters].

What was stressed by these young people was that it all seemed 'so natural'; in other words, working in the shop was 'second-nature' to their every-day lives. While they were aware that their experiences of childhood differed from the Western norm of childhood, most young people characterised their work roles as developing in the context of family needs and circumstances, rather than in terms of a purposeful mode of socialisation (James and Prout 1996). When I asked young people if their parents had told them that they needed their help, they commonly responded in the following ways:

Sui   No, they've never said, 'we need you'. You don't need to say it really.

Fai   If you ask me, yes, they needed us, but they're not saying it in that way. It was understood.

Typically, children who started working at a young age started out doing 'easy things' in the kitchen, such as washing dishes, peeling prawns and potatoes, and other tasks which were considered suitable for young children. Because of the close intertwining of home and work, tasks performed for the business comprised an important part of family life. For many families who lived above their businesses, family meals were cooked in the take-away kitchen, and eaten around the dictates of business hours. When asked how and when housework was done, young people who lived above their shops, as Fai did, seemed somewhat amused by this question: 'Well, there is no housework as such; the shop *is* the house' (Song 1995).

The availability and potential productivity of children's labour tended to increase as they grew older, and their work responsibilities increased over time. This was usually signalled by their learning new skills in the kitchen, such as cutting vegetables and meat with knives, or using woks, which are quite heavy and not easily handled by young children. As children grew older, they were able to move from 'the back' (the kitchen) to 'the front' of the shop, to work at the counter. Although parents with very limited English language proficiency could take orders at the counter (the dishes were numbered), children who were fluent in English were better able to deal with customers. Not only did the increased diversity and responsibility of children's work roles over time mean that children could relieve their parents of some work pressure, but their availability as mature workers meant that families were much less reliant upon paid employees and more distant relatives.

For most of the children (in twenty-two of the twenty-five families), their daily lives were fundamentally structured by their parents' reliance upon them for language mediation and various forms of labour, while for the children in a minority of families (three of twenty-five), their parents' reliance upon them was minimal. Most children tended to work fairly regularly in their shops, for instance in the evenings, after school, or during weekends. Those who had to be at their shops when they opened (usually 5.00 or 5.30 p.m.) had lives which were very structured by shop hours.

Many of the young people reported a strong sense of being needed by their parents because of the 'caring' work they performed, which included accompanying parents to appointments with doctors, solicitors, bank managers, and teachers (on behalf of their younger siblings). One daughter, Sue, recalled the difficulty of having to divine 'adult' information and knowledge in her efforts to mediate for her parents, especially in business meetings, which required very detailed translations:

> It was a lot of work, especially, at a young age, when you don't know that much about the outside world, mortgages, etc. You just don't know the background to all that. And all of a sudden you're flung to the deep end. Your parents often show a letter in the middle of a transaction, or from a source, and your Chinese isn't at the level where you can explain exactly what's going on.

Therefore, the performance of 'caring' work for parents was significant in terms of children's intense sense of responsibility for their parents. As a result, many of them reported common themes around a 'loss of childhood', given the responsibilities that 'caring' work and working in the shop had entailed – a finding which corresponds with a recent study of young people's participation in Chinese and Korean family businesses in the USA (L. Park 1999). As one respondent, Anna, put it, 'A lot of that feels like a loss of childhood, almost. I don't feel in a sense, we were ever really young, because we were working so young'.

It would be simplistic and erroneous to understand children's labour participation in these families only in terms of economic rationality or in terms of parents' need for their children's labour and language proficiency. Chinese parents' reliance upon their children as workers was motivated by a range of difficulties that hiring outside employees entailed for families, such as affordability, trust and privacy. Outside employees, both Chinese or British, 'spoiled' the family basis of these enterprises. In order to gain a full understanding of how children became involved in providing their labour, we need to privilege their own views and experiences of working with and for their families.

'We should help out'

The majority of respondents believed that children *should* help their parents in their shops. In very few families had parents and children actually discussed their respective expectations and concerns about working together. Nevertheless, the children in these families suggested that they were subject to a kind of binding and unspoken contract to 'help out', and their beliefs about 'helping out' were embodied in what I call a 'family work contract' (FWC) (Song 1999). These family work contracts were not explicitly agreed contracts in the usual, legalistic sense. Nevertheless, the relations of production in these families, and the norms which governed these relations, constituted a contract of a different kind. That is, the duties involved in these

FWCs were diffuse, based upon trust, and not premised upon explicit consent to specific obligations (Fox 1974: 153).

A family survival strategy

Chinese young people's beliefs and understandings about their FWCs were consistently elaborated primarily in terms of the need to contribute to a family survival strategy. In contrast with the norm of parents engaged in waged work in Britain, shop ownership was commonly regarded as the culmination of a family survival strategy among many Chinese families in Britain. According to Paul:

> We did accept the fact that this is how Chinese families cope if they was [sic] to immigrate to England. It was the only way. Like my mum and dad can't speak English. What can they do? The best way is to open a restaurant or take-away. I don't see any other way, to be honest, to survive. I accepted it completely.

As Paul emphasised, his parents had few work options apart from the take-away. Family work contracts emerged out of a collective strategy in which every family member was expected to help out.

This collective sense of responsibility for survival was keenly felt, not only because of material survival pressures, but also because of experiences of racism at school, university and employment, and young people's experiences of racism while working at the take-away counter (see Parker 1995). According to Stephen, 'They'll [customers] say things like, "You're in our country, chink, and you should be serving us." Things like that. So generally, we tend to ignore that, to avoid trouble.'

Belief in a 'family work contract'

'Helping out', as part of a 'family work contract', differed in important ways from the terms of formal employment. These young people understood their family labour in terms of familial *interdependence*, rather than just having to work for one's parents. The sense of mutual need and support developed over the long-term, as families migrated, adjusted, and worked together. Another key way in which 'helping out' was distinguished from formal employment was that it was not contingent upon remuneration. As a 'home ethic', helping out was generally seen to be unconditional, and based upon family ties. This understanding of helping out was manifest in most young people's belief that they should not expect to be paid for their labour (though some were happy to accept some modest remuneration; see Song 1999 for more detail).

The relatively widespread consensus that children should help out in their take-away businesses reflected the complex balance of both moral and material imperatives underlying these Chinese families' FWCs. Most respondents talked about the strength of 'family' and family obligations in ways which suggested the powerful ideological pull of such terms and the potentially double-edged nature of family ties (Rapp *et al.* 1979; Finch 1989). As Sue noted, 'with your family, you have to work extra hard, because it's your family, whereas if you're in nine-to-five, you don't kill yourself over it'.

Helping out and Chinese cultural identity

The fact that many first generation Chinese families from Hong Kong's New Territories have relied so heavily upon take-away businesses, as well as the fact that Chinese people are often popularly linked with the Chinese food they sell to the wider British public, have meant that 'the take-away' has been, and continues to be, an absolutely central part of many Chinese people's cultural identities and experiences in Britain.

In addition to survival pressures and an understanding of the family obligations underlying the FWC, expectations that children should help out emerged in a context where there was an awareness that other Chinese children in Britain also helped out in their take-away businesses. Because of the prevalence of Chinese families running take-away businesses, working in 'the take-away' signifies a particular social and economic status for Chinese people in British society. Not only do children provide labour in these businesses, and fulfil their family obligations by doing so, but these children also sell an 'ethnic' food to the wider public.

By selling Chinese food to predominantly white customers, these Chinese families trade upon 'cultural difference' in Britain (Parker 1995). For young people, working in the take-away evokes issues of what it means to be Chinese in Britain. Furthermore, 'serving' customers could be harrowing and stressful: many young people reported that some of their white customers treated them as if they *should* serve them, and they were all too aware of the colonialist tinge to these interactions across the take-away counter.

In response to the ill treatment and denigrating stereotypes foisted upon them by their customers, Chinese young people tried to conceive of the work they performed in their take-aways in a more positive, rather than a negative, light. The sense of upholding a widespread Chinese practice in Britain – helping out as part of the FWC – was important in providing these young people with a sense of Chinese identity in Britain and of belonging to a Chinese 'community', even though some of these families had little contact with any such community.

In addition to the desire to counter undesirable racial stereotypes, another factor which could explain why these young people attributed positive meanings to their FWCs, as emblems of Chinese cultural identity in Britain, was that many white British people were seen to be unsympathetic, and lacking in understanding about Chinese people's situations in Britain. This could be very alienating for Chinese young people, as explained by Sue:

Quite a few friends had birthday parties, always on Saturday evenings. We could never go because we had to help out in the shop. Some of my friends just couldn't understand it; they thought it was quite barbarious [sic], actually. They don't understand how my family operates, that we were from a different world from them. Our fathers do not have a nine-to-five job, we don't have evenings and weekends free, holidays.

In fact, most Chinese young people actively defended their FWCs. They were keenly aware that while their work was normatively prescribed among Chinese families running take-aways in Britain, it was proscribed in British law and social norms. Many respondents noted that although most customers 'understood' their labour participation in the take-away, they were also aware of legislation barring children under the age of 16 from working any substantial hours.

When asked about working in their family businesses, it often seemed that these Chinese young people assumed that I (and the wider public), as a non-Chinese researcher who did not grow up working in a take-away, disapproved of their labour participation. On a number of occasions, I had the strong sense that respondents had prepared to defend their work roles in the interviews. For instance, when asked if she thought that children should help their parents in a family business, Lisa replied,

I know you think, oh, the children shouldn't help. Maybe I think they should because I've been through it. Say you eat, you're there [in the shop], and naturally, you help your parents. Having your life at home, and having the shop, it's all the same thing. You have to be doing something constructively as well.

Chinese young people's cultural identities were thus heightened by the recognition that their family lives diverged greatly from those of most other Britons. Despite many individuals' feelings of vulnerability, exposure, and their experiences of being stereotyped in offensive ways, they did not passively accept imposed meanings of being Chinese. As Fernandez-Kelly and Schauffler have noted, 'Some identities protect immigrants; others weaken them by transforming them into disadvantaged ethnic minorities' (1994: 663).

Therefore, helping out, as part of a family work contract, was not only crucial to the survival of these family businesses, but also enabled Chinese young people to interpret their labour in positive, rather than negative, ways. Since they encountered, in their view, ethnocentric disapproval of their labour participation in their family livelihoods, their support for their FWCs could be seen as a positive affirmation of their identities as Chinese people in Britain.

In contrast to James Watson's observation from the late 1970s that 'The Chinese caterers, including even the younger migrants, have not begun to redefine themselves as a consequence of exposure to British society and culture' (1977: 205), I would argue, twenty years later, that helping out in their take-aways has been formative for Chinese young people's cultural identities in Britain. Much of the literature on the 'second generation' in Britain, particularly in relation to Asian young people, has situated and explored issues of young people's identities in relation to their parents' cultural practices and their ties (e.g. the idea of being 'between two cultures' (Watson 1977)), if any, with their countries of ethnic origin (see Stopes-Roe and Cochrane 1990; Drury 1991; Brah 1992; Modood *et al.* 1994; Shaw 1994). However, none of these studies has addressed the relationship between cultural identity and the performance of work, and of family labour in particular.

Negotiating children's labour participation

Despite the widely reported belief in helping out, many young people reported a constant tension between *wanting* to help out and feeling that they *had* to help out. As Pue-lai put it, 'It's really hard to say pushed or not, but thinking, oh yeah, your father's earning, and you have to help as well, so I help'. Some young people reported feeling resentful about how much they were needed by their parents and their family livelihoods. Annie struggled with the sense that helping out *seemed* to be 'compulsory' and non-negotiable, even though she knew it was not. For some daughters, helping out could be a particularly ambivalent experience, given that they tended to perform much more domestic housework and childcare than their brothers (see Song 1995).

We cannot simply assume that family members are unproblematically committed to working in ethnic businesses, based upon enduring and 'natural' norms of family obligations and feelings of affection (Qvortrup 1985). Although researchers on ethnic businesses have pointed to the positive contributions of unpaid family labour for the success of these businesses, feminist research has challenged the putatively benign characterisation of family labour, in particular of women working unpaid for their families (see Hartmann 1981; Finch 1983; Phizacklea 1988; Delphy and Leonard 1992). Nevertheless, the fact that children are subject to their parents' authority does not preclude the possibility that they may want to provide their labour, even though they may be ambivalent about doing so.

Not surprisingly, guilt was a prevalent theme which was raised by virtually all the respondents. Most respondents reported that they felt guilty if they didn't want to help out. According to David, 'It would be hard for me *not* to help. 'Cause basically by nature, I'm really helpful. If I'm not doing anything, I feel guilty. 'Cause I can do it. Yeah?' Not only did their parents work extremely long and arduous hours, but these young people knew that they should contribute their labour to a livelihood from which they themselves benefited.

The young people in virtually every family reported that their parents regularly reinforced their expectations that children should help out, though to varying degrees of explicitness. One of the most common ways in which parents communicated such expectations was by either 'guilt-tripping' children, or by citing traditional Chinese adages about children helping their parents. Young people were often 'guilt-tripped' about the sacrifices which their parents had made for the benefit of their children, or parents would compare their children's labour commitments to those of other model Chinese children. One daughter, Pue-man, described a commonly used 'guilt-trip' technique of her parents:

> My mum's got a lot of friends with take-aways. She's always saying, whoever, whoever's son is working for his parents, and he's giving up his studying, and how they've sold the shop, and he's gone back to studying, and I think I'm not gonna waste my life like that. And sometimes she compares us to her friends' daughter: 'She's been working until she's 30'. And I said I'm not gonna be like her. She always compares us with people who have children who work.

Interestingly, 'guilt-tripping' was not exclusively practised by parents. Siblings within families could differ in their commitments to helping out, and this often resulted in some feeling aggrieved about their less willing and committed siblings. As such, some who had 'good' family reputations for helping out could attempt to make their 'bad' sibling(s) feel guilty (Song 1997).

In addition to the potentially oppressive nature of parents' expectations, young people's ambivalence about their FWCs stemmed from their acute awareness of their families diverging from 'Western' norms of family and work: an ideal which did not involve children in a family livelihood or in performing an array of 'caring work' on a day-to-day basis. These young people tended to experience tensions between two polarised ideals of 'family' and identity: one Chinese and one British. In spite of the critical dismissal of the notion of being 'between two cultures', I found that this idea, or very similar elaborations of it, was articulated by many of the young people in this study. In fact, most of these young people tended to see themselves as being informed by *both* Chinese and British cultures (see Song 1999 for more on this).

A common source of tension which arose in upholding family work contracts was the need for young people to subordinate their own needs and desires to collective, family needs (see also Auernheimer 1990, for Turkish young people in Germany). For instance, many of the respondents in the sample struggled with the fact that they had very limited social lives. This was particularly the case at weekends, when most social activities, such as parties and dates, were planned by their peers. Because of time constraints and their need to be at their shops, their Chinese friends or partners sometimes joined in helping out, so that this labour was performed in what was partly a socialising context. Given that weekend nights were usually the busiest of the week, working together in the shop was one way of spending time together; after closing hours, some young people went out to late-night clubs or restaurants where they could congregate with other Chinese people in the same situation. In this respect, the rhythms of their social lives were very distinct from those of their non-Chinese peers.

However, children's socialisation seems to have been an important factor in shaping the degree to which young people experienced tensions in relation to helping out. The majority (thirty-one of forty-two) of the Chinese young people in this study were born in Britain, while ten were born in Hong Kong, and one in Yemen (however, of the thirty-one young people born in Britain, five were sent back to Hong Kong and partly raised there before returning to Britain). Individuals born and raised predominantly in Hong Kong and those born and raised in Britain (or brought to Britain by primary-school age) tended to have different expectations about family and work. Children who were born and raised in Hong Kong, who were in the minority, tended to have strikingly similar views about helping out: many of them said that they had *expected* to work in Britain with their parents. Some of them had witnessed and experienced poverty in the New Territories, where they had been raised. Children raised in Hong Kong tended to report much less tension around upholding the FWC, because they had been more accustomed to children working in Hong Kong (Easey 1979). Nor did these young people articulate concerns about the implications of helping out for their cultural identities.

In contrast, children who were partially or wholly socialised in Britain (who referred to themselves as 'BBCs': British-born Chinese) tended to report more ambivalence and difficulties associated with helping out, especially in terms of their families' atypical family and work lives, which were largely merged (see also L. Park 1999). For example, in Colin's case, he disliked customers being able to see his family's sitting room, which he considered to be his family's 'private' space, from 'the front' of the shop (the counter). Another example of private space being intruded upon by work was that some families had telephone lines for take-away orders in their living quarters – in sitting rooms and even bedrooms in some cases.

Typically, British-born Chinese individuals also reported that as they had grown up, they had resented their parents at times, not only for relying upon them or for putting pressure on them to help out, but for not being like 'other' parents. Such feelings could be especially intense for 'BBCs', like Anna:

> It was difficult coming to terms with the fact that they were not like other parents. Talk to them, get advice, take you on holiday, etc.. But they always had your best interests at heart. You had to realise their constraints, and that they didn't fit the ideal of parents.

Although most young people (including BBCs) actively defended their FWCs as a way of life, some of these young people were still coming to terms with negative senses of identity (in relation to 'the take-away') which they had internalised. According to Jacqui:

> Throughout my childhood and adolescence, I questioned why certain things were the way they were. My own identity came into question, and I questioned how living above a shop could be normal. Normal is like what I saw on the telly, or my friends. It was quite a bizarre thing coming home to a shop. But beyond that, the fact that I was Chinese-British, and

living a sort of typical background to what the British see the Chinese as being, was quite a problem for me at one stage, partly because I saw myself as being British, and tried to push away my Chinese identity. . . . I remember one time, I was about 16, and I went to this girl's birthday party, and her house was really nice, obviously middle-class, her father had a business, self-employed. I remember having a lift home, and I was the last one to be dropped off, and I saw all their houses, and it was really strange seeing all these really nice houses, and then he dropped me off, and mine was above a shop. Nowadays, I'm quite open about saying that I've lived in a Chinese take-away all my life, but it can be a disadvantage with some people, who back off.

Conclusion

The centrality of children's labour in Chinese take-aways stemmed from a combination of factors, such as their parents' limited command of English and educational qualifications, the labour intensive nature of these businesses, and the unusually intense intertwining of family and work lives. I found that the dominant Western paradigm of 'dependent' children and 'breadwinner' parents, and of clear divisions between work and family (or home), was not applicable to these Chinese families. Chinese parents were not the sole economic providers or decision-makers in most of these families, for these parents relied heavily upon their children in various ways. This is not to deny these parents' authority and power as parents; however, children who performed 'caring' work were acutely aware of their parents' dependence *upon them*, and knew that they were crucial both to their parents' adaptation to life in Britain and to the survival of their family businesses.

Although the moral and material pressures for family members to provide their labour apply more generally to all small family enterprises, the intertwining of normative and material expectations in immigrant family businesses (in a context where they are subject to various forms of racism) may be even more intense (Kibria 1994). Their status and experiences as immigrants and ethnic minorities in Britain are therefore fundamental for the formation of family values and cultures, as embodied in their 'family work contracts'.

More comparative research on the productive and 'caring' roles of children in immigrant families is needed, both in Britain and the USA. Just as there is inconclusive evidence of the extent of children's labour participation in Korean businesses in the USA, there is very little documentation of the ways in which children in small Asian businesses in Britain may contribute to the running of their family livelihoods.

Although this chapter does not address the policy implications of children's labour participation *per se*, this exploration of Chinese children and their labour participation has policy implications for ethnic minority families and children, immigrant adaptation, and 'race relations' more generally. The case of Chinese families running take-away businesses raises thorny questions about how scholars and policymakers should conceptualise and categorise the issue of 'family labour', as performed by ethnic minority children who are the children of immigrants (or who are immigrants themselves). Unquestionably, children's labour in a family context is much more difficult to detect and monitor than their waged work outside the home.

It seems that in the case of children whose parents speak little or no English, the wider society does not object to children fulfilling their roles as language mediators, but at the same time they are much more likely to view children's labour in family businesses in a pejorative and negative light (because they are productive enterprises on which the family economy depends). And yet it is important that we remember that it is difficult to draw clear boundaries between a 'labour of love' (Finch and Groves 1983), such as the 'caring' work described above, and the many quotidian forms of labour performed in the 'work' setting, such as a Chinese take-away business. After all, the 'caring' work performed by many Chinese children was also experienced, in many ways, as work, albeit within the context of a family work contract. One thing is clear, however: policymakers and social workers should not be hasty in making top-down judgements about the assumed misery and suffering of such children. Although there is bound to be a proportion of children who do genuinely suffer as a result of unrealistic and unfair demands made upon them, we must not lose sight of the many children who have been successful in coping with their demanding lives or of the fact that many children are understanding about their parents' reliance upon them.

Note

1 The centrality of wives' labour has been noted in a number of different types of family businesses (Bertaux and Bertaux-Wiame 1981; Delphy and Leonard 1992; Bechofer *et al.* 1974; Scase and Goffee 1980), and ethnic businesses (Baxter and Raw 1988; Westwood and Bhachu 1988; Song 1995; Kim and Hurh 1988; Min 1998).

6 Children's labour of love?

Young carers and care work

Saul Becker, Chris Dearden and Jo Aldridge

Most children will care *about* and sometimes care *for* family members and significant others. This caring needs to be encouraged and nurtured if children are to value care-giving both during childhood and later in adult life. Indeed, *learning* to care, and showing and providing care, are part of a child's socialisation and are a prerequisite for healthy psycho-social development.

But what of those children who take on significant, substantial or regular caring tasks and responsibilities which have a negative impact or outcome for their own well-being, their psycho-social development and their transition from childhood to adulthood? It is this group of children – those who undertake significant unpaid care work within the home – who are the focus of this chapter. These children are generally referred to in the United Kingdom as 'young carers'.

Young carers can be defined as:

> children and young persons under 18 who provide or intend to provide care, assistance or support to another family member. They carry out, often on a regular basis, significant or substantial caring tasks and assume a level of responsibility which would usually be associated with an adult.
>
> (Becker 2000: 378)

The person receiving care is often a parent but can be a sibling, grandparent or other relative who is disabled, has some chronic illness, mental health problem or other condition connected with a need for care, support or supervision.

Young carers provide similar levels of support to adult carers but their experiences differ because those under the age of 18 are legally defined as children and, as such, are not expected to take on significant or substantial caring roles. However, community care policy and legislation in the UK assume that family members will provide, unpaid, the bulk of care in the community, with the state stepping in to fill the gaps (Griffiths 1998; DoH 1989). In some families this results in children and young people adopting caring roles, often, although not exclusively, in the absence of an adult in the home. While adult carers can be seen to be conforming to societal norms in supporting family members, children who act as carers transgress such norms. In theory at least, childhood is viewed as a protected phase, with adults and the state supporting and protecting children and young people until they make the transition into adulthood.

There is now a considerable body of research in the UK, and also developing internationally (Becker, Aldridge and Dearden 1998), which shows that when children undertake significant care work within the home, and where they and their families lack appropriate health and socialcare support and adequate income, then many young carers experience impaired well-being, health and psycho-social development in ways that include physical injury, stress-related symptoms, poor educational attendance and performance, restricted peer networks, restricted friendships and opportunities, and difficulties in making the smooth transition from childhood to adulthood. This chapter reviews the main research studies on young carers in the UK and identifies the implications of children's unpaid care work for future policy and practice.

It is important to emphasise at the outset that not all children in families where there is illness or disability will become young carers. Indeed, in the majority of such families it will be rare for children to take on significant, substantial or regular caring responsibilities. In many families another adult may provide care, support or supervision, from within or outside the family unit. The family may receive services and support from health organisations, social services, and the voluntary or private sectors (the so-called 'mixed economy of care') that work with families as part of the state's framework and provision for health, social and community care, or as part of the welfare infrastructure which exists to protect children and support families. Good quality, reliable, and affordable professional support, especially when combined with adequate family income, can help prevent many children from having to undertake significant care work within the home and can reduce the labours of those already heavily involved in this type of work.

Children's unpaid care work

Can we consider the caring tasks and responsibilities performed by young carers to be *work*? Let us answer this in a number of stages.

There are approximately one million people in England paid to work full- or part-time to provide social care, as many as the number employed in the NHS. Of these, about a quarter work in local authority social services departments while the remainder are employed in the private (for profit) sector and voluntary sector. Those who provide home-based care (from all sectors) total about 170,000 people (compared with about 450,000 who work in residential or day care services for adults) (Becker 2001 forthcoming). Home care services staff are the people who go into the homes of ill, elderly, disabled and other vulnerable adult groups, generally to provide domestic or personal care support; in other words, they are paid care workers. The vast majority of these staff (as well as the majority of all staff who work in social care) are unqualified. Most are women. And most are poorly paid.

An example of a home care worker is a Community Care Assistant. Scanning the job adverts in the social work press and especially local and regional newspapers will show that there are almost always vacancies for this kind of care work. A typical job description for a Community Care Assistant (to be employed in a social services department) goes like this:

Nottinghamshire County Council. Community Care Assistants (25 Posts). 20–25 Band £5.11 per hour.

Are you a caring, reliable and flexible person? . . . Community Care Assistants provide services to vulnerable people in their own homes which is a challenging but rewarding career and staff are supported through NVQs and other training by the Department's Investors in People programme. Community Care Assistants provide personal care and domestic support services to people of all ages, including families with children, and from different backgrounds and cultures and therefore an understanding of Equal Opportunities is required. Although staff work usually on a one to one basis with service users in their own homes they are supported and managed by a Senior Community Care Assistant and Home Care Manager.

(*Nottingham Evening Post*, 15 March 2000: 43)

Another advert states the kind of hours expected:

Nottingham City Council. Community Care Assistants SCP 8 £5.12 per hour.

. . . You will be responsible for providing a high standard of personal care and domestic support for people of all ages, disabilities and from all sections of our multicultural community, in order to maximise service users' independence within their own homes. We expect that you will have a flexible approach to the post and will be prepared to work weekends and bank holidays on a rota basis. In addition you may be required to work occasionally in the evenings. You will be expected to participate in training opportunities relevant to the post.

(*Nottingham Evening Post*, 15 March 2000: 39)

These posts are for Community Care Assistants to work within two local social services departments. Staff employed to similar job descriptions within the private and voluntary sectors can usually expect poorer employment conditions, and even lower wages, with few if any opportunities for training and personal development.

As Clough argues, 'looking after other people has always been badly rewarded'. He suggests three reasons for this. First, 'such work is not thought to require skills; surely it's only what people do within their own families? Second, it is the work of women: it requires instinctive, feminine characteristics. Third, we cannot afford to pay more' (Clough 2000: 71).

As we shall see later, many children perform exactly the same kinds of care work required of Community Care Assistants. The difference though is that children do this work most often with little choice or alternative; their labour and commitment is rarely recognised by professionals; they have no supervision; no opportunities for training and personal development; no specified hours or terms of employment; and they are unpaid. They do care work as 'a labour of love'.

Children are not the only people who perform this labour of love. There is an extensive literature on adults who care for other family members – informal carers – and there is comprehensive data on their characteristics. This literature is more developed in the UK than elsewhere, although there is now a growing international recognition of the role and importance of informal carers (Becker 1997, 1999). Today, nearly six million adults in Britain provide unpaid care to other family members; that is 13 per cent of all people aged 16 or over (Office for National Statistics 1998). About a quarter of adult carers provide more than twenty hours of unpaid care per week, with around 800,000 people providing full-time care of at least fifty hours a week. Research has highlighted the experiences and needs of adult carers, including the effects, impacts and outcomes of caring (Glendinning 1992; Becker and Silburn 1999). Moreover, there is a developed literature on the gendered dimension of caring: 'in most societies at most times, the sexual division of labour has given responsibility for the care of people who are frail or vulnerable to women – within families and on the basis of love or duty' (Baldwin and Twigg 1991: 117). Thus, of those caring for at least twenty hours per week, 63 per cent are women (OPCS 1992).

Feminist analysis of paid care work in general and informal care in particular has helped raise awareness of the sexual division of care labour. However, the literature that grew out of and contributed to this analysis rarely if ever recognised the other power dimension around the division of unpaid care work within the family, namely the children's dimension. So, research, policy and practice throughout the 1970s and most of the 1980s failed to identify, acknowledge and respond to the fact that in many families unpaid care work was provided not by adults but by children and young people.

It would be inconceivable to employ children as Community Care Assistants or other care workers; there would be a public outcry as well as all the other ramifications. However, within the 'private' domain of the family children do provide unpaid care work; but their labour is not defined as work. Because unpaid informal care is a 'private' family matter, governed by its own relationships and rules, it is referred to in the UK as 'caring' and in the USA as 'care-giving', not care work. While this language has helped to distinguish the informal unpaid carer from the paid care worker, it has simultaneously helped to obscure and hide children's contribution to both caring *and* care work.

The growing awareness of 'young carers'

Since the mid-1980s there has been an increased awareness in the UK of the existence of children and young people as carers, although even today there is little recognition that the care they provide is actually unpaid care work. Research, by focusing on the characteristics and experiences of young carers (as a group of children who are also carers), has given little attention to the significance, the social meanings, and outcomes, of children's unpaid care work. This chapter is an attempt to redress this imbalance.

Early research in Britain sought to establish the extent of the 'problem' of caring among children (O'Neill 1988; Page 1988) and, while failing to indicate potential numbers of young carers, did stimulate further research into the needs and experiences of such children. Small-scale qualitative studies, such as those by Bilsborrow (1992) and Aldridge and Becker (1993a) identified the experiences of young carers, often drawing on their own words. Aldridge and Becker (1994) also conducted the first study of parents with an illness or disability who were supported by their children. Other studies have sought to ascertain the experiences of, or effects on, children in families where a parent has a specific illness or disability, such as Parkinson's disease (Grimshaw 1991), mental health problems (Elliott 1992), multiple sclerosis (Segal and Simkins 1993), and HIV/AIDS (Imrie and Coombes 1995).

As awareness of young carers' issues has grown and support for them has increased, it has become easier to identify them in larger numbers and to conduct more detailed quantitative studies. By contacting specialist support services it has been possible for researchers to generate statistical information about larger numbers of young carers. In 1995 the first national survey was conducted (Dearden and Becker 1995) and information was collated on 640 young carers supported by specialist projects. This survey was replicated in 1997 and generated data on more than 2,300 young carers, including information relating to social services' assessments of young carers (Dearden and Becker 1998). These two national surveys are discussed in some detail later in this chapter.

Alongside the growing body of research into young caring has come increased professional awareness of and support for young carers. In 1992 the first two pilot projects to support young carers were established. By 1995 there were thirty-seven such projects and by the end of the decade over 115 (Aldridge and Becker 1998). The majority of specialist support projects are located within the voluntary sector but most receive some form of statutory funding.

The projects offer a range of services and are valued highly by young carers and their families alike, especially those families who resist professional assistance or are not entitled to it. Without the support of these projects a quarter of young carers and their families would have no outside support at all (Dearden and Becker 1998).

Young carers projects offer a range of services based on the identified needs of the children themselves. Most provide information and avenues for accessing other forms of support as well as counselling, advocacy and befriending services. Providing leisure activities for young carers is also a priority for most of the projects and is valued highly by the children themselves. Activities allow young carers some respite from caring and the opportunity for fun 'time-out' as well as the chance to meet and mix with other children in a similar situation. This also gives parents 'time off' from their children, an opportunity to have some privacy and time away from worrying about or having to deal with their children's needs.

Aside from service provision, young carers projects are also involved in awareness-raising strategies in order to ensure the needs and rights of young carers are identified and met both within statutory and voluntary agencies. Projects are also keen to work in collaboration with, or advise, other agencies in order to meet these needs, and some aim to influence local policy and practice. Young carers projects are increasingly located within carers' centres or other carer support groups.

Research by the Department of Health (DoH 1996a, 1996b) has suggested that the services offered by young carers projects are equally valued by health and social care professionals for their 'specialist' response to the needs of young carers and their families, as a way of locating appropriate access to statutory services and of raising the profile of young carers.

The Department of Health issued guidance to all local authority social services departments regarding their duties to young carers, a move which was followed by the Department of Education. Other developments at the end of the 1990s, not least the National Carers Strategy (DoH 1999), helped put young carers firmly on the policy and professional agendas. The Carers Strategy outlines a number of government policy commitments to meet the needs of young carers in Britain. Internationally too, there is growing recognition of the contribution children make to caring, with a developing body of research in the USA, Australia and elsewhere, and policy initiatives and services being developed in a number of countries (Becker, Aldridge and Dearden 1998).

The extent and nature of children's care work within the family

In the UK, almost three million children under the age of 16 (equivalent to 23 per cent of all children) live in households where one family member is hampered in daily activities by any chronic physical or mental health problem, illness or disability. In Europe as a whole, nearly a quarter of all children (16 million in total) live in households of this type (Becker, Aldridge and Dearden 1998: xii). It is impossible to calculate with any accuracy the proportion of these children who take on, or do not take on, significant caring responsibilities within the family. However, Office for National Statistics figures (Walker 1996) indicate that there are between 19,000 and 51,000 children in Britain who take on 'substantial or regular care' and who would thus be classified as 'young carers' under a Carers Act definition based on the quantity of care provided and its regularity. The 'real' figure will be higher if the definition of a young carer is constructed more broadly, to include the *significance* to the family of the care given, and the *impacts* of care work on children's well-being and psycho-social development. Because of the negative nature of these impacts and outcomes a number of organisations, including the Family Rights Group (1991), Children's Rights Development Unit (1994) and Social Services Inspectorate (1995) have argued that young carers should be responded to and considered as 'children in need' under the Children Act (see later for a discussion of this Act).

Figure 6.1 illustrates the extent of care work among children. Within the child population as a whole the number of young carers is relatively small (but no less important for that). By way of comparison with other groups of children defined as 'in need', there are more children in Britain providing substantial or regular care than there are on the Child Protection Register (32,000), but fewer than the number 'looked after' in fostering or residential units (78,000) (DoH 2000a).

Many small-scale studies have provided a fairly uniform profile of the characteristics, experiences and needs of young carers. The findings of these studies have provided a picture of who young carers are, what they do in terms of care work, and the outcomes that caring has for their lives. The results of these small-scale studies have also been confirmed by the two national surveys of

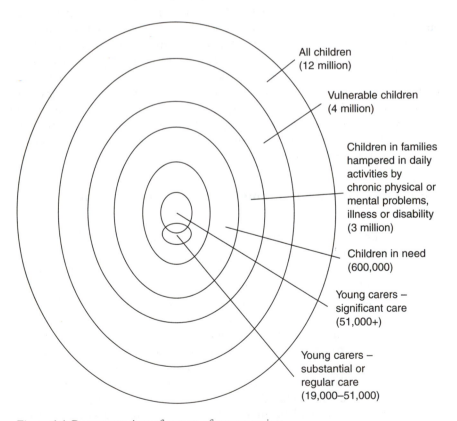

Figure 6.1 Representation of extent of young caring

Sources: Department of Health 2000a: 5; Becker *et al.* 1998.

young carers mentioned previously (Dearden and Becker 1995, 1998). The later study, *Young Carers in the UK*, provides a profile of the characteristics, needs and experiences of 2,303 young carers aged 18 or under, all of whom are supported by specialist young carers projects.

The average age of young carers supported by projects in 1995 and 1998 remains the same, at just 12 years. Over half are from lone parent families and most are caring for ill or disabled mothers. In 1998, 86 per cent of young carers were of compulsory school age; 57 per cent were girls and 43 per cent were boys; 14 per cent were from minority ethnic communities.

Most young carers (63 per cent) in 1998 were caring for someone with a physical illness or disability, followed by mental health problems (29 per cent of young carers), learning difficulties (14 per cent) and sensory impairments (4 per cent). The proportions do not add up to 100 per cent because one in ten young carers is caring for more than one person.

The nature of care work undertaken by children ranges along a continuum from basic domestic duties to very intimate personal care. Most (72 per cent) young carers, like other children who are not carers, do some level of *domestic work* within the home. However, where young carers differ substantially from other children is in the extent and nature of the personal care work which they perform, and in the significance and outcome of the adult-like responsibilities which they take on for other family members.

Over half of the young carers in 1998 were involved in *general care*, which includes organising and administering medication and injections, lifting and moving parents. About 43 per cent provided *emotional support and supervision*, particularly to parents with severe and enduring mental health problems. Almost a third took responsibility for other *household responsibilities*, including translating (where English was not the first language), dealing with professionals, the family's money management and so on. One in five provided *intimate care* including toileting and bathing. A small proportion, about 7 per cent, also took on *child care* responsibilities in addition to their caring roles for other family members (Table 6.1).

Table 6.1 The percentage of young carers performing various forms of care work, 1995 and 1998

	1995	1998
Domestic work	65	72
General care (giving medication, lifting etc.)	61	57
Emotional support and supervision	25	43
Intimate care (toileting, bathing etc.)	23	21
Child care to siblings	11	7
Other household responsibilities (translating, dealing with professionals, money management etc.)	10	29

Source: Dearden and Becker 1995, 1998.

In many families children are involved in exactly the same types of care work as other (unpaid) adult carers. But most young carers are also undertaking the same kinds of care work that other adults from outside the family (such as Community Care Assistants) are being paid for. Where children are concerned, this care work often leads to negative consequences, as we shall see in the next section.

The outcomes for children of undertaking care work

Small-scale studies and the two national surveys of young carers have produced very similar findings on the impacts of caring on children and the outcomes for their well-being and psycho-social development. Taken as a whole the research literature on young carers shows that these children are likely to experience:

- restricted opportunities for social networking and for developing peer friendships (Bilsborrow 1992; Aldridge and Becker 1993a; Dearden and Becker 1995, 1998)
- poverty and social exclusion (Dearden and Becker 2000)
- limited opportunities for taking part in leisure and other activities (Aldridge and Becker 1993a)
- health problems (Becker, Aldridge and Dearden 1998)
- emotional difficulties (Elliott 1992; Dearden and Becker 1995, 1998)
- widespread educational problems (Marsden 1995; Dearden and Becker 1998; Crabtree and Warner 1999) (Table 6.2)
- limited horizons and aspirations for the future (Aldridge and Becker 1993a 1994)
- a sense of 'stigma by association', particularly where parents have mental health problems or misuse alcohol or drugs, or have AIDS/HIV (Elliott 1992; Landells and Pritlove 1994; Imrie and Coombes 1995)
- a lack of understanding from peers about young carers' lives and circumstances (Aldridge and Becker 1993a, 1994; Dearden and Becker 1998)
- a fear of what professionals might do to the family if their circumstances are known (Aldridge and Becker 1993a, 1994; Dearden and Becker 1998)
- the keeping of 'silence' and secrets, again because of the fear of public hostility or punitive professional responses (Aldridge and Becker 1993b)
- significant difficulties in making a successful transition from childhood to adulthood (Frank, Tatum and Tucker 1999; Dearden and Becker 2000).

Since 1995 there have been some small improvements in the overall position of young carers in the UK. For example, fewer are providing intimate personal care such as bathing, showering and toileting – the type of care work found most unacceptable by both parents and their children (Aldridge and Becker 1993a) – and fewer young carers are missing school or experiencing educational difficulties. However, these improvements are slight. The incidence of intimate care has reduced by only 2 per cent (from 23 per cent of all young

Table 6.2 The percentage of young carers of school age experiencing educational difficulties or missing school, 1995 and 1998

Age group	1995	1998
5–10	20	17
11–15	42	35
All 5–15	33	28

Source: Dearden and Becker 1998.

carers in 1995 to 21 per cent in 1998), while the overall incidence of educational difficulties has fallen by just 5 per cent (from 33 per cent of all young carers in 1995 to 28 per cent in 1998). This is in spite of a Department of Health national initiative during 1996–7 to raise awareness of young carers (DoH 1996a, 1996b).

Young carers' transitions to adulthood

While we are now more aware of how care work affects young people still classified and (in theory) protected as *children*, we have until recently had little knowledge of whether providing significant or substantial care work influences young people's transitions into *adulthood*.

In their study *Growing Up Caring*, Dearden and Becker (2000) investigated the ways in which care work influenced sixty young carers' transitions into adulthood. They show that children and young people who adopt significant caring responsibilities can be affected not only during their childhood, but also as they make the transition from childhood to adulthood.

Young carers' transitions to adulthood can be influenced and affected in a variety of ways. While parental illness or disability can occasionally *directly* influence their children's transitions, it is usually an indirect influence. The most obvious direct influence is parent–child separation. This can happen as a result of parental death, hospitalisation or local authority care proceedings. Sometimes young people feel they can no longer remain with their parents *because* of their illness; this is usually where a parent has mental health problems.

The indirect influences and effects are many and varied, sometimes positive, more usually negative. A large proportion of the young carers had missed school and gained no or minimal educational qualifications. This affected their transition from school into further/higher education and the labour market. Missing school was often linked to an absence of or inadequate service provision to sick or disabled parents, resulting in them often being left alone for long periods or having little support at times when help is most needed. Young people were sometimes reluctant to leave sick parents alone because they feared the consequences for them.

Almost all of the young carers lived in families that were in receipt of welfare benefits. Many were living in poverty. None of the parents with illness or disability were in employment. Even previously affluent families may become poor if they rely on benefits for a prolonged period of time. Half of the young carers lived with lone parents. The combination of lone parenthood and illness or disability makes entire families vulnerable to poverty and social exclusion. The absence of a second adult in the home also resulted in children and young people within families taking on additional care responsibilities. Where that lone parent had health problems, these responsibilities included the provision of care work and support. Charging policies for social care services served to exacerbate poverty and resulted in some families cancelling services which were deemed too expensive or which were seen as poor value for money.

The emphasis on continuing education coupled with the lack of jobs for young people often exacerbated poverty. For those young people with caring responsibilities part-time work became difficult, sometimes impossible.

Care work can be stressful, particularly for young people living with parents who experience pain or mental distress, or who have a terminal or life threatening illness. In a few cases stress and depression were severe enough to lead to physical and psychological ill health for the child.

Helping to care for and support parents with ill health sometimes results in maturity, self-reliance, independence and responsibility. The young people in Dearden and Becker's study exhibited a range of skills and competencies that aided transitions into adulthood. Many viewed the acquisition of these qualities and skills in a positive way. However, at the same time, many young carers were denied educational and employment opportunities because of their caring circumstances: a 'Catch-22' situation. The skills and competencies that they acquired therefore had opportunity costs, and providing care and support to family members in the absence of professional, external, acceptable support services cannot be considered as a proper way for young people to acquire these skills.

Dearden and Becker concluded that a range of factors determine the quality and outcome of young carers' transitions to adulthood. While the family structure and the nature of parental illness or disability are important and inter-related influences, they provide only a partial explanation for young carers' experiences of vulnerability and transition. Other factors, external to families, have the major influence. The receipt, quality and timing of professional services and support, and the level and adequacy of family income, are critical. These interact with familial factors in complex ways, and in the importance of the various influences may well differ for each family. None the less, the authors conclude that it is the absence of family-focused, positive and supportive interventions by professionals, often combined with inadequate income, which causes the negative outcomes associated with caring by children and young people. The main factors that influence young people's caring experiences and transitions to adulthood are thus: service receipt, family income, the nature of parental illness or disability, and family structure. In the next section we consider the legislation available to help meet young carers' needs for support and services.

Legislation which supports children who are also carers

The Children Act

The 1989 Children Act proposes that children are best cared for within their own families and that intervention should only occur when necessary to safeguard the child's welfare. The emphasis is on 'parental responsibility', the combination of rights, powers, duties and responsibilities which parents have. The Act also stresses the 'welfare principle' which makes the child's welfare paramount. This principle would be applied in any court proceedings. Furthermore, courts must listen to the wishes of children subject to their age and understanding.

Section 17 of the Children Act (1989) states that local authorities have a duty to 'safeguard and promote the welfare of children within their area who are in need; and so far as is consistent with that duty, to promote the upbringing of such children by their families'. A child is defined as being in need if:

1 she/he is unlikely to achieve or maintain, or to have the opportunity of achieving or maintaining, a reasonable standard of health or development without the provision for her/him of services by a local authority
2 her/his health or development is likely to be significantly impaired, or further impaired, without the provision for her/him of such services, or
3 she/he is disabled.

While the Act does not specify what constitutes a 'reasonable' standard of health or development, there is some debate as to whether young carers should be considered as children in need of services and as children who may not have an equal opportunity of achieving a reasonable standard of health in relation to non-caring children. As we have already seen, the research evidence shows that many young carers are vulnerable to a range of health-related and developmental difficulties, and experience a series of negative outcomes.

If a child is defined as being in need, social services are able to provide a range of services and interventions, including: advice, guidance and counselling; activities; home help (including laundry services); assistance with travelling to use a service provided under the Act; and assistance to enable the child or her/his family to have a holiday. These, and small amounts of cash, can be provided to the family, rather than specifically to the child in need, if it will benefit her or him.

Young carers and the Carers Act

Young carers may be assessed as children in need under the Children Act if they meet their local authority criteria, but their needs as *carers* may be overlooked.

While the NHS and Community Care Act offers carers the opportunity to request an assessment of their needs, the Act is intended specifically for adults; young carers were not considered when the Act was drawn up. As a consequence, young carers have been unable to access this legislation but have been referred instead to social services children's sections for assessment of their needs under the Children Act. The Carers Act 1995 has closed this loophole, since it applies to all carers, regardless of age. For the first time, the needs of young carers as carers can be assessed.

The Carers Act is concerned with carers of any age who are providing, or intend to provide, a substantial amount of care on a regular basis and entitles them to an assessment of their needs when the person for whom they care is being assessed or re-assessed for community care services. The result of a carer's assessment must be taken into account when decisions about services to the user are made. The *Practice Guide* to the Act recognises that 'denial of proper educational and social opportunities may have harmful consequences on [young carers'] ability to achieve independent adult life'. Consequently, 'the provision of community care services should ensure that young carers are not expected to carry inappropriate levels of caring responsibilities' (DoH 1996c: 10–11).

However, while the Act imposes a duty on local authorities to recognise and assess young carers' needs, it does not oblige departments to provide any services to them. Thus, the needs of young carers may continue to be neglected, even where they are acknowledged, because of an overarching concern with budgets and the management of limited resources. Another limitation of the Carers Act is that it requires carers to request assessment, which necessitates a knowledge of their rights and entitlements.

However, the major benefits of the Act, as it relates to young carers, are in the way it gives formal recognition to this group of children and provides for an assessment of their needs as carers. Moreover, the Act allows for a wider interpretation of the definition of a 'young carer'. While the Carers Act refers to carers as people who provide a 'substantial amount of care on a regular basis' the term 'substantial' is not defined. The *Practice Guide* clarifies the definition of a young carer and acknowledges for the first time that young carers should not be defined solely by reference to the amount of time they spend caring. The guidelines state: 'there may be some young carers who do not provide substantial and regular care but their development is impaired as a result of their caring responsibilities' (DoH 1996c: 11).

The needs of young carers identified under this piece of legislation will be met under local authorities' duties under section 17 of the Children Act; in other words, they will be treated as children in need. This will also be the case for those young carers who do not provide a 'substantial' amount of care but who are considered, nevertheless, to be in need of services which will promote their health and development. Thus, young carers – those who provide a substantial amount of care or those who provide less care but whose health or development is nonetheless impaired as a result of their caring responsibilities – can be defined as children in need and can expect support and assistance via the Children Act, even in the absence of resources available to deliver services under the Carers Act.

The assessment of young carers

Although young carers have rights under the Children Act and Carers Act, very few have ever been assessed by social services. Of the 2,303 young carers surveyed by Dearden and Becker (1998), only 249 had received any form of assessment of their needs under the two acts. These figures are particularly low considering that all of these young carers are supported by specialist projects and therefore have someone to act on their behalf (should they require it) to request an assessment of their needs. They are also low considering that one in five young carers still perform intimate caring tasks and almost a third have educational difficulties. The process of assessment by social services of young carers was found to be variable, ranging from very poor to excellent. The majority of assessed young carers were unaware that they had been assessed by social services even after the event, and few had been actively involved in the process.

While the process of assessment is variable, the outcomes tend to be positive. Among the young people assessed, services were either introduced or increased following assessment, and most children and families were satisfied with these outcomes. It is the availability of such external support services which has a key influence on what young carers have to do within the family, and why.

Recent policy has improved the assessment procedure for *children in need* to incorporate three domains: the child's developmental needs, parenting capacity and family and environmental factors (DoH 2000a 2000b). Future assessments of children should therefore take into account the needs of young carers, the needs and capacities of their ill or disabled parents and environmental factors such as poverty, housing and so on. This should, in due course, result in better assessments of existing young carers and support for the wider family.

Childhood and care work: issues for policy and practice

Young carers' experiences of care work, and the impact on their well-being, development and transition to adulthood, challenge common understanding of what childhood is about. Because young carers are involved in adult-like tasks which require maturity, responsibility and often a high degree of exper-tise (and which would often attract a fee or salary if undertaken by adults from outside the family), there is a question as to whether it is appropriate for children to be involved in significant care work at all, or whether there are appropriate ages at which children might reasonably be expected to take on these responsibilities. So, for example, at what age should children be allowed to toilet a parent or to carry them up and down stairs? Could we define an age for these and other tasks or responsibilities? Even if it was possible to determine an 'appropriate' age, would it be desirable to do so?

The key issue here is that for healthy psycho-social development and transition to adulthood children should *gradually* increase their responsibilities within, and outside, the home. Being responsible from an early age for care work, especially intimate and personal care – those labours which would usually be associated with (paid) adult work – can seriously compromise a child's well-being and development and can lead to a number of negative outcomes, not least impairment in their transition to adulthood.

How can these negative outcomes be tackled and reduced, for the benefit of young carers now and in the future? There are a number of ways forward which need to be addressed by policy makers and professionals in health and social care, education, employment, social security and elsewhere.

First, the definition of a young carer needs to be broad and inclusive, but also as precise as we can make it. There has been considerable confusion in policy and professional circles, and also in the literature, about what constitutes a young carer. There is a compelling case that a definition should not just be based on the *amount* of care work provided by children but should also relate to the *significance* of that care to individual families, and to the *impacts* of care work on children themselves. Definitions are important. To be defined as a young carer opens the door to a set of specific rights, not least the right to a detailed assessment of need, which itself is the gateway that gives access to services and support under children's or carers' legislation.

Second, awareness-raising and training on young carers' issues needs to be widespread and on-going. Professionals need to recognise and understand that their involvement and their positive interventions with families and children can make all the difference to the well-being of all family members and can prevent children from having to take on care work in the first place. Professionals also need to ensure that young carers and their families are aware of, and understand, their rights to assessments under the various pieces of legislation and their rights to services and support. Currently few young carers are being assessed under any Act. Where children have been assessed and have received services or support this is usually beneficial and reduces their own involvement in care work. In some cases it will prevent children taking on care work.

Third, assessment processes will need to be viewed by families as a positive step. Disabled parents must feel that their needs and rights will be taken into account and promoted, and that their parenting abilities will not be questioned. Equally, young carers must feel that their abilities as carers are acknowledged and valued and that they are not patronised or ignored in decision-making processes.

Fourth, many families receive inadequate social care services, or none at all. This results in children and young people undertaking inappropriate care work. Even where services are provided they are sometimes seen as inappropriate, intrusive or too costly. Service providers need to examine the level and types of services available and also the point at which these are offered. Early interventions may prevent inappropriate roles from becoming established.

Fifth, although awareness, research and policy relating to young carers have developed, there has been little development in policy or practice regarding disabled parents. This skewed development has meant that while support for young carers has increased, some local authorities feel that the 'problem' has been solved and have done little to support ill and disabled parents in their parenting roles. This has led some commentators to suggest that highlighting the experiences of young carers serves to undermine disabled parents (Keith and Morris 1995), and that providing services to young carers deflects attention and scarce resources away from their disabled parents (Parker and Olsen 1995).

Services that support disabled adults in their parenting role are rare. While most local authorities now acknowledge the existence of young carers and mention them in community care or children and families service plans, the needs of disabled parents are rarely *specifically* mentioned or responded to. Additionally, the social security system does not recognise the particular needs of ill or disabled parents who have adolescent children. Assumptions are made regarding the responsibility of families and parents to support their children for increasingly long periods of time. Poverty, illness, lone parenthood and lack of support may make this difficult.

Sixth, social services, health, education and the voluntary sector all have a responsibility to prevent young caring from occurring, by early recognition and positive interventions which focus on the needs of the whole family. If interventions are instigated early and are positive and supportive, then young caring should not become entrenched within families nor be condoned by professionals.

Seventh, while support of the whole family should be seen as a priority, rather than a focus on parents or children in isolation, young carers projects do offer a highly focused way of recognising, valuing and responding to the specific needs of children who undertake care work. However, there is scope for young carers projects to take a more active role in supporting the family as a whole. Moreover, young carers projects should operate alongside, and complement, support services for ill and disabled people. The existence of such projects should not detract statutory organisations from their duties to arrange or provide services to ill or disabled people and to children in need as laid down by law.

Eighth, young people with caring responsibilities experience educational difficulties and disadvantages. Schools can compound these by failing to recognise the specific educational, social and developmental needs of young carers. Where children and young people do miss school, there needs to be a better, more even range of responses between punitive interventions (such as threats of court action) and collusion (by condoning unauthorised absences).

Ninth, health, social services, education and other organisations, agencies and professionals need to consider the best way of working together to deliver a seamless package of support to adults and children within families where there is illness, disability, drug or alcohol misuse, mental health problems and the like. There is also a need for national standards for the quality and quantity of health and social care support to young carers and their families. There is currently no uniformity across regional boundaries in what families can expect in the way of help and support. Families should receive help that is based on their needs, rather than where they live.

Tenth, employment and education policies in particular need to be better co-ordinated to recognise the specific needs of young carers and the 'Catch-22' situations that many of them face. In some families caring might make financial sense in the absence of grants and awards; the skills and competencies young carers develop (which some identified as important for transitions) go largely unrecognised and unrewarded in the labour market; access to education and paid work is impaired as a result of caring.

Eleventh, each family must be considered and treated as unique, with its own strengths, weaknesses and needs. Professionals must acknowledge, value and respect the reciprocal and interdependent nature of caring within families and support these relationships through a range of policies and services. Care must be taken to acknowledge and value the diverse cultural, religious and social expectations and experiences of families from minority ethnic communities while acknowledging the rights of children to a secure and healthy childhood.

Finally, children and young people have rights, and some may choose to become carers for their parents. In such cases they should have the right to services and benefits which will assist them in their role as carers. Children and young people should not, however, feel compelled to care because of a lack of alternatives.

Conclusion

Young carers need security in childhood and independence in adulthood. They need to be able to make the best of their own lives, their childhood, and the educational and other opportunities available to young people in a modern society. To secure these, the emphasis in policy and practice should be on preventing children from taking on inappropriate care work in the first place, and stopping these roles from becoming institutionalised where and when they have already begun. Policies and services which identify and respond to the needs of all family members, but in particular those which support ill or disabled parents to enable them to prevent inappropriate caring roles from developing, will offer the best way forward.

But what of those children already heavily engaged in care work? Here policy and practice should try to ensure that these children have the opportunities for a healthy and happy childhood, and that their own well-being and future as adults is not compromised by their care work and family responsibilities. This challenges us all to think critically about how services to ill and disabled parents, and to existing young carers, should be structured, what they should do, and how they should fit together. Such a re-think would mean fundamental change to the existing structures for young carers' services, and the emergence of new and empowering services for ill and disabled parents. It would also require a re-appraisal of what we mean and understand by terms such as 'caring' and 'care work'. To date, children's caring responsibilities within the home, by being defined as 'caring', have hidden its importance and significance as care work. But to define these caring responsibilities as work poses major challenges to how we understand, and then respond to, children's unpaid labour of love.

Part II

International perspectives on children's work and labour in the industrialised world

7 School-work, paid work and the changing obligations of childhood

Jens Qvortrup

In a remarkable statement, the fifth Family Report to the German Federal Government says that:

> the costs of the educational system . . . are of the same immediate importance to society and economy as expenditure on traffic infrastructure because of the superior consequences a qualified labour power potential has as an instrument for fundamental economic policy. Thus these expenses cannot primarily be regarded as an element in equalisation of family burdens.
>
> (Bundesministerium 1995: 291, my translation)

The statement is remarkable because it is one of the rare cases – perhaps the only one – where it is openly admitted in an official political report that the costs of schooling are not an investment primarily to the advantage of children and their parents. Therefore, the report argues, they do not belong to those items on the budget that are open for negotiations about redistribution between different groups in society. Instead they must be understood as a general expense in line with traffic, research, defence, public administration and the like, to be regarded as beneficial for the common good and therefore shared by all taxpayers. The German report in other words argues that educational expenses do not have a status comparable with transferred resources, such as cash payments in terms of child support and tax reductions, or in-kind support such as kindergartens.

The reasons for this position are not only that education and schooling are assets which benefit everybody in society, but also that it has so far been overlooked that parents themselves, more or less directly, contribute massively to the whole process of human capital formation. The monetary value of this contribution is estimated at DM 445,000 per child (Bundesministerium 1995: 291–3). Moreover, a calculation of the distribution of expenses between parents and the public purse demonstrates that public funds are merely 10 per cent of the overall costs. This tiny part is what the taxpayer adds financially to the upbringing of children, which means that parents have themselves to provide the remaining 90 per cent; itself a considerable burden since (in 1996) only one household in four includes children under 18 years in Germany (Statistisches Bundesamt 1997: 65).[1]

To the traditional notion of 'family burden settlement', the Family Report in other words adds the idea of 'family achievement settlement' (see also Olk and Mierendorff 1998a, 1998b) and thus also opens up the discussion about contributions of the family to society, with the purpose of bringing about a fairer balance between families with and without children. This is a remarkable step. Yet, in my view one thing is missing in the Family Report: only parents are acknowledged as partners of public authorities and as agents of human capital formation. Children are not mentioned in this capacity, which perhaps would be too much to expect. This is however what I am going to examine in this chapter. What I want to suggest is that there is an intricate relationship between children's activities, family economy and family size, and that children's activities play a crucial role in this equation.

Most observers seem to agree that children in pre-modern society were useful and an asset to the family economy, to such an extent that the Australian demographer Caldwell (1982) could conclude from numerous and extensive studies that there was a positive net wealth flow of resources from children to adults; something he saw as conducive to a high level of fertility. Now, he argues, the situation is completely reversed: it has now become an obvious economic disadvantage for families to have children, children are not in general seen as useful, and thus the fertility level is very low. I think Caldwell is right: this is how it appears and this is also how it works in practice. Parents do currently face a situation in which they have to incur losses in terms of money, time and careers to raise children. The question is, however, is this necessarily so? It is my argument that it merely appears to be so because we have failed to appreciate the part of the equation which deals with children's activities, in other words to recognise the importance of children's school work as a major input into the modern social fabric. I am therefore going to argue that in principle nothing has changed in terms of intergenerational wealth flow.

Now, as before, there is a division of labour and obligations between generations implying that children are obliged to do *socially necessary work* and that the adult generation must provide for their elders (two elements previously identified as fertility motivations). If this intergenerational reciprocity were still taken seriously and, in particular, if children's school work was acknowledged as a part of those 'family achievements' to be compensated for, it is not at all certain that the wealth flow would have been reversed. In Germany one of the main authors of the Family Report, Franz-Xaver Kaufmann, while not going so far as to include children's activities as an achievement which has an economic value, does suggest that children have been forgotten in the modern version of the generational contract (see Kaufmann 1996).

An acknowledgement of children's school work as a part of human capital formation, and thus as a factor to be taken seriously in discussions about transfers between social groups, might lead to a better economic position for families with children. Whether this would also lead to an increase in fertility and in the end make provisions for the elderly easier to manage in the future remains to be seen. This is the broader framework of this chapter, but one that has to be dealt with elsewhere. For the purpose of this chapter I am going to concentrate on children's school work and how it has been misunderstood.

Children are not 'trivial machines'

The historical *faux pas* leading to this situation was that parents or children were not, in the transition to modernity, materially compensated for their loss when, as Kaufmann has indicated, the state expropriated children's labour from their parents.[2] In Kaufmann's interpretation the problem was that parents incurred a loss, whereas he does not discuss the changed working modus of children, let alone consider their usefulness in their new obligatory occupation as pupils.

Now, are children still useful today? This is the question. Many contemporary researchers would answer that they are, by demonstrating children's extensive work for wages outside school and home, perhaps even in the family doing chores (see Morrow 1994, 1996). This is without doubt true but, as I shall argue, *this work is somehow residual and anachronistic*. The children's work that I will be focusing on is school work, because this is the part of children's work which is constituent to modern society.

Nobody is likely to deny that children's school work is an activity in the abstract sense that it involves brain, muscles and use of time, but it is not customary to regard it as an activity which contributes to forming human capital, let alone to producing and hoarding wealth in society. At the same time nobody would dare to suggest that schooling – understood as the totality of educational activities taking place in schools – is without such a value. These activities are however exclusively credited to the teaching staff, whose task it is to transfer knowledge to children. In this sense children are logically reduced to a medium into which knowledge is placed, and few thoughts are invested into how knowledge is produced and processed; yet how does one imagine it to be received, embodied, carried through the medium and made active without the help of the child's own capacities and competencies? It does not seem to make much sense to contemplate this process without taking children's active involvement into account. As Niklas Luhmann (1991) has rightly pointed out, this medium – this 'trivial machine', as he calls it – cannot exist in practice in terms of living organisms. To use a Marxian phrase, children are in this imagery the objects of simple production, characterised – like a 'trivial machine' – as vehicles for reproducing what was put into them and nothing more than that.

I doubt that anyone would subscribe to such an interpretation, so why am I describing it? It is because – despite its patent absurdity – children's school activities are nonetheless typically not recognised as useful in the sense that just and equitable consequences are drawn from acknowledging it in terms of a relationship between *obligation and reward*. I am doing it furthermore because revealing absurdities may force us to think deeper about ongoing processes. If the view of children as 'trivial machines' – like computers – is rejected, what then are children's roles in the process? If, in other words, we recognise that children are actually doing something more than acting as receptacles, we will have to define what that is. If they are not merely a medium for simple production we must explore to what extent they are taking part in extended production: that is, production the result of which is more than was invested into it, a corollary of which seems to be that something must have happened on the part of the children themselves. Perhaps even more interesting: if it is thus acknowledged that somehow extended production does take place, for instance in terms of a broad understanding of Corsaro's concept of 'interpretive reproduction' (see Corsaro 1997) – that is, if children are themselves adding to human capital formation in contributing to the enhancement of knowledge – should we not then be inclined to also include them into our systems of reward and distribution? By asking this question I am of course implying, as I did to begin with, that the issue is one which cannot be dealt with in a void, as merely an exercise in definition, but is intricately related to issues of welfare as intergenerational distribution.

Children's system-immanent activities

It is however important to understand the changing historical nature of children's work in terms of the meaning it assumes in various stages of economic development or modes of production. The renowned comparative sociologist Erwin Scheuch many years ago said that, 'similar indicators in different countries may be interpreted as functionally different, while different indicators may be interpreted as functionally equivalent' (Scheuch 1969: 173, my translation).

In the context of children's activities this means that one must be careful not to automatically interpret their work as being qualitatively equal, even if it appears to be so; in other words, it may very well happen that forms of children's work which look completely different may indeed be the same in qualitative terms, and vice versa. To be more concrete, although many children until this very day are still working manually, we have no guarantee that the work has any correspondence with manual labour a hundred or more years ago, other than the fact that in both cases children use their hands. Manual work does not necessarily have equivalence of meaning or, in Scheuch's words, functional equivalence.

In my view this is the mistake made by many researchers into child work or child labour; they appear to be saying – indeed often they launch the view *expressis verbis* – that there is a *historical continuity* in child work in the sense that children now are working manually as before. It cannot be denied that they actually do perform manual work now as before, and therefore in a sense the researchers are right; it is also true as revealed by many researchers – sometimes to the surprise of media and politicians – that this type of child work still looms large in quantitative terms. Therefore, whatever one's assessment of children's manual work, the study of it is and remains important. Yet I believe it deserves a more profound understanding, and in particular I find the continuity thesis questionable.

In the first place, although quantitatively significant, children's work is rather modest in terms of time invested compared with their school work. Children's extra-familial manual wage work is concentrated into relatively narrow age groups, say 13 to 17, perhaps in some cases from 10 or 11 years of age, while school work starts much earlier, from 5 or 7 and continues for another eight or ten years depending on the country concerned.[3] The Danish historian Ning de Coninck-Smith suggests that, in terms of manual work, the current mean work hours *per week* – four to six hours – corresponds to the *daily* work hours in 1900 (de Coninck-Smith 1997: 154). Thus it is an obvious point that the number of hours children work in school throughout their childhood adds up to dramatically more than the hours worked after school. From a historical point of view, I would suggest that a quantitative relationship between children's manual work and their school work has tentatively developed, as shown in Figure 7.1.

Figure 7.1 illustrates the secular trend in children's main activities over the past two centuries. It indicates that manual child work and school work have both been factors in children's lives throughout this period, and indeed for much longer. Two centuries ago, child manual labour was by far the more widespread, while school work represented only a small fraction of children's routines. Today manual child work is still with us, but has declined from being children's predominant form of activity to being a

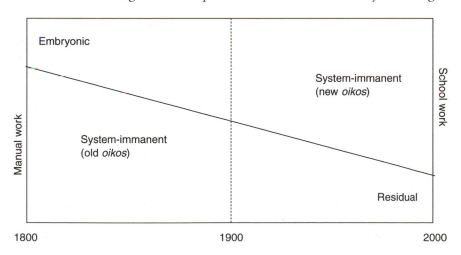

Figure 7.1 The development of children's obligatory activities

residual one; a remnant of times past to be replaced by school work as children's predominant activity today.

Much more important, however, is that from a qualitative point of view manual work has lost ground, although for other reasons. What I am arguing is that we have to understand children's socially necessary – and therefore, in practice, *obligatory* – activities in relation to prevailing or dominant ways of production, and by using the term obligatory activities I am abstracting from their particular forms.[4]

As is well known, *economic development in general* has entailed a movement from manual activities to abstract or symbolic ones, corresponding to a movement from producing use values to producing exchange values, and from simple to extended production. Quite a number of trades and crafts which were previously indispensable have disappeared, and it is presently almost impossible to find any occupation that can be carried out without knowledge of and competence in abstract symbols: letters, numbers, digits and so on. While people in general worked with their hands two centuries ago, it is a dwindling number who do so today; and even those that do must have some knowledge of the symbolic instruments. It is the demands of this new economic way of production which have forced new forms of obligatory work upon both adults and children.

The correspondence between the prevailing economy and children's obligatory tasks has been demonstrated by Coleman (1993), who shows children's embeddedness in this process in terms of an almost *parallel development of men leaving agriculture and the proportion of children remaining outside school*. These highly instructive time series cannot help but alert us to the nature of children's participation in economic development. They are a warning against theories which discursively ignore children's role, since they are always likely to have played an integrated part in it. Indeed, integration into any economy has been the rationale behind all historical struggles over children's time. Children's obligatory tasks have and always had a correspondence to the prevailing forms of production: they have a *system-immanent* nature. It is not by chance that the bulk of children's activities have changed from one system–immanent type to another. Nor indeed is it by chance that children's school work eventually came to occupy more and more of their time as the *prevailing form of production demanded greater capacity for abstract reasoning and communication in symbolic terms*. For adults, the struggle over children's time was a struggle to expropriate the value of their work with the purpose of obtaining control over their labour, something to which no planning or governing body could afford to be indifferent.

So far I have argued that children's school work has become dominant in quantitative terms and that this happened because the new economy could not survive and prosper with forms of children's activities which did not meet its immanent requirements. The problem is, however, that the consequences of this qualitative change have not been acknowledged. In particular this has been detrimental to families with children, both demographically and financially. I shall therefore deal more with this schism between the popular image, and what I see as children's real position.

Children's exclusion from the modern *oikos*?

My use of the term 'obligatory' work must not be understood in a purely formal meaning. I am rather suggesting that children have always – disregarding any legal underpinning – been forced to take part in what was deemed necessary by any prevailing economy (or as I shall call it shortly: any *oikos*). Therein lies the historical continuity of children's participation. In hunting societies children hunt; in fishing societies they fish; in agricultural societies they undertake farm work; in embryonic industrial society they work in factories; and in developed industrial society children do school work.[5] What are superficially different tasks are similar in the sense that they are *all* system-immanent because they pertain to prevailing ways of production, however different the specific forms of work and ways of production are.

Until the arrival of modernity this is fairly easy to appreciate because the *oikos* was what it originally meant: a household or, in the words of Eucken, 'a simple centrally directed economy' (see Brunner 1978: 86), in which production, consumption and planning were in the hands of the head of the household; but also a household in which each and everybody had a role – apart perhaps from the very young and the very old, who nonetheless were legitimate claimants on all resources provided. Only with modernity was this transparency lost because the central and, in the end, controlling body of the production process changed from being the household to the state. The local or the extended *household* turned into the *family* and the societal household became the *oikos*.[6]

Interestingly enough, this was also the time when classical child labour ceased to be the predominant form of child work; when schools became massively accepted and attended, fertility rates started their almost incessant decline, the old were disconnected from the extended family and children from the *oikos*. There is really nothing new in this; all of it is basically reflected in a number of dichotomies, the most famous of which is Tönnies' *Gemeinschaft* and *Gesellschaft*, which were both embodied in the *oikos* 'des ganzen Hauses', but now have been split up so as to leave *Gesellschaft* to the firm and the state, while *Gemeinschaft* belongs to the family. Brunner mentions interestingly that the concept of the family became common in Germany only in the eighteenth century (Brunner 1978: 89), while according to Ariès the 'invention' of childhood occurs slightly earlier in France.

I am taking the liberty of availing myself here of the concept *oikos* as a supra-concept, one understood as any prevailing economic organisation. At any time *oikos* involves production, consumption, circulation and the division of labour; only their forms change.[7] The transition to the modern *oikos* represented an enormous centrifugal expansion, resulting in many production units (firms) and even more units of consumption (families); in a proliferation of the division of labour, which could no longer be contained within the confines of the locality; in unprecedented levels of circulation of labour, goods, services and wealth; and all of it held together by a planning body, the national state, which was also charged with collecting taxes and redistributing revenue. Even in a capitalist market economy with private property rights, the state remains the controlling body through which labour force planning is done and the balance of the economy checked. The character of each prevailing *oikos* cannot, however, be decided merely by law but depends as much on the strength of the relationship between the actors and agents at any given time.

Among the peculiarities of the modern *oikos* – or rather how it is depicted in academic and political discourses – is that children are disconnected from it. In fact, this was the gist of Ariès' message about the birth of *childhood*. Both in popular imagery and in terms of legitimate claims, children are excluded from production and the division of labour; as consumers they merely have claims on their parents with whom they constitute a family but no *oikos*; and finally in terms of circulation they appear as objects rather than subjects – objects in the sense of raw material or potential human capital to be formed as future labour power without acknowledgement of the contributions they make while children.

Does this imagery correspond to reality? By and large it does not, I believe. Only as far as consumption is concerned are children *in reality* outside the modern *oikos,* because they do not independently dispose of 'common equivalents' (money).[8] This is the problem; and until children are rehabilitated as agents in the division of labour, and childhood integrated as part of the modern *oikos*, we do not have much of an argument for granting them status as legitimate claimants of societal resources. For parents the problem is that they are left with the obligation to provide for children, while having lost any claims on them as producers or as providers for their old age. This means that what was previously a motivation for childbearing has vanished. Children's activities may have a positive impact on the family economy, but not to an extent that even remotely balances parents' expenditure on children; meanwhile provision for the elderly has in terms of intergenerational reciprocities become alienated from (covenant) modalities of solidarity and obligations.[9]

> The thesis here maintained will be that the declining birth-rate has resulted from a ripening incongruity between our reproductive system (the family) and the rest of modern social organisation. . . . The incongruity has been frequently recognised, but there are two contrasting views as to its nature. First, the view of the cultural lag theorists, who maintain . . . that eventually it will adapt itself to the new situation. Second, my own view, that the kind of reproductive institution inherited from the past is fundamentally incompatible with present-day society and hence can never 'catch up'.
>
> (Davis 1937: 290)

It seems to me that Kingsley Davis, as the sixty years that have passed since he wrote these words have shown, is correct in asserting that there has been *a ripening incongruity between our reproductive system (the family) and the rest of modern organisation*. It is indeed a fact that this modern organisation does not assume responsibility for the family and its children. In a similar vein of thought Kaufmann has suggested that: 'The problem lies more in the . . . *structural disconnection of economy and family*: modern business is, unlike previous household economies, indifferent towards the problem if its labour force carries parental responsibility or not' (Kaufmann 1996: 16–17; my translation and italics).

Now, between Davis' pessimistic, functional realism and Kaufmann's radical Christian morality, there may be another interpretation which allows children a position in the modern *oikos*. This interpretation does not contest Davis' and Kaufmann's observations, which empirically have much support; rather it is an interpretation which looks for the logic of children's participation within any *oikos* – or in Polanyi's (1971) words, in any 'substantive economy'.

In terms of *production*, children's obligatory tasks were in the traditional *oikos* or pre-industrial economy decided by their parents – or rather by the paterfamilias – who in a local, subsistence economy purportively knew best how to make use of children's time and work; as responsible for the *oikos* the father had to decide what children were obliged to do in terms of useful work. In exchange children had a claim on resources for consumption.

In principle the basic mechanisms for giving obligatory tasks to children have not changed, although the exchange of results has. The state has now taken over from the paterfamilias as the main agent for deciding where and how children must use their obligatory time; it does so because it has the responsibility for securing the long term functioning of the economy or *oikos*. Thus no country is without an educational system, although there are variations in how far the state decides to go in fulfilling this responsibility. The state is, as it were, conscripting its children to do obligatory work in accordance with the demands of the modern *oikos* but, in contrast to the pre-industrial *oikos*, children have no legitimate claim on any revenue from the current decision making agent or employer: the state. They do get something, not as deserving participants in the division of labour, but rather for reasons predicated on the necessities of reproducing the labour force and preserving a socio-political balance. These are however tasks which are left to the parents, which means that children's material satisfaction is made contingent on their parents' position in the division of labour. State interventions do occur to varying degrees, but nowhere with reference to children's school work. On the contrary, educational investments are typically understood as a contribution to meeting children's needs, to enhancing the general well-being of families with children and to augmenting human capital; a view which, as we saw, is partly challenged by the fifth Family Report.

To what extent can one argue that children are still a part of the division of labour? In addition to a number of new divisions of labour in the wake of the change of *oikos*, including educational, occupational, geographical and gendered divisions, an overlooked form is one which has to do with the flow and duration of production. I call it the *diachronic division of labour*. In previous ways of production, processes were contained within the locality and aimed at producing use values; the number of hands the resources went through was small, and the time of production was relatively short and *converged towards synchronicity*. Currently, the opposite is the case. Any end-product has typically passed through many heads and hands, and the total production period from idea to goods or services is long. There is in other words a *growing diachronicity* in the production process. Therefore, just as children previously were part of the synchronic division of labour, their school work should presently be understood as part of the diachronic division of labour. In the first place, it takes a long time to produce a labour force that will become part of an adult labour market. The process begins in school. Next, children are not goods to be processed: as human capital they actively take part in processing themselves, and it is hard to believe that a new labour force can be processed without the active involvement of the children's own intelligence, capacity and competence. Children, thus, are active partners in the diachronic division of labour even during their childhood, because without their activities in school no production can take place later on. It is in other words not only as adults that they become useful.

Thus, the peculiarity of children's school work is that on the one hand they are producing a labour force, which in itself as a product eventually enters supply–demand equations in the labour market. But on the other hand their school work is indispensably, albeit with a delay predicated on the diachronic nature of modern economy, a precondition for the production of other goods and services, and therefore far from useless.

Finally, in terms of *circulation*, children are now as before – and this is a corollary of my analysis – both producers and consumers of wealth flows. This is obvious not only in the short run in the market for products designed for children, or the interchange with the state in producing human capital, but also in the long run in their roles as a conventional labour force and in making provisions available for older generations (although not for their own parents).

What I have been arguing is therefore that children during the transition from the old to the new *oikos* did not lose their usefulness, but that the new *oikos* took advantage of the historical transformations to reconsider and reformulate its obligations. The previous mechanism of reciprocity, according to which children had both obligations and claims on the prevailing *oikos* (parents, family, locality), was replaced by a new mechanism whereby children and their families were faced with a predicament in which children's new obligations came without reciprocal claims on the new *oikos*. The claims they had were now, as before, directed to their parents who in the meantime had lost their status as decisive agents of production and therefore could no longer count on children as partners; nor could they fully meet the needs of children without facing comparative disadvantages *vis-à-vis* both families without children and other age groups.

None of this was a result of conscious planning nor a conspiracy against families with children. In fact there were many other changes which made this step reasonable, perhaps even desirable, from the point of view of children and parents. Even if it is now acknowledged that children did often play a useful role in material terms in the past, it was a major advantage for millions of children to spend their time in schools rather than in factories. The dedication of child savers (see Platt 1977) to rescuing children from child labour and from the streets, and the concomitant redefinition of the child through develop-mental psychology and the work of progressive educationalists, produced a fertile soil for changing attitudes towards children, as convincingly described by Zelizer (1985). Another aspect of this was an upgrading of the family, imply-ing an underscoring of parents' care and in principle exclusive responsibility, which included existential, moral and economic responsibilities. There was nothing new in this but it did become more visible, not least in urban settings where the family as a 'haven in a heartless world' (Lasch 1977) became the last resort for children, even as the locality based on mutuality had lost its material underpinnings. The precondition, as Brunner says, for the new meaning of the family in terms of a particular emotionality is its disconnection from the total-ity of the old *oikos* and its emergence into the narrow urban small family (Brunner 1978: 89).

To sum up, my arguments for seeing children's school work as part and parcel of our current *oikos* are the following: first, children are not 'trivial machines' and therefore some human capital formation must take place through their activity; second, children are obliged to devote an enormous amount of time to compulsory education; third, their school work is system immanent; fourth, their activities are an integrated part of modern society's diachronic division of labour; and finally, they are now, as before, an indispensable part of the overall circulation of goods, services and wealth flows.

One might argue that these points are speculative, and it is certainly true to suggest that they need more elaboration. On the other hand, however, I would suggest that an argument that children's school work is not useful is no less speculative. I therefore challenge anyone to prove that school work is actually not useful. Where, in other words, does the burden of proof lie?

Consequences

This lack of recognition of children's school work poses a major problem for the family. Children are producing for and in the modern *oikos* but without a legitimate right to share the results. They have claims on parents, whose incomes must bear the strains of supporting children. Welfare states may socialise these costs, but as we saw earlier, in Germany only 10 per cent of all the resources directed towards children come via the public purse.

Thus throughout modernity parents have had the obligation to provide for their children, but the children's labour has been expropriated by the state. The benefits of children's school work are in the long run shared by everybody in society; particularly by business, for whom an educated labour force is supplied more or less free of charge. On the other hand, of course, for children to be supported in obtaining knowledge and the capacity to act as citizens and workers is, in itself, of value. On balance however, it is my thesis that children and their parents were the losers in this exchange, as the calculation in the fifth Family Report indicates.

Although many positive features were involved in the strengthening of the family and its ideology, it is easy to forget what was really new; namely that the status of the family underwent a metamorphosis from being the core unit in the old *oikos* to its new place as the repository for rest and recuperation for individual members in the new. Under the old *oikos* children were a part of the hierarchy – although certainly at the bottom of it – while under the new order parents became small wheels in a new hierarchy, from which children were completely disconnected.

The primary reason that this was accepted was that the new system permitted a dramatic increase in wealth and prosperity for everyone, including children. The price to be paid was – besides the misjudgement of children's school work – a dramatic reduction in the proportion of children in the general population and an increased risk of their impoverishment (Preston 1984; Ringen 1997; Sgritta 2000). This has, however, implications for my thesis, which suggests a positive relationship between the recognition of children's main activities, per capita incomes in families with children, and the number of children born.

Scholars as different as Ariès (1962), Caldwell (1982) and Kaufmann (1996) seem to agree that scholarisation was the event which most dramatically changed childhood, and at least the latter two appear to be saying that it had a major influence on the economic situation of families with children; Caldwell focuses chiefly on intergenerational relationships, while Kaufmann deals more with differences between families with and without children. None of them however grant children status as contributors.

As the fifth Family Report proposes, it is high time that the contribution of parents to human capital formation was acknowledged. If this contribution was converted into monetary terms, it might potentially create more equitable relationships between families with and without children, and thus in the end bring children back into the intergenerational contract, but now at the level of the new *oikos*. In my view it makes sense also to consider children as major contributors, and my proposal is thus supplementary to that of the Family Report. An argument for acknowledging children's school work as useful both here and now and for the future, and beneficial for the common good, is in the same vein providing an argument for equalising resources in intergenerational terms.

Whether this transfer of resources to parents will actually result in an increase in the birth rate in the long run remains to be seen.[10] It seems in my view beyond doubt that the fertility rate is a sensitive indicator of people's experience of security. If, however, the fertility level rises as a result of an equalisation of resources, there are other benefits to be achieved; first of all in the long run in terms of improved chances for rescuing future old age pensions.

In this sense the circle is closed. What in the old *oikos* was a well understood contract between three generations, because the middle generation provided for both the younger and older ones, will have a chance to become re-established under the conditions of the new *oikos*. It will again become a three-generation contract, because all adults will experience wealth flowing upwards, and not merely those without children. It is of crucial importance for the functioning of the three-generation contract that this is also felt by parents and potential parents.

Caldwell was right in suggesting that the wealth flow made a downwards turn at the time when children were placed in schools. There is however no reason why the tide of this flow cannot turn once again. The potential consequences of this are in my view positive: an improved family economy, a slight increase in fertility rates and a much better basis for the provision and care of the elderly.

Children's manual wage work versus their school work

I have used my chapter to deal with the nature and meanings of children's system-immanent work – that is, manual labour in the old and school work in the new *oikos*. Given the importance now attached to children's waged work after school, it is worthwhile to conclude with some reflections comparing the two forms more directly; the more so since I have argued that children's contemporary wage work is both residual and anachronistic.

Most importantly, it must be stressed once again that this charge does not mean that I see wage work as valueless or useless, nor unworthy of further research. Indeed, I see no reasons for contesting the main results of research on this issue, for instance that it is of benefit to the family economy and provides children with work experiences and the capacity to handle money. Furthermore, given that children's wage work is a reality, it is also necessary to address issues of their rights at work. This includes both the right to be protected against unhealthy and exploitative conditions and the right to negotiate wages and employment contracts.

Having said this, I also believe that we have to acknowledge the ambiguity with which children's wage work is met *vis-à-vis* their school work. Children's paid work appears to some extent to be wanted by children, encouraged by a considerable number of firms and at least tolerated by many parents, whereas it is normatively a twilight activity, resisted by the trade unions and legally opposed by the state. Thus, on the one hand, despite the fact that it is often opposed and usually unlawful, it is nevertheless the kind of work, perhaps the only kind of work, for which children get some normative recognition, at least among children and some parents. Further-more, it is definitely the only one which gives them in exchange money as 'a common equivalent', access to the consumer market, some freedom *vis-à-vis* parents and status among peers. The promises given by adults that school work involves some future exchange are neither well-understood nor well-received among children, who otherwise are told that they must eventually grow into autonomous persons. On the other hand, the recognition of children as manual workers in the midst of a society marked by abstract and symbolic work may be the final confirmation of the way we regard children as immature. Manual labour is nowadays emblematic of discarded and primitive stages of social development, and therefore suitable to the image of children as developmentally incompetent and incapable. At the same time, denying children the right to dispose of money may likewise be interpreted as a lack of trust, while adults may fear that children are neither sufficiently competent nor responsible in using money.

If ambiguity reigns as far as children's wage work is concerned, their school work is simply not recognised as useful since, typically, it is seen as part of children's socialisation rather than as a constructive activity. And in contrast to children's wage work, there is no way that it is related in a positive way to family consumption. It therefore appears that, although everyone demands that children invest time and energy on education, their school activities are largely less prestigious than wage work after school hours. It is however not by chance that schooling is no longer a contested terrain. The struggle for children's time and activities is currently profoundly different from what it was one or two hundred years ago. Despite the fact that children may be normatively and pecuniarily better rewarded for engaging in gainful work after school hours, it can hardly be denied that, comparatively speaking, it is now children's manual work which is in the defensive position. Children's school work is no longer the privilege of an elite minority but a universal claim, while it is the agents of manual child work who are fighting their battles on the fringe of the dominant economy.

Table 7.1 sums up the contexts and characteristics of children's obligatory work that have been discussed in this chapter. By and large, I am suggesting that children's wage work in modern society belongs to the 'old *oikos*'. Since it is in many respects similar to unskilled manual adult labour, it may be argued that it is to the same extent part of the 'new *oikos*', that is, the contexts in terms of production, division of labour, form of labour, circulation and perhaps locus of activity. However, children's wage work is in modern society not an obligatory task; it is optional, even if it may be demanded by parents and felt to be necessary by children. There is furthermore no relationship between children's obligatory work – their school work – and their claims on or rights to societal resources. The economic responsibilities for children are no longer connected with the beneficiaries of their work – the state or society as a whole – but now (as before) with parents, who no longer specifically enjoy the fruits of their children's work. Whatever the argument in favour of children's wage work, it is

Table 7.1 Children's obligatory activities: contexts and characteristic differences and similarities between old and new *oikos*

	Oikos	
	Old	*New*
Production	Simple/use value	Extended/exchange value
Division of labour	Synchronic	Diachronic
Form of labour	Manual	Symbolic
Circulation	Local	Societal/global
Locus of activity	Locality	'Society'
Claims/rights to resources	Yes	No
Obligations to work	Yes	Yes
Economic responsibility for children	Parents/locality	Parents
Beneficiaries of child obligatory work	Locality/family	'Society'

bound to be residual because their school work will not go away. On the contrary, it is likely to become even more demanding of children's time and effort. Children's waged work therefore unequivocally remains a spare time activity over and above that required by the demands of schooling, as Kanitz (1970) has already observed.

Irrespective of the reasons that children may give for working for wages, among them their objection to schooling as boring and inappropriate to modern society's reward system, ideally – from a child's point of view as well as theoretically more satisfying and consistently system immanent – I would suggest two small changes to the pattern shown in Table 7.1 under the new *oikos*: namely that 'no' is made into a 'yes' under 'claims/rights' and that 'parents' are changed into 'society' under 'economic responsibility'. These two small alterations would however mean a fundamental change, if not a revolution. They would admit that children's school work is socially necessary and a contribution to human capital accumulation. This admission would logically provide children and their advocates with a licence to negotiate with the state or other public authorities over their legitimate share of social production as a reward for what they contribute to the social fabric. It would be an acknowledgement of their useful work in line with that of their parents, as suggested by the fifth Family Report.

Notes

1 The value of parents' taxes is included in the 90 per cent; thus the 10 per cent mentioned is the contribution of all taxpayers barring parents.
2 'With the introduction of the general school obligation, child labour eventually disappeared without an awareness of the consequences for families. In reality it

was to do with a state legislated expropriation of parents as far as the labour force of their children was concerned' (Kaufmann 1996: 15).

3 I am here not dealing with *écoles maternelles*, let alone kindergartens.

4 I use the phrase 'ways of production' rather than 'modes of production' to avoid confusion with a strict Marxian understanding of the latter.

5 This description is admittedly shorthand; there are many other children's activities which are cultural in nature but nonetheless indispensable. Thus, Schildkrout describes the situation in the Muslim city of Kano, Nigeria, where women (through the so-called *purdah*) are secluded, and

> Children are the links between the secluded women and the outside world . . . they can act as intermediaries between the male and the female domains . . . perform errands, carry information, buy and sell food, including the ingredients for daily cooking, and help women in their income producing activities. . . . Although *purdah* makes women more dependent on children than they would otherwise be, such uses of child labour are not restricted to Muslim societies in West Africa. It is simply that in these societies the use of children in this way, which occurs elsewhere, is what enables the seclusion of women to persist and to be valued as a sign of high status of men.
>
> (Schildkrout 1980: 486; see also Caldwell 1982 for similar examples)

6 Please note the comparative perspective even at this level: households understood as *oikos* continue to exhibit similarities in terms of the meaning of tasks, while at the same time the *discontinuity* is apparent as far as the concrete operations are concerned.

7 One could probably have chosen instead to use Polanyi's framework 'economy as an instituted process', which underlines the continuity in the various forms of economy (Polanyi 1957). He here distinguishes between 'substantive economy' and 'formal economy'; the latter relates to the special case of economy (e.g. a market economy), while the former – as explained by Dalton in his Introduction to the book – means that

> every society studied by anthropologists, historians, and economists has an economy of some sort because personal and community life require the structured provision of material goods and services. This is the minimal definition of economy which calls attention to similarities among economies otherwise as different as those of the Trobriand Islands, an Israeli *kibbutz*, a twelfth-century feudal manor, nineteenth-century Britain, and the present-day economy of the Soviet Union. *These very different economies have in common that they make use of natural resources, technology, division of labor and, frequently, practices such as external trade with foreigners, the use of markets, and some form of money. But the specific institutionalisation of these features may vary radically among economies.*
>
> (Dalton 1957: xxxiii, my italics)

The term *oikos* is easier to handle than 'substantive economy'; see also Polyani (1957: 16), where Polanyi himself refers to the Greek *oeconomia* – the etymon of 'economy' – as the principle of *householding*. A similar distinction is made by Coleman, who talks about a change from a *primordial* structure to a *purposive* structure, 'the world of corporate actors'. See Coleman (1993, chapter 22).

8 The irony is of course that the only way in which they get some independent access to the modern consumer world is by availing themselves of activities that are not system immanent, namely manual work for wages!

9 A conflict of interest has arisen that pits

> *The interest of parents or potential parents in spending their resources on themselves*

versus the interest of the broader social order in spending their resources on the next generation. This conflict of interest arises only when the intergenerational family is no longer the basic building block of the society, and persons in one generation are not dependent – financially or psychologically – on the success or failure of their own progeny, but on the overall success or failure of the generation that succeeds them in the society as a whole. This conflict of interest exists principally in the most advanced societies in Europe and America.

(Coleman 1990: 604, original italics)

10 I do not deal with the practical political question of to whom the transfers are to be addressed – parents and/or children – or the age at which children can be trusted as receivers. My main message is that the family should be granted a larger share, although I admit that for children it is also important to obtain capacity as consumers.

8 Hidden sources of knowledge of children's work in Norway

Anne Solberg

Over the last few years children's work has received growing attention within both the social sciences and society at large. There is today a theoretically and methodologically sophisticated body of knowledge of young people's work experiences, often combined with a serious social commitment to addressing the implications of this for children. The present situation is enviable compared to that of two decades ago when I discovered working children on the coast of northern Norway, and took on the task of bringing them into sociology. At that time 'work' and 'adulthood' were almost synonymous. Correspondingly, 'play' and 'socialisation' defined 'childhood'. Those studying former times and distant people were by and large the only scholars to connect 'work' with 'childhood'.

In this situation, with only rudimentary theories to build upon and very few colleagues to exchange ideas with, I soon found myself in quite an isolated position in which I was left mainly with my informants for conversation. However, little by little I became aware that there is a potential for gaining knowledge about social reality by studying ones own research relations in ways largely unused by social scientists (Solberg 1996).[1] The aim of the present chapter is to throw light on some hidden sources of knowledge of children's work, which we usually do not bother to account for but which nevertheless may have a formative influence on the outcome. Looking back at my own first steps in researching children's work, it is obvious to me that many of the time-consuming fumblings and long detours that it seemed to involve were efforts to break through prevailing ways of conceiving children's work in particular, and the early period of human life in general. Nevertheless, within this general process I want to discuss the four routes through which I became increasingly aware of the role of work in children's lives, routes which, in different ways, allowed me to go beyond the prescribed ways of thinking of the time and reflect upon this from a different perspective.

The first of these routes took me from curiosity about a peculiar empirical observation to attempts to make this observation more valid by placing it within the framework of 'proper' social science. This route towards treating children's work with greater rigour proved a risky one since it meant bringing my observations within 'authorised' ways of thinking about children: ways of thinking that did not necessarily allow human beings the space for social action. My resolution of this was to look more closely at what was going on, with the intention of letting the diversities of social life generate a basis for questioning these authorised views. The second route involved accepting that social phenomena cannot be seen as existing outside, or unconditioned by, ourselves as research instruments. Consequently, our own varied life experiences have an impact on our scientific work. In my case, this arose from a number of exchanges which took place between my private and professional life while I was studying children's work, and which brought a productive flexibility to my conceptualisation of the activities of children.

The third route involves a movement through statistics. Through my work on public statistics on domestic labour, I became increasingly aware of the position of children in contemporary thinking. From this work, I observed that children were present in the statistics only as objects to be worked upon and this motivated me to produce data of my own. Copying the standardised ways of generating statistics of domestic labour for the adult part of the population proved productive for my decision to treat children's involvement in the daily running of the household as *work*. Finally, reflecting on the making of texts is the fourth route to knowledge that will be discussed. I shall explore some of the ways in which I have become aware of an inherent 'adult voice' in the representation of childhood and work, and how through this awareness I have managed to avoid passing on unwanted influences in my analysis of children's work.

The awareness of children's work through close observation

My sociological interest in children and childhood arose in the 1970s, while I was engaged in a community study on the coast of northern Norway. While observing the fishermen at work on the quay on one of the first evenings of my stay, I noticed something which made me curious: three or four boys, the youngest not more than 9 or 10 years of age, seemed to be taking part in the work. Moving closer to them, I could see what they were engaged in. As the fishermen were cleaning the fish and cutting off the heads, the boys picked them up, threaded them on a stick and then removed the outer parts so that only the tongues were left. The boys would later on, I was told, offer their products for sale to the local households since I learned that fried cod-tongues were considered to be a delicacy. For a period of time I left the tongue-cutters on the fringes of my research interest, as a peculiar phenomenon, and continued to concentrate on what I perceived to be the real working life of the community, the work in which the adults took part. Gradually, however, tongue-cutting became my main research interest and its study became my first step in a long-lasting research interest in children's work.[2]

From the very beginning I evaluated the cutting of cod-tongues positively for a range of reasons. First, this was in line with my own observations of the boys in action. I *saw* how eager and willing they were to work. Second, this was also the view of the local people. When I showed my interest in the matter, I was told stories about children who had entered working life at an early age and earned large amounts of money. Endurance and industry were emphasised as important virtues, and early signs of these qualities were highly appreciated. The cutting of cod-tongues was mentioned with particular enthusiasm.

The discovery of boys cutting cod-tongues stimulated my sociological curiosity and rather quickly I took on the task of transforming this peculiar and seemingly insignificant activity into a serious matter worthy of sociological inquiry. This turned out to be a risky business, however. For a time my curiosity in the activities of these boys vanished and I soon found myself 'locked' into both a process of abstract thinking and a set of implicit assumptions about what children's life was and should be like. Returning to academia which viewed favourably permanent settlements on the outskirts of Norway, the tendency was to see children's work in the fisheries as a crucial element in the preparation for future adult life. My concern, however, was to direct attention to the significance of children's work for the present as well.

My most pressing task was to redefine the image of children's work and to this end no further observations were necessary. I wanted to replace the older images of working children drawn from the earlier period of industrialisation, images that I had stored in my memory since my own early childhood, with this recently discovered image of boys at work. Against the depiction of pale and unhealthy child miners deprived of play and schooling, I wanted to present a picture of the strong and healthy tongue-cutters, engaged in easy work, getting plenty of fresh air and generally enjoying what they were doing. It was a matter of course for members of the communities in which these boys lived and worked, and increasingly for myself, that work was a much sought-after activity and that the prime motivation of children was money. At the time, this did not seem to be an issue that needed further exploration. Rather the core issue was that they were not obliged to work, but did so voluntarily. When I learned that the tongue-cutters, in many ways, formed an economic elite among the children, I added another positive mark to my evaluation.[3]

The Swedish sociologist Rita Liljestrøm (1979) provided support for my next step in establishing children's work as a matter of serious sociological enquiry. She was concerned about children's contemporary societal position, their segregation from adulthood in general, and their non-participation in work in particular. A similar critique, although undertaken at a more concrete level, was also developed by two Norwegian educators (Linge and Wille 1981). In their study of day care for children, Linge and Wille make a number of suggestions for changing the daily running of day care provision in order to compensate for the lack of what they saw as the real participation of children. Their recommendations contained two main principles. On the one hand the staff should offer children the opportunity to undertake useful tasks, like setting the table, answering the telephone and taking out the household refuse. Inventing tasks to make the children feel they shared in the running of the day care household would not, according to the educators, have the same positive implications for either the children's upbringing or the on-going quality of their lives. On the other hand, their recommendations also contained a warning not to give children too much responsibility. While children's involvement in the running of their day care provision should be real, the tasks should be properly adjusted to a level appropriate to the children's development.

In my study of the fishing community, I made use of both these principles as schemas of comparison. A considerable number of the things that were often pointed out as missing in the critical accounts of modern childhood were to be found in my fishing community. Being a child on the coast of northern Norway seemed to mean integration into the central parts of community life. Besides obtaining informal education for work within the fisheries in the future, the working children possessed, in my evaluation, a particular welfare dimension in their lives which was lacking from the lives of children in contemporary society at large. They were permitted entry into activities that had a high degree of significance to the community. Participation in the fishing industry was certainly not invented to make the children feel useful; rather, the activities went on as part of the broader business of the community, among which the significance of the boys' tongue-cutting was obvious to everyone.

If I had left my interest in children's work here, this still rather abstract picture might well have persisted. However, as I continued to look closely at social reality, a further serious challenge to my analysis appeared, since I learned that there was a scarcity of work and that the majority of children did not have access to it. As it became apparent that work was unequally distributed, it appeared that the segregating elements to work and community life were now more distinctive than the integrative ones, and that for some children work could be a cause of exclusion as much as of inclusion into the life of their communities. The notion of what constituted the 'real' role of work in children's lives was also challenged when I added another community to my sample. In this community, the fishermen used a different technology, in which children were involved in baiting long fishing lines. Here, the children formed a far more significant part of the local work force than did those who cut tongues and, while tongue-cutting was the exclusive work of boys, baiting these lines meant work for both sexes and for an age range from those still at school to the old.

Baiting the fishing lines was obviously 'real' participation in the activities of these communities, and there was plenty of it to go around. But I also became interested in whether or not the workload was properly adjusted to a child's level of development, given that a child was expected to work at this for two or three hours each weekday; and that from time to time the children didn't fully enjoy their work commitments. Decisions on how frequently to go out fishing were taken by the fisherman on the basis of weather conditions and the prospect of catches. A certain number of long lines had therefore to be finished at a certain time. Within this framework, it was a matter of course not to make too many exceptions based on the children's ages. To me, the almost complete absence of age grades as a structuring principle in including the children in work strengthened the picture of children as socially integrated.

The material conditions for children's participation in work were obvious in the fishing communities in northern Norway. Simple tasks that needed to be done by hand were available and the working time was flexible. At the same time, letting children perform these work activities seemed to presuppose the conception that these tasks were appropriate for them. In understanding this 'circle' it seemed important to understand *why* work occupied such a central position in their lives. Further concepts of childhood and what were considered 'proper' activities in children's lives could hardly be grasped directly. A more fruitful route seemed to be the need to explore the particular working life of the local children, its material conditions and its concrete shapes. When I embarked upon the fieldwork that allowed me a closer look at children while working, this helped increase my awareness not only of the diversity in their ways of living but of the variety in ways of looking in the first place.

The awareness of children's work through everyday reflection

As I finished my analysis of children's fishing work and moved with my family from northern Norway to a suburb of Oslo, where I had no expectations of finding children who worked, I was very soon surprised to discover that they did. The first time I noticed this was when someone rang on my doorbell to sell flowers. It was a boy of about 11 or 12 years old and he reminded me of the boys in the fishing communities selling cod-tongues. His height was about the same as theirs and he was similar to them also in his way of approaching me. Enthusiastically, the flower seller convinced me, as the tongue-cutters had previously done, that what he was selling was just what I needed that day.

Accepting his offer, I took the opportunity to ask some questions about his work and, from what he told me, the business in which he was engaged seemed to bear some important resemblances to the tongue-cutting business. Just like the tongue-cutters, the flower-sellers were closely connected to a broader chain of work, mostly involving adults. Neither group was regularly employed but they worked by some sort of arrangement with adults, and how these adults made their work arrangements was decisive for children's employment. 'If you want to sell flowers, you have to be around when the flower-car comes', they told me. 'If the man in the car recognises your face, or you come with someone else he knows, you will be allowed to sell.' After becoming acquainted with the flower-selling business, I then became aware of numerous young sellers coming to my door, offering a variety of products, such as 'snowballs', magazines and lottery tickets. In my neighbourhood I ran across other categories of children working as well, most of them roughly the same age as the flower-sellers. I noticed children putting advertising leaflets in the letterboxes and assisting somewhat older boys and girls in delivering newspapers. I also noticed some self-employed children and young people collecting empty bottles.

Why hadn't I previously noticed all these young workers surrounding me? These activities were certainly not, as with tongue-cutting and baiting, totally unknown to me. However, my stay in the fishing communities seemed to have sensitised me to observing children rather differently from the ways I had done before. While studying children's work in northern Norway, I had felt that it was necessary to pay close attention to the process of production simply to learn what was going on. This focus on 'doing' implied a certain ignorance of the 'doer' (Solberg 1996). Looking in the same way and with the same intensity at the familiar activities of children in a suburb of Oslo made them appear to me more 'work-like' than I had previously acknowledged.

This shift became explicit to me on one of my first visits to a local vegetable shop. Entering, I recognised a girl of about 10 years of age 'assisting' the shopkeeper. She was allowed to weigh the goods as well as to take payment and to give the change back. It was obvious to me that she enjoyed what she was doing, looking seriously engaged in making the calculations correctly. From time to time her supervisor nodded to her, discretely but undoubtedly with appreciation. I had great pleasure in observing them. The shopkeeper showed an admirable patience in guiding without interfering and it seemed to be a very good experience to be allowed to pretend to be a shop assistant in this realistic manner. I remarked with a smile to the shopkeeper, to praise them both, that she was lucky to have such a clever helper. After leaving, I realised that paying attention to the child had prevented me from fully recognising the products of her activities. Whether she enjoyed attending to the customers or not, or whatever the reasons the shopkeeper let her, the girl had still weighed the vegetables and given the customers their change. She had assisted the shopkeeper. I felt no need to use quotation marks around the notion of work.

At about the same time I had a similar experience in my own kitchen. I was busy preparing dinner and, being very hungry, had placed my 4-year-old daughter on a chair in front of the sink so that she could scrub the potatoes. My attempt to keep her busy and not worrying me was successful; she seemed content and cried out 'finished!' at the same moment as the water started to boil in the casserole. I remember I hesitated for a moment before I put the potatoes into the water; they were not as clean as I used to make them, but I nevertheless put the lid on quickly and was pleased to be a step closer to having the dinner ready. Then it struck me. Ingrid had washed the potatoes.

Embedded in my discovery of the variety of productive activities performed by children was a broadening of my notion of work. In the fishing community, children's status as workers was apparent to me through the signs of equality that they shared with the adult workers. In recognising door-to-door selling as work, my concept of work was still a rather narrow one in which children were the last link in a chain of adult participants. Even if these activities took place on the fringes of what we speak of as 'the labour market', the connections with ordinary paid work were distinct. However, when the selling of lottery tickets was referred to as 'work', the concept expanded significantly. A variety of contracts were covered: voluntary work contracts with charitable organisations, and sales undertaken as part of their obligations as members of school brass bands or local sports clubs. My choice to label both categories as 'work' was partly connected to the fact that both involved money. But the children's way of making use of the work contract also blurred the seemingly significant division between 'voluntary' and 'obligatory' sales activities. Some of those who *had* to sell welcomed this duty as an opportunity to make some money, and appreciated any chance they were given to sell more than their share.

I realised that my way of perceiving children's leisure time activities was different from how I perceived the involvement of adults. In this respect, I recalled my mother's complaints about having to produce prizes for lotteries in my school marching band during my own childhood. Colleagues and neighbours frequently emphasised their own efforts in connection with their children's participation in leisure-time activities. While some of them openly complained, others underlined the rewards to be gained from taking part. However in doing so, they all maintained and strengthened the picture of themselves as the producers. Even if I had no difficulties in remembering my own worries about selling lottery tickets, these memories circled solely around my feelings about the duties that this involved. In the same way, I had mainly paid attention to the likes and dislikes of the young sellers coming to my own front door. By moving my attention onto the activity itself, I found that the contribution of the children to the running of the organisation became clearly visible.

In doing so, I realised that I had generated a 'thinking tool' that turned out to be very useful. I became aware of how my concept of what could be said to constitute children's work had expanded during my observations, and that this widening was closely connected to the way in which I looked at it. Accordingly, I pushed myself to consider seriously whether there were other tasks undertaken by children that might be hidden from me. Thinking of contributions to the running of institutions, I was suddenly aware of an institution to which we all belonged and all assumed responsibility for running: the family household.

On reflection, I find my own reluctance to recognise housework as production, when performed by children, quite thought-provoking. I was well informed about the efforts of feminist researchers to uncover domestic activities as work and the Norwegian Central Bureau of Statistics was at the time a pioneer in the publication of information on the time-use of the population. Here formal as well as informal work was included. This basis obviously was decisive for my 'discovery' of household activities as *work* when children were involved also. To understand why my recognition of work in the family came so much later than my recognition of work outside the family, we have to bear in mind that the obstacles to looking at children's relations within the family were far greater. I shared the dominant view of society at large, as well as in the accounts of feminist researchers, that those who mattered in the division of labour at home were the adults. In this perspective, if children were present at all, they appeared mainly as work objects, either burdens upon adults or possibly elements which influenced how housework was conducted. The way I looked at children and work in the domestic sphere was particularly difficult to change because, unlike the children on the quay in northern Norway, this was so familiar to me that it formed part of the deeper layers of what we take for granted.

The awareness of children's work through statistics

There did exist a few studies indicating that children's contribution to the daily running of the household was worth counting (White and Brinkerhoff 1981; Walker and Woods 1976). Their results, however, were ambiguous. Part of the reason for this might have been the different methodological approaches these studies involved. So if children's production of goods and services at home was hidden, not only from social scientists and parents but also from children themselves, it was essential to find a mode of questioning that would allow children the opportunity to make these activities explicit. Designing a questionnaire covering eighty highly specified work tasks, a colleague and I carried out a survey of 800 11–12 year olds for information (Solberg and Vestby 1987). The results indicated that children in all parts of Norway were familiar with most of the housework tasks specified in the questionnaire and that most of them frequently took part in these activities.

Looking into this statistical material, a decision to study housework as *work* guided the development of my next phase of analytical thinking. But it proved somewhat difficult to pursue the 'workish' activities: those that were related to work but not normally included in more orthodox accounts of children's work. Rereading my analysis now, I recognise a distinct emphasis on the *products* of children's contributions: cleaning floors and making lunch for school, for example. However, I can also identify a circling around notions of necessity and usefulness, as if I doubted what the figures indicated. To what extent were the activities undertaken by children necessary? And would others take over if children refrained from doing them? It seemed reasonable to argue that, if the children were not there, someone else would have to perform most of the tasks that children did. Only in the case of two tasks did there seem to exist elements other than 'pure' production: tidying one's own room and baking cakes, pizzas and the like. High scores on frequency and time–use indicated that here we were dealing not only with the product of children's labour but also with *ways* of being at home; activities that were not generally included in the calculations of the total time–use.[4]

I thus came to the conclusion, one which I would now advocate quite forcefully, that children must be seen as belonging to the division of labour in the family. I related our informants' housework activities to similar work tasks performed by adults, as recorded by the Central Bureau of Statistics (NOS B 378; NOS C 10). Comparing the proportion of children and adults who had carried out various housework activities on a particular day, as I have done in Table 8.1, produced a picture of the two generations as occupying a surprisingly equal position.

The findings of the Central Bureau of Statistics influenced my investigation of children's housework throughout the research process. Making use of a

Table 8.1 Housework at home: the percentage of children and adults doing housework in the course of a day

	Children	Adults
Preparing food	71	63
Washing up	38	52
Cleaning	49	51

Source: Central Bureau of Statistics 1983; Time Budget Survey 1980-1; Solberg and Vestby 1987.

standardised way of classifying work provided me with a vocabulary – and a line of thinking that went with it – which was undoubtedly helpful to my project of breaking out of the dominant ways of thinking about children and their work. But accepting this standardised way of handling information also brought some unwanted constraints. This was the case with the question of gender differences. There seemed to be a 'requirement' to explore the working position of boys and girls to see if the traditional gender division of labour between men and women also applied to children. Initially this was exactly what struck me but comparing the male and female components of the two generations in the same tables made me notice something other than the well-known differences between the genders. As Table 8.2 illustrates, in comparison to the distinctive differences between men and women, the gender distinctions among children actually 'shrank'. The figures point to the four categories of family members as forming a hierarchy, with women at the top and men and children at the bottom. The women are pictured here, as we are getting used to seeing them, as the main producers of goods and services in the home. However, the position of men does not comply with the familiar picture of them as their wives' sole collaborators. They can also be seen as a group of assistants, but they are not the only ones.

Table 8.2 Housework at home: the percentage of women, men, girls and boys doing housework in the course of a day

	Women	Girls	Boys	Men
Preparing food	90	75	66	43
Washing up	78	45	30	30
Cleaning	82	53	46	27

Source: Central Bureau of Statistics 1983; Time Budget Survey 1980-1; Solberg and Vestby 1987.

The awareness of children's work through language

My efforts to maintain a way of looking at children's work activities which focuses on what they are *doing* also had implications for language. At the time when I was studying children's fishing work, there was no particular attention among social scientists to how we read and write; this was to emerge over a decade later (Atkinson 1990; Clifford and Marcus 1986). Yet the growing emphasis I wanted to place on children's *activities*, on what children were doing and how this was taking place, meant that a concern with children's positions as subjects seemed to follow as a matter of course. On reflection, it is now obvious that I had some linguistic support in attempting to do this. The discovery of children within the local fishing industry implied the possibility of adopting a vocabulary that belonged to a life of work. That vocabulary enabled me to represent children as *ordinary* industrious people (Waksler 1986).

Something similar happened in the study of children's housework. When I placed children in statistical columns originally designed for adults by the Central Bureau of Statistics, I could make use of the terms which I was familiar with from discourses on the division of labour in the home. Then children as well as adults became *producers* of goods and services at home. But when I moved my attention to activities on the margins of the labour market, like the selling of lottery tickets and the provision of care for smaller children, there was no language available which covered the activities of both children and adults. The conventional mode of talking and writing about children's involvement circled around their likes and dislikes, while the mode of expressing how adults took part emphasised effort and contribution. By recognising these differences I took some steps towards one of the central issues in the emerging sociology of childhood: how to break through our taken for granted, adult-centred way of perceiving children and the early period of human life (Alanen 1988; James and Prout 1990; Thorne 1987).

In a subsequent study my awareness of language was further sharpened. Some of the words I was about to use as I was producing a text had connotations which were not suitable for my purpose. I broke some rules about proper language and *invented* some modes of expression, which are worthy of illustration here. The study focused on everyday routines in families with school age children in which mothers, fathers and children spoke separately about their daily life through open-ended interviews (Solberg 1990, 1994). My interest was in the position of children in the family, covering not only their contribution to the running of daily life by doing household tasks, but also 'hidden work' (Wadel 1979) like managing on their own and organising their own activities. It was while writing about children managing on their own that I experienced some problems with the prevailing language.

During work days the children who participated in the study usually spent several hours at home without adult company and in doing so made use of the home in different ways to that of the rest of day. Accounting for children's use of the home after school, I made efforts to depict these events in line with the children's own ways of presenting them. Some seemingly common and 'innocent' words, which I used initially, turned out to fit uncomfortably into an analysis in which I wanted to emphasise sociability and the inventive use of the dwelling. Describing the children returning from school as locking themselves into an 'empty' house and staying there 'alone' seemed quite inappropriate. The dwellings were certainly not 'empty' and my informants not 'alone' when they were accompanied by their friends when they entered their homes. In response, I decided to choose a different term, one that shared some characteristics with *empty* but which also pointed to the potential for activities within the home. I thus let the children return from school and lock themselves into a *vacant* house.

Gradually I recognised that this little word 'empty' was a central element in everyday talk and accounts about children and home. The emphasis on 'emptiness' was, I noted, accompanied by worries about the unwanted effects of social change, particularly on the well-being and development of children. Empty homes were talked and written about as requirements that often went unmet, as the term 'emptiness' conveyed a sense of parents failing to meet the 'needs' of their children or families failing to come together. Although these problems were emphasised as serious, they remained largely unexplored; the assumption was that we as adults shared a common knowledge of the 'needs' of children, but this paid no attention to the work children undertook when occupying *vacant* houses.

Conclusion

This chapter has sought to uncover some hidden sources of knowledge in the social sciences in relation to children's work and labour. Taking my own research as its focus, it has explored how processes that I experienced at the time as a series of detours now appear, on reflection, to have been productive steps in the development of knowledge about children as actors, makers and producers.

In different ways the efforts which have been highlighted here have been primarily about making breaks with prescribed ways of thinking and writing at the time I was conducting my research. Making such breaks presupposes a certain distance from the phenomenon under study. In my case it was the *exotic* nature of children's work which made me notice it in the first place. Subsequently, I also latched on to something unfamiliar about the phenomenon within my own neighbourhood, as I found myself looking at the children who worked there differently from before. In this respect, I saw children who sold lottery tickets in and around the places where I lived in the same way as the cod-tongue cutters of northern Norway. Turning my attention to the households, I kept a distance from the familiar, from washing up and cleaning, by handling the data in a somewhat irregular way. I insisted on restricting my analysis to the efforts being made, the frequency with which children took part and their use of time. In this pursuit, I rejected requests from my colleagues to go into questions which were proper as far as they were concerned, in relation to children.

Looking back I see now that I also brought an element of this strangeness to the making of texts about children and their lives. My visit to the fishing community opened the possibility of making use of a vocabulary connected to working life. Actors in the local context 'supported' this choice by recognising children as persons producing goods and services. Social science colleagues were also ready to accept the cutters of cod-tongues as part of the work force. But by adopting phrases like 'division of labour at home' and making space for children in the 'domestic work force', I created a picture of family life which to most people was somewhat strange. As I see it today, this textual strategy was only partly successful. Some of my readers obviously widened their ways of perceiving children within the family. To some others, the unfamiliar seemed to be read as irrelevant.

The purpose of all these reflections is educational. I have used my own research history to show that social scientists use sources of knowledge that they ordinarily do not account for, either because they are unaware of doing so or because they think it is not important. Then these sources become hidden. Making them explicit may influence other researchers to make use of them, or recognise that they do so. Of course, my experiences from studying children's work in the late 1970s and on into the 1980s cannot be applied directly to the study of children's work today. Our theoretical and method-ological basis is now more advanced. Nevertheless, my reflections may still be valid since there may be some questions built into them which are worth considering for those still studying children's work today. I will finish by indicating some of them.

One question to ask is whether there are some 'risks' connected to the present situation where child research has moved from the periphery to play a more central role in the social sciences. As I have shown in the case of the fishing community, my efforts to make children's work into 'proper' science made me withdraw from fieldwork for a period. It was when I took the time to 'immerse' myself in the diversities of small jobs for children, some of them seemingly insignificant, that I was able to establish the tools needed for questioning current theories. Later on, it was children's detailed accounts of their daily lives that brought the necessary material for questioning the assumptions about children inherent in the way we talk and write about them. Is there a possible risk that the theoretical basis available today offers a too 'comfortable' frame of reference for empirical investigations? Is it worth considering how to increase the chance of challenging the dominant theories of today by the meticulous and detailed analyses of odd activities?

Another question is whether we fully acknowledge and make use of everyday reflections as a source of knowledge? To me, doing child research has repeatedly underlined the fact that *how* I look is decisive for *what* I see. On reflection I recognise that I probably took a number of important analytical steps towards that understanding, not so much while I was actually researching at my office or in the field, but in my private life. Moving from the University of Tromsø to the University of Oslo did not imply any significant challenge to my conception of childhood. However, my new suburban surroundings offered opportunities to reflect on my previous thinking, which I so far had taken for granted. Since we are positioned in our own culture as adults, and most of us also as parents, we may have difficulties in finding the necessary distance to reflect upon adult ways of perceiving children and childhood. This probably touches upon our deeper layers of awareness. These conceptions may be more accessible to change in a context similar to the one in which they were basically formed.

Notes

1 This attention to our own research relations also involved the question of how young informants may influence the research encounter (Solberg 1996: 60–2). See Christensen and James (2000) for a fuller discussion of the potential in the recognition of a reflexive stance adopted by children who participate in the research.
2 The cod-tongue business – and other kinds of children's work – are presented at more length in Solberg 1997.
3 The point that working children may form a well-to-do part of the child population was later supported by others, for example Morrow 1992.
4 These *ways* of being at home were later explored in a study of how children take part in the organisation of daily life, and how they make use of the home (Solberg 1990: 94).

9 Adolescent part-time employment in the United States and Germany

Diverse outcomes, contexts and pathways

David M. Hansen, Jeylan T. Mortimer and Helga Krüger

Youth employment in the United States is not a recent phenomenon. Prior to 1925, the majority of adolescents entered the labour force before the age of 15 as full-time workers. With the introduction of compulsory secondary education, full-time employment among high-school age youth dramatically declined; adolescents remained full-time students at least until the age of 16. However, in the United States between 1940 and 1980, adolescents increasingly combined school with work. The growth of the service industry greatly enhanced part-time employment opportunities and changed the nature of work in adolescence. Part-time employment among youth in the United States is now a normative context of development. By the late 1980s, approximately 70 per cent of adolescents aged 16–18 were employed during the school year (Manning 1990; more recent studies confirm the prevalence of this experience in adolescence, Carr 1996).

In view of its popularity, researchers have attempted to understand the benefits and costs of working while in school. The changed nature of youth employment over the past several decades has led some to question its value for adolescent development (Steinberg and Dornbusch 1991). Others have explored various dimensions of adolescents' jobs and how the quality of employment influences specific outcomes (Mortimer, Harley and Johnson 1998). Whereas employment during adolescence at one point in history may have provided opportunities to learn vital skills for adult work, current research provides a complex, and sometimes contradictory, picture of the value of youth work.

One group of researchers view the costs of employment as outweighing any benefits adolescents gain by working (Greenberger and Steinberg 1986; Steinberg and Dornbusch 1991; Steinberg, Fegley and Dornbusch 1993). They point out that workers have less favourable attributes than non-workers, including lower Grade Point Averages (GPA) and more frequent use of alcohol and drugs. Though such associations are troublesome, there is much debate about whether they result from processes of selection into employment, or whether they should be construed as the consequences of working.

A different picture of adolescent employment emerges when researchers consider the quality of adolescent work. There is evidence that working in a high quality job protects adolescents from behavioural problems otherwise associated with employment, such as substance use (Bachman and Schulenberg 1993). Substantial evidence for the value of part-time employment comes from the Youth Development Study (YDS), a longitudinal study of urban youth in the upper Midwest. In general, young people working in higher quality jobs were found to gain confidence and develop positive occupational values. Moreover, several studies have shown that adolescents who work more intensively during high school have higher incomes and other positive labour-market outcomes in the years immediately following (Mortimer and Johnson 1999; Ruhm 1995).

How can these diverse findings and conclusions be understood? This chapter attempts to disentangle this complex picture by focusing on the manifold consequences of employment, the contexts of work, and the alternative pathways available to adolescents in the United States in their pursuit of full-time work. We will see that employment comes to have different meanings from the vantage of these perspectives.

In the first section, we argue that employment can have different long- and short-term consequences. In the long term, employment can serve as anticipatory socialisation for future adult work. In the short term, part-time employment may have immediate behavioural consequences; these may be particularly deleterious if engagement in work detracts the adolescent from school and encourages premature adult-like behaviours.

The second section of this chapter focuses on the varying contexts of adolescent employment. We believe that the extent to which employment overlaps with other domains in the adolescent life space is critical. Comparing different contexts of adolescent employment suggests potential solutions to the dilemma of protecting youth from potentially negative effects of working, while simultaneously incorporating them into the social world of adults.

The third section explores what may be considered dual pathways to full-time work, emphasising schooling and part-time employment during high school. After a review of common pathways in the United States, educational and occupational pathways in Germany are examined as a means of highlighting American and European differences in young people's experience of work. The fourth and final section attempts to understand differences in the societal debates about adolescent work in view of variation in the macrostructural contexts in which it occurs.

While some recent research addresses part-time employment that occurs following graduation from high school, the focus of this chapter is on the work experiences of adolescents primarily between the ages of 14 and 18. Youth employment prior to the age of 14 is generally treated as 'informal' in the United States and is beyond the scope of the current project. Although diverse terms are used to identify young people, the terms 'youth' and 'adolescent' are used interchangeably. Finally, it should be noted that research on adolescent work benefits from longitudinal designs. Unless otherwise indicated, the findings described in this chapter are based on panel studies.

The diverse outcomes of adolescent employment

The consequences of adolescent work for youth psychosocial development and socio-economic attainment are central to the debate in the United States. Whether part-time employment is viewed as a salutary or a maleficent agent is determined, in large part, by whether the focus of attention is on long-term anticipatory socialisation, or on short-term behavioural and attitudinal outcomes. Attending to one set of outcomes while neglecting the other fails to address the complexity of employment experience among youths as they move toward adulthood. Let us now examine each of these kinds of outcomes in greater depth. (This chapter features findings from the Minnesota Youth Development Study; for a thorough review of research on the implications of part-time employment in adolescence, see Committee on the Health and Safety Implications of Child Labor 1998).

Anticipatory socialisation

Part-time employment in the formal labour market signals the assumption of a new social role for adolescents, a point of entry to the occupational world. It is reasonable to suppose that by providing experience of work-related skills, employment during high school helps adolescents navigate successfully toward the 'adult' work role. Thus, the features of work (work quality), not only its quantity, deserve attention. Despite prolific research on work intensity and work status, researchers know little about the quality of experience of adolescents while at work (Finch, Mortimer and Ryu 1997).

In contrast, empirical investigations of adult work primarily focus on work quality as a key predictor of positive outcomes. In particular, the complexity of work, the variety of tasks, self-direction, job content, and the perceived meaningfulness of work have implications for adult mental health and well-being, including job satisfaction and various dimensions of work motivation (Kohn and Schooler, 1983; Mortimer, Lorence, and Kumka 1986; Oldham 1996). Reflecting poorer work quality, stressors on the job are associated with decreased physical health (Baker and Green 1991) and other negative outcomes (Oldham and Gordon 1999).

General job skills

Through part-time employment, United States youths develop general job skills that are useful for future adult employment. These include the ability to follow directions, to get along with co-workers, to be on time, to take personal responsibility for their work, and to manage money (Mortimer, Pimentel, Ryu, Nash and Lee 1996). Jobs that create an environment for the development of these skills place adolescents at an advantage when seeking full-time employment.

According to the parents of teenagers, a primary benefit of adolescent employ-ment is that it teaches autonomy and self-reliance (Phillips and Sandstrom 1990), orientations that are perceived as vital for adult work. Reflecting this belief, parents overwhelmingly approve of part-time employment for adolescents (Aronson, Mortimer, Zierman and Hacker 1996). Parents also report that their own child's job provides opportunities to learn new skills and attitudes not taught in school.

Adolescent jobs have been described by researchers as consisting of menial and repetitive tasks, indicative of poor work quality. However, adolescents themselves may not perceive their jobs in this way. Using longitudinal data from the Youth Development Study, Mortimer and her colleagues assessed the qualitative features of youth jobs (Mortimer, Finch, Dennehy, Lee and Beebe 1994), focusing on their potential to develop job skills. Over the course of the high school years, adolescents worked in jobs that required the use of more complex skills, involved more training, and greater supervisory responsibility (Mortimer *et al.* 1994; Mortimer *et al.* 1998). Mortimer *et al.* (1994) also reported that most students gave generally favourable descriptions of their work experiences; these descriptions remained stable during high school. For example, adolescents generally viewed their jobs as providing ample opportu-nity to use their skills and to learn new ones. These perceived features of work remained stable despite the increased demand for more complex work skills over the four years of high school. While adolescent jobs may be characterised as less desirable by adult standards, novice workers continue to view them as providing learning opportunities and challenge, even as the jobs themselves become increasingly complex and require greater responsibility.

Although jobs that provide an opportunity to learn new skills tend to be associated with positive outcomes, work autonomy may not always be beneficial. Among high school age males, self-direction on the job is associated with more depressed mood (Shanahan, Finch, Mortimer and Ryu 1991). Adolescents who have more discretion in decision-making may not feel adequately prepared for such responsibility. Taken together, these findings suggest that adolescents can benefit from high quality work experiences that provide sufficient structure.

Occupational value formation

Social scientists are concerned with the development of occupational reward values because of their relation to occupational choice and attainment. Persons entering the labour force try to choose occupations and experiences that are in line with the occupational values they deem important (Mortimer 1974; Mortimer and Kumka 1982). As adolescence is considered to be an especially formative period in the development of vocational identity (Erikson 1968), it stands to reason that work experiences during this phase of life would be a potentially important part of this process.

The assessment of occupational values in adolescence focuses on the importance of the perceived rewards that are offered by a job (Mortimer and Lorence 1995; Ryu and Mortimer 1996). Extrinsic reward values concern the external rewards derived from the job, such as opportunities for advancement, income and prestige. Intrinsic reward values relate to the personal or internal rewards derived from the work experience itself and include opportunities to work with people, be of service to society, and to express one's interests and abilities. Jobs offer a variable mix of experiences that can either detract from or enhance the extrinsic and intrinsic dimensions of occupational values.

Using longitudinal data from the YDS, Mortimer *et al.* (1996) reported that the opportunity to learn new skills had a positive effect on occupational value formation. Those adolescents who perceived their jobs as providing opportunities to learn skills related to a future occupation came to see work as a potential source of both intrinsic and extrinsic rewards. There was also evidence that as adolescents entered the labour force, work stress fostered extrinsic value formation. Taken together, these findings indicate that adolescents, like adults, develop work values that reflect the quality of their occupational experiences. Further, the findings contribute to the evidence that the characteristics and content of adolescent jobs are important factors in the anticipatory socialisation of youth for adult work roles.

Proximal socialisation

The immediately observable behavioural impacts of working may not be as positive. Researchers who view adolescent employment as a negative socialising agent point to the number of hours worked as the primary culprit. While the number of hours worked per week (work intensity) during the school year is frequently found to be associated with undesirable behaviours, the causal process linking intensity and these outcomes is complex.

Academic achievement

A particularly salient concern among researchers is that working interferes with the primary 'occupation' of adolescence, that is, education. If working detracts from academic pursuits, there could be serious ramifications for future educational attainment and for adult employment. In the United States, considerable emphasis is given to academic performance in secondary schooling because of its importance in attaining higher education. A high grade point average (GPA) is especially important for those youths who wish to pursue a college education.

Comparing work patterns over a one-year period, Steinberg, Fegley and Dornbusch (1993) reported that those adolescents who entered the labour force at a higher level of intensity spent less time on homework, earned lower grades, and were less engaged in school prior to entering the labour force compared to those who remained non-workers throughout the study. Of greater relevance to the debates surrounding adolescent employment, Steinberg and his colleagues

(Steinberg *et al.* 1993) also examined changes in GPA as a function of change in employment status and intensity. Mixed findings were obtained. Among students employed for between one and twenty hours per week in the first year, those who increased their hours to twenty-one or more had a significantly lower GPA in the second year than those who became non-workers. (In these analyses, prior grade point average was controlled.) However, these students, who were employed for from one to twenty hours per week in the first year constituted just 28 per cent of the panel. Among the remainder (those initially out of the labour force or working more than twenty hours per week), the pattern of employment (change or stability in the intensity of work) had no significant effects on grades.

Thus, while there is some evidence that work intensity may lead to deleterious academic outcomes, not all data support this pattern. Mortimer, Finch, Ryu, Shanahan and Call (1996), on the basis of the YDS, reported that, overall, working long hours was not associated with a decrease in grades. Only in the second wave of data collection (grade 10) was there an association between long hours of work and decreased grades. However, in wave 4 (grade 12), those employed for twenty hours or less (moderate levels) had a higher GPA than adolescents who were not employed.

Substance use

A consistent finding from both cross-sectional and longitudinal designs is the positive relation between working and substance use (Bachman and Schulenberg 1993; Hansen and Jarvis 2000; Mortimer, Finch, Ryu and Shanahan 1996; Steinberg *et al.* 1993). Those adolescents who work longer hours are more likely to use alcohol and drugs. A number of explanations for this robust pattern have been offered (Mortimer *et al.* 1996). First, adolescents who work may be exposed to older workers whom they emulate. This may be particularly relevant in the United States and other countries where alcohol use is permissible for adults but legally restricted for adolescents. Adolescents are thus exposed to 'adult' behaviours and mimic these patterns. A second explanation is that working adolescents are thought to have more disposable income with which to purchase (illegal) substances. Third, adolescents may use alcohol, cigarettes, and drugs as a means of coping with work stressors. Finally, adolescents who are employed for more hours may become more independent of parents, and less subject to parental monitoring and control (McMorris and Uggen forthcoming).

While the causal mechanisms underlying the increased used of alcohol among adolescents who work more intensively are not entirely understood, this effect is indeed worrying. Still, it is important to know whether this is a harbinger to a long-term pattern of frequent, or excessive, alcohol use, or whether it is simply a short-term reaction to the experiences of working. Youth Development Study data indicate that four years after high school the youths who worked less intensively during high school effectively 'catch up' with their more intensively working peers, yielding no difference in drinking behaviour between them (McMorris and Uggen forthcoming; Mortimer and Johnson 1998). If this pattern is replicated for other substances, the effect of working may be best described as earlier initiation rather than increased, long-term use.

Work intensity, cumulative work hours, and duration

As we have seen, investigators in the United States (and Canada) focus on work quantity (the number of hours worked per week). However, cross-sectional measurements of adolescent work hours may not reflect students' experiences over longer periods of time. Mortimer and Johnson (1999) examined the impact of part-time work during high school on a series of behavioural outcomes. Adolescents were placed in five employment categories, reflecting their cumulative work experience through high school. These categories were based on the duration of employment (separating students who worked throughout most of the time of observation and those who worked relatively few months) and its intensity (the average number of hours worked per week during the duration of employment, either more than twenty, or twenty or less). Five employment patterns emerged: low duration, low intensity; low duration, high intensity; high duration, low intensity; high duration, high intensity; and non-working.

Confirming the findings of other studies, adolescents who pursued high intensity employment (twenty hours per week or more, on average) had higher rates of alcohol use, irrespective of work duration. However, a greater quantity of work experience was not always linked to the most deleterious outcomes.

Of special interest, low duration–high intensity employment was found to be especially problematic for girls, associated with frequent alcohol use, smoking, and other forms of troublesome behaviour. Even though these girls had less work experience than their high duration–high intensity counterparts, these behavioural indicators suggested considerably more problems for them. The high duration–low intensity pattern, in contrast, was associated with low levels of problem behaviours, despite the accumulation of many hours of work through high school (commensurate with the low duration–high intensity group). Young people who limit their hours of work are able to combine their employment with other beneficial activities; those who work intensively (more than twenty hours per week) pursue other activities with greater difficulty (Shanahan and Flaherty forthcoming). These findings demonstrate that the pattern of youth employment, including its continuous or sporadic quality, must be considered if we are to understand fully its impacts on adolescent development.

The research portrays a complex picture of adolescent work. On the one hand, there is ample evidence that part-time work experience serves an anticipatory socialisation function. Adolescents who work benefit by gaining general work skills that are potentially useful in future jobs. Occupational values, developed through early work experience, contribute to vocational maturity in making occupational decisions and selecting future careers. On the other hand, adolescents who work longer hours are more likely to use alcohol and drugs, get in trouble at school, and engage in other forms of troublesome behaviour.

These findings entail a number of implications. First, adolescent work in the United States may be better conceived of as contributing to a general 'work readiness' socialisation rather than to occupationally-specific socialisation. This is in contrast to the situation in European countries with strongly institutionalised apprenticeship programmes. Second, while the immediate behavioural impacts of working may appear to be alarming, their significance for later life adjustment needs further assessment. As we have seen, rather than signifying a long-term propensity toward alcohol use, YDS findings indicate that intensively employed adolescents initiate drinking at a younger age, but soon become indistinguishable from their peers (Mortimer and Johnson 1998).

Third, the diverse consequences of employment may be clarified by consideration of their meaning in relation to the transition to adulthood. Bachman and Schulenberg (1993) conceptualise teenage employment as part of a syndrome of precocious maturity. That is, adolescents who are employed, and especially those who work more intensively, have assumed adult-like work behaviour, and may come to take on an adult identity. The ensuing behaviours may be evaluated rather differently. On the one hand, youths who are employed may actually become more like adults, assuming desirable, 'adult-like' attributes such as being responsible, independent, better time managers, and so forth. If parents' reports are correct, these are widespread positive sequelae of employment. However, youths may also take on what they perceive to be adult-like ways of spending their leisure time: drinking alcohol, smoking cigarettes, and 'getting into trouble' (e.g. partying), highlighting the paradox of attaining adult status in the work domain but not in the leisure setting.

Considering the costs of youth employment (e.g. precocious development) while ignoring its benefits can lead to the conclusion that contemporary youth work is harmful and exploitative. While some may promote restricting youth employment in an effort to protect youths from the deleterious effects of early entrance into an 'adult' role, restrictions that are overly severe could deny young people the potential benefits of working. Excluding them from occupational experiences could diminish their readiness for adult work. Thus the dilemma: finding ways to adequately protect youths from harm while simultaneously including them in the adult social world (Eccles *et al.* 2000).

The diverse contexts of adolescent employment

Development is clearly a joint function of the person, the immediate environment, and the broader social context. The developmental value of overlapping contexts is perhaps best understood within the ecological framework (Bronfenbrenner 1979). Bronfenbrenner argued that inter-connections between life contexts are developmentally beneficial, particularly when the individual is making a transition into a new role or setting. For example, children benefit when their parents are interested, and participate, in the school context. Consistent with this proposition, adolescent work will probably have its greatest developmental benefits when there are clear linkages between contexts (Hansen and Jarvis 2000; Mortimer and Krüger 2000; Steinberg 1983).

Bronfenbrenner's insight suggests one possible solution to the 'exclusion versus incorporation' dilemma. The particular context in which the adolescent job occurs could make a difference in the experience of employment and its outcomes. Specifically, the risks of employment may be reduced when it is linked to contexts that are generally protective of youth (e.g. school or family), providing an appropriate balance between exclusion and incorporation. Although the potential value of merging work with other contexts has been acknowledged (Steinberg 1983), this hypothesis has not been examined systematically in the US context.

Obtaining a part-time job for the first time can signal to the adolescent and to adults that there has been a change in the young person's social status. This new role that the adolescent assumes, the 'worker' role, may be the only new primary role that is embraced during this period (Steinberg 1983). While adolescent jobs in the United States are not typically linked to other contexts in which adolescents spend their lives, there are employment settings that offer various degrees of overlap.

Historically, youth employment in family-owned farms and small businesses was common. Employment in family enterprises currently persists in areas reliant on farming and in urban settings among recent immigrants. The prevalence of employment in a family business or farm varies widely by region. For example, in the wave 4 of YDS (1991) only about 5 per cent of the urban (Minneapolis, Minnesota) youth reported being employed in a family business or in a job where their parents worked. In contrast, Steinberg (1983) reports that approximately 15 per cent of youths in a sample from the states of California and Wisconsin work in a family business. Hansen and Jarvis (2000), in a cross-sectional study of Midwestern youth, reported over 30 per cent of adolescents worked in a family setting. The wide variation in the prevalence of family-based employment suggests variability in the experience and outcomes of work. Working in a family business can maintain, and strengthen, crucial links with the family, while working in a non-family business does not support these links.

In a comparison of the Iowa Youth and Families Project, drawn from economically depressed communities in rural Iowa, and the St Paul Youth Development Study (YDS) data, Shanahan, Elder, Burchinal and Conger (1996) examined whether adolescent earnings have different consequences for family relationships in the two settings. While earnings were not significantly related to affective ties between parents and children or to advice giving in the urban setting, in the rural setting relations with parents improved as the child made more money. The investigators interpret this pattern as resulting from the more communal character of youth employment in rural communities. Teenagers in the rural setting were much more likely than their urban counterparts to use their earnings for what the authors called 'non-leisure spending', purposes that supported the economic welfare of the family as a whole. Youths in the urban setting were more likely to use their earnings for individualistic pursuits.

Hansen and Jarvis (2000) compared young people employed in a family business (e.g. where a parent or relative owned the business) with those employed outside such businesses. Adolescents who worked in a family business perceived greater parental support. Moreover, adolescents working in other enterprises reported being more autonomous than those working for relatives. Furthermore, in the same study, males who worked in a family enterprise reported the least drug use: less than females employed in either a family or another employment context or males in non-family employment. Males may especially benefit from closer links with the family when they are employed. Because of its reliance on cross-sectional data, the conclusions of this study, while suggestive, deserve further assessment. For example, it could be that male adolescents who choose to work in their families' businesses and farms have lower levels of drug use prior to the initiation of this employment.

Other employment contexts provide an overlap between school and work. Although most research concerns adolescent employment in naturally occurring settings, youths whose work is connected to school – through school-supervised internships, job shadowing, or other school-to-work programs – describe their jobs in more favourable terms than adolescents whose jobs are found in the 'free labour market'. In a cross-sectional study comparing young people employed through school-supervised programmes (SSWE) with those not employed in a school-supervised setting (NSWE), Stone, Stern, Hopkins and McMillion (1990) showed that youths in a SSWE reported that their jobs allowed more initiative, were more varied in responsibility, were more challenging, and were more satisfying. Similarly, youths in a SSWE were more likely to view their jobs as teaching them how to learn on the job, and to report that their job influenced their career choice.

Thus, emerging evidence suggests that linking work with other primary contexts, such as school and family, can be beneficial to and protective of youth.

The diverse pathways of transition to adulthood

Let us now consider the broader context, what Bronfenbrenner refers to as the macrosystem: the structural pathways in the transition from school to work, which vary greatly across societies (Mortimer 1999; Mortimer and Johnson 1999; Mortimer and Krüger 2000). The United States, compared to countries such as Germany or Japan, has a relatively unstructured transition pathway from school to work (Hamilton 1990; Mortimer and Johnson 1999). While youths who receive college degrees can rely on college placement services to help them find work, those who do not go through college have to find employment on their own (Foundation 1988). Because of the unstructured nature of the school-to-work transition, the connections between part-time employment and adult work are not clear.

Recent initiatives in the United States (e.g. the School to Work Opportunities Act) have attempted to remedy this situation (Borman, Cookson Jr., Sadovnik and Spad 1996). However, most youths in the United States must negotiate the transition without formal help. This stands in stark contrast to other countries. For example, in Germany strongly institutionalised vocational training programmes structure early school and work trajectories, and the connections between them (Mortimer and Krüger 2000).

How do adolescents in the United States negotiate the school-to-work transition? More specifically, what pathways to adult employment are available to youths in the United States and how does this compare to the experience of youths in Germany?

Employment and economic attainment

Clearly, educational attainment does have ramifications for occupational success (Kerckhoff 1990). The manifest purpose of education is to provide knowledge and skills for successful adaptation to adult occupational roles (Mortimer and Krüger 2000). However, education is not the only pathway to adult occupational attainment. Experience in the work role can also serve as an important pathway to occupational attainment.

One of the most consistent findings in the research literature is that part-time work among adolescents has positive consequences for subsequent employment up to ten years after graduating from high school; it also reduces the amount of time youths spend unemployed (Carr 1996; Mortimer and Johnson 1999; Steel 1991; Stern and Nakata 1989). Marsh (1991) reported that the number of hours worked during high school was associated with a decreased risk of unemployment in the two years following graduation. Other researchers have found similar patterns (Mortimer *et al.* 1998; Ruhm 1995; Steel 1991), though the causal impact of work experience remains controversial (Hotz, Xu, Tienda and Ahituv 1998).

Employment during high school can also affect future economic attainment (Mortimer and Johnson 1999; Ruhm 1995). Data from the National Longitudinal Study of Youth (NLSY) indicate that having a job in the senior year of high school predicts earnings, wages, benefits and other indicators up to nine years following graduation (Ruhm 1995). For the NLSY sample, those who worked at higher intensities during high school experienced greater economic gains than those working at a lower intensity. Data from the YDS indicate a similar pattern to that of the NLSY sample for males but not females (Mortimer and Johnson 1999). High intensity male workers reported the highest annual earnings four years beyond high school. Among female workers, higher income after high school was accounted for by prior socio-economic differences.

Research further indicates a continuity of work experience between high school and the years that follow (Mortimer and Johnson 1999). Data from the YDS revealed that students who worked at a high intensity during high school entered full-time employment more quickly following high school. Low intensity employment during high school was associated with continued part-time employment (which, in turn, was linked to higher educational attainment). Taken together, research clearly demonstrates that youth employment in the United States is a pathway to adult work, despite the absence of formal institutional linkages. How prominent the adolescent work pathway is (compared to the educational pathway) may depend, in part, on the socio-economic resources of the youths.

Data from YDS show that ninth graders who had little interest and lower levels of achievement in school were more likely to take on jobs characterised by high intensity work. There were also significant relations between parental education and high school work experiences (Mortimer *et al.* 1998). Specifically, adolescents from families with lower levels of education reported more 'adult-like' work experiences, of both a positive and negative character. These youths reported that their jobs offered greater access to extrinsic occupational rewards (e.g. higher status among their friends, better advancement opportunities) and greater opportunities for learning job-related skills. They also were more psychologically engaged in their jobs. However, they also reported more work-related stressors, experiencing work as simultaneously more demanding and more involving, and thus more 'adult-like'. For young people from lower socio-economic backgrounds, work may constitute a means of gaining adult-like work skills. For these youths, greater investment in work during high school may coincide with more immediate goals of adult employment after high school.

From their study of African-American youth, Entwisle and her colleagues (1998) also concluded that those from poorer family backgrounds obtained employment that was higher in quality than their working counterparts who were less disadvantaged. They argued that these youths, who had little interest in academic pursuits, may find work experience during high school as an alternative path to obtaining adult employment. Given that grades achieved in high school show no relation to occupational success for those who seek full-time employment immediately following high school (Rosenbaum, Kariya, Settersten and Maier 1990), it is no wonder that these young people make a greater investment in work.

Thus, socio-economic status appears to have a clear influence on the experience of early youth employment. Though educational attainment is the surest route to occupational attainment, part-time employment may serve as an alternative pathway to full-time work for those with little propensity toward school. Young people from lower socio-economic backgrounds may take on work that is more adult-like in a positive sense (providing more learning opportunities and responsibilities), but they also experience more negative aspects of adult work (e.g. work stressors). In contrast, youth from more highly educated backgrounds, and those who themselves are more interested in school, tend to limit their investment in employment during their high school studies by pursuing low intensity and less engaging work.

In the United States then, youth employment may provide two distinct pathways. One pathway leads directly from high intensity high school employment to full-time adult employment. For the second pathway, low intensity employment may serve as a complement to the academic pathway. Attention will next be given to how the varied pathways in the US compare with those available to German youth.

German realities: welcomed versus tolerated adolescent work

A comparison of the issues and debates surrounding adolescent employment in Germany and the United States illuminates the importance of the broad macrosocietal context for understanding the implications of youth employment for development and attainment. The German debate on students' part-time work assumes quite different contours depending on the context in which that employment occurs. In one context, part-time work is accepted, desired, and welcomed; in the other, it is seen, as in the United States, as involving a problematic coupling of activities.

The German school system offers three levels of qualification. First, adolescents may finish general education at the level of the *Hauptschule*, at the age of 15 or 16 (25 per cent of the cohort do this). Second, they may finish at the level of the *Realschule*, at 16 or 17 (34 per cent of the cohort). These two streams feed into vocational education, which prepares students for specific occupations in a highly regulated labour market. Third, students may finish their education through the *Gymnasium*, at 19 or 20 (about 35 per cent of the cohort), and then take up an apprenticeship or go on to university. Only about 6 per cent of the cohort drop out with no formal qualification (Alex and Stoos 1996; Bundesministerium für Bildung 1995; Heinz 1996; Krueger 1999).

The difference in the way adolescent work is perceived and evaluated relates to whether it takes place within or outside the formalised pathways to adult occupations. The minority who pursue the higher educational path (historically, more advantaged youth) expect to stay in full time education (in the *Gymnasium* or university) prior to entering professional and managerial occupational positions. The majority of young people, even in recent cohorts, take a different path: through the vocational education system which typically involves apprenticeship placement (between the ages of 16 and 20). Having completed this training, the young person moves into one of 498 formally regulated middle and lower level occupations in the German economy (Stooß 1997).

While undergoing their general education (in the *Hauptschule, Realschule* or *Gymnasium*), adolescents may undertake part-time employment. The German debate, in so far as it envisages this experience, in some respects parallels that in the United States. Students sometimes perform jobs similar to those undertaken by American youth: working as newspaper deliverers, baby-sitters and so on (young people are not permitted to work in the industrial or service sectors). Since the German programme of study is more strenuous than that of a typical US high school, however, students have relatively little time for such commitments.

As in the United States, it is thought that such work makes positive contributions to becoming an adult, by instilling confidence, independence, reliability and the like. However, the more highly qualified young people (those who attend the *Gymnasium*) are considered to be full-time students until they complete their university studies and enter the labour force. There is a strong consensus that they should dedicate their time to learning, not to working. Their living conditions should be conducive to optimal preparation for work through studying. Only when they have finished their studies should they actually enter the labour market. To ensure that students are not distracted by the need to work, they do not have to pay tuition fees, even at the university level. Every placement is tuition free in the conviction that qualified youths should not be excluded from higher-level opportunities because of a poor family background.

However, at a somewhat later stage (from 19 to 26 years of age), while attending university, many students supplement their standard of living and educational grants (provided by the government for those from low income families) by various part-time jobs; in 1993, 53 per cent of university students did some kind of paid work while studying (Griesbach and Leszczensky 1993). These jobs tend to be frowned upon, especially when they are not linked to the students' programmes of study and when they are perceived as delaying the students' graduation. According to some news accounts, up to 70 per cent of students work part-time, and there have been calls for high tuition fees to force students to concentrate on their studies and finish them in a shorter length of time (for an overview see BUS 1999).

Paralleling the emerging American focus on the quality of adolescent work, recent commentators distinguish between 'bad jobs', which young people only pursue for the money, as they are not connected to future labour market positions and internships, nor jobs that will help students to establish informal networks for further labour market promotion, and 'good jobs' that offer these advantages. This debate, in the context of the highly regulated German occupational structure, takes a different form from that in the US. In the US, good adolescent jobs are considered to be those that foster general job skills and positive orientations towards work by providing learning opportunities, good supervisory relations, and psychological engagement without undue job stress. In Germany, even those jobs that are seen as 'good', are viewed with some concern since they signal an erosion of the once-secure pathways from university to the (now shrinking) professional and managerial labour market. In their absence, university students attempt to establish their own informal networks.

University students' growing engagement in 'good' – and therefore tolerated – jobs is greatest in fields with more open labour markets such as business management, economics, new technology, computer science, psychology, and sociology. Those planning to be teachers, physicians, and lawyers rely on other, more fully institutionalised pathways (Bundesministerium für Bildung 1995).

It is with respect to the much larger group of German youths who pursue vocational training following their general education that adolescent employment receives widespread approbation. Indeed, the debate is not about whether these young people should work; working in an apprenticeship position is considered to be a fully legitimate and desirable pathway to adult employment. Instead, concerns focus on the availability of placements, particularly in times of economic downturn when it may be difficult to place all aspirants to apprentice positions; as well as on the adequacy of those placements in preparing youths for future labour market realities.

In apprenticeship, the link between school and work is formally institutionalised. The adolescent spends a day or two each week in school and the remainder of the week working in a firm. During training, the employer pays the apprentice a low wage, which does not provide full economic independence from the family of origin. The low level of payment underscores the fact that the apprentice is not primarily a labourer but a learner (Hamilton and Hurrelmann 1994; Krahn 1991).

The state pays the apprentice's schooling costs, including high salaries for teachers whose university training is roughly the same as that for top-level specialists within the respective branch of the company. Work within the firm is under the supervision of a certified *Meister* (a master journeyman or craftsman with extensive work experience and further qualifications in pedagogy). The *Meister* must have 'key qualifications' that ensure the capacity to transmit knowledge and skills that are needed in the occupation, so as to develop skills that can be utilised in the firm as well as in other firms which include the *beruf* (Fels 1989; Marsden and Ryan 1991). The university education of school teachers for educational and vocational training is supposed to guarantee the transfer of the most recent knowledge, research findings and standards for development within the field.

What is most pertinent from a comparative perspective is the rigid division between adolescent work and learning for most young people in the United States, where only a small minority participate in school-supervised work programmes. In US schools, most adolescents take general academic classes which have little vocationally-relevant content. In the workplace, their activities are directed to the smooth functioning of the operation, not to the education of the worker. In the most stereotypical adolescent jobs, in the fast food industry, fragmented work procedures (Taylorization) are carried to an extreme (Leidner 1993). This stands in stark contrast to the complete amalgamation of school and work experiences in the German apprenticeship system. As a result of the apprentice experience, young people are expected to become more responsible and reliable, and to internalise positive work values, a result which is similar to the perceived benefits of youth employment in the US. In short, concurrently attending school and a workplace is an intensive learning combination which is not usually found in the US.

Part of the success of the apprenticeship system, as evidenced by its high reputation in Germany, stems from the mutual benefits derived by the individual and by society. For the apprentice, there is job-specific learning that leads in due course to a good job that offers economic independence and the development of a work identity. For the firm, workers are produced who can provide not only the skills needed for the present job by meeting quality standards but also the key competencies that will be needed for innovation and future job development in the firm.

Internal criticism of the German training system is primarily directed to a perceived lack of correspondence (congruence) between training and developments in the labour market. Some express concern that the number of apprenticeships in the dual system falls and rises in line with economic up- and down-turns. Among young people who come of age during times of high unemployment, many will fail to obtain an apprenticeship and will suffer permanent occupational disadvantage (Blossfeld 1987). Notably absent from the German debate is any concern about the immediate problem behaviours or deviance, linked to adolescent employment, that figure so prominently in the American critique. On the contrary, problem behaviours are linked to the failure to obtain an apprenticeship position (Dietz *et al.* 1997).

Conclusions

Consideration of the controversies and debates in the US and Germany reveals that the social meaning and consequences of adolescent work are highly variable, depending on the macrostructural context in which it occurs. There are important points of convergence, most notably recognition that employment in adolescence represents an initial point of entry to the adult world of work with positive consequences for becoming an adult. There is little disagreement, even among work's most adamant critics in the United States, that the experience of working heightens understanding of the world of work and how to conduct oneself in this domain. The positive functions of employment in building work motivation and responsibility are recognised in both societies. These longer term consequences of employment are unquestionably desirable.

There is convergence also with respect to the emerging recognition that it is not so much employment that is harmful or beneficial (in either context), but rather that it is the type of work that is important. Germans want the apprenticeship experience to be clearly linked to occupational realities and to ensure a smooth transfer from school to work. Considerable effort is directed to assuring high quality training in both the work and school portions of the experience. They worry that when adolescents have odd jobs, such as baby-sitting, yard work and so on, there is no clear connection to future jobs and such activities serve to distract students from what should be their primary academic concerns.

Similarly, in the US there is growing recognition among researchers that adolescents' work experiences vary in quality, and that these differences have significant implications for their developing self-concepts, work motivations, values, and mental health. In both societies, class-specific dual pathways to adult work can be observed, one emphasising formal education, and the other early work.

It is also widely recognised in both contexts that the manner in which work is integrated and balanced with other activities in the adolescent's life is of crucial importance. Germans believe that it is not work itself that affects the adolescent's development into a well-functioning adult but the type of work that is done, the arrangements for balancing commitments across multiple domains, and the links between these arrangements and subsequent educational and occupational opportunities.

Likewise, it is evident from the YDS that most adolescents who work balance their employment with involvement in many other activities (Shanahan and Flaherty forthcoming). Moderate work (that is work restricted to twenty hours per week or less) and the multifaceted patterns of time-use which such work allows are associated with higher levels of post-secondary educational attainment (Mortimer and Johnson 1998). Indeed, working under some conditions is found to be associated with stronger, not weaker, educational performance.

The two societies differ, however, in the extent to which desirable balances of school and work activity are pre-set and constructed. In the US, through negotiation with employers, parents, and others, adolescents construct their own balances. Through such negotiation, clearly different levels of work investment and varying quality of work experience emerge, with distinct linkages to subsequent educational and occupational attainment. In Germany, the amount of time devoted to school and to work is set in advance by the structure of the apprenticeship itself.

It is with respect to perceptions of the short-term behavioural consequences of adolescent employment that we see greatest divergence in the debate. In the US, critics worry about precocious adulthood, drinking, smoking, early dating, withdrawal from school and premature family formation. In Germany, these behaviours are not linked to early work, but to its absence, which signifies a failure to become integrated into the apprenticeship system and, as a result, into adult society. The ecological perspective well illuminates this difference. In Germany, adolescent work placements are clearly linked to the educational structure, especially in the predominant form of the apprenticeship. At the University level, 'good' jobs are those which connect young people to future occupational prospects. In the United States, in contrast, most adolescents work in the service sector or retail trade in jobs that have little connection to family, school, or other developmentally beneficial socialisation institutions, or to future adult job placements.

These divergent patterns, and consequences, of adolescent work are rooted in the historically and culturally varied past. The establishment of the German apprenticeship system occurred at the beginning of the twentieth century, a time of high unemployment, insecurity for workers and instability in the state. Many young people were turning to communism. Germany remembered the socialising and stabilising success of the pre-industrial guild system of training in the skilled trades and crafts, and transformed it into a state-based system of preparation – in the years between the completion of foundational schooling and military service – that would prepare young men for both their long-term working life in a highly regulated occupational structure and the duties of citizenship (Kerschensteiner 1901; for young women see Kleinau and Mayer 1996).

The American background is of course very different. In accord with its emphasis on occupational opportunity, westward expansion, and the strong demand for labour, and lacking the legacy of a strong guild system, the United States is unique among post-industrial nations in the extent to which its educational system is non-vocationally specific (Kerckhoff 1996). Unlike students in Germany and other countries, young people finish schooling with generalised diplomas and bachelors' degrees. Only at the highest levels are educational programmes vocationally specific (e.g. degrees in engineering, medicine, academic fields); certificates and diplomas issued by vocational schools tend to lack widespread recognition. Vocational schooling programmes, as part of high school curricula, are on the wane.

In this context, young people in the US are encouraged to attain the highest level of education they can. A recent critique of the American educational system calls American youth 'ambitious but directionless' (Schneider and Stevenson 1999). Those who do not plan to graduate from college are offered little in the way of programmes that will help them find their place in the world of work. For many, paid jobs in the youth labour market provide an alternate route to adulthood, but also disconnection from school and family, and from the kinds of jobs that would be considered desirable in adulthood. These institutional connections in the one society, and their absence in the other, may be key to understanding the distinct emphases in the debates over adolescent work.

10 Child labour in the Federal Republic of Germany

Heinz Ingenhorst

Child labour as a concept is seemingly unavoidably associated with images of exploited children in Third World countries. This association between the Third World and extremely exploitative forms of child labour is often used by people in general, and politicians in particular, as a way of either denying or trivialising the continuing existence of child labour in the German Federal Republic. The general tone of comment is either to claim that in a highly developed and industrialised country such as the Federal Republic of Germany there is absolutely no exploitation of children through work, or that children's employment is limited to a few part-time jobs here and there; the sorts of jobs that most Germans take on during their years at school and ones that in any case hardly merit the description of proper employment. But a closer analysis reveals that child labour is part of the normal social life of the Federal Republic of Germany today, although it is hardly ever discussed seriously.

What is child labour?

It is clear that children have always been involved in various forms of work, so many indeed that there is no definition of child labour that covers all of these forms. There is no one single type of child labour and so we have to be prepared to differentiate between its various patterns, and refrain from defining child labour either universally or outside the context of its specific content, values and norms. Throughout this chapter, child labour is defined as work undertaken by children and youths aged between 13 and 16 years old, who are therefore also students in years 8, 9 and 10 of full-time schooling. These male and female school students are regarded as children under the Youth Protection Law of the German Federal Republic, since they have not yet completed their compulsory full-time schooling: nine years in Nordrhein-Westfalen and ten years in Berlin. Thus young people working while still at school are legally defined as children, while child labour here is defined as work undertaken in exchange for money, generally in the form of a wage, carried on outside the parental home or household.

Half of all male and female pupils do have jobs

According to a series of investigations into child labour in the Federal Republic of Germany undertaken between 1987 and 1994 in Nordrhein-Westfalen (Ingenhorst and Wienold 1988, 1991), Hessen (Ingenhorst *et al.* 1994) and Berlin (Senatsverwaltung für Soziales 1994), it can be reliably estimated that about half of all pupils in years 8 and 9 have jobs. Not only is paid employment prevalent among this age group, the children's reports of their jobs show widely varying working conditions and therefore offer a systematic and detailed insight into the day-to-day forms of child labour that exist in an advanced industrial society like the Republic of Germany.

This research illustrates that the experience of earning money often begins at an early age, since around one in five of all children in year 6 report holding a paid job. Moreover, by the time students leave full-time schooling, more than four-fifths will have had some experience of earning money through work; an experience that can vary considerably according to criteria such as the pressures involved in working, the risks that employment may involve, the regularity and nature of hours worked and the level of pay. Average hourly rates of pay are around 10 DM per hour (US$4) (Ingenhorst *et al.* 1994), but the amount of money a school student can earn through working varies considerably, ranging from 1,500 to 2,000 DM per year (US$600–800). This average aggregate level of pay exceeds the amount children generally receive in pocket money by as much as 600 DM (US$250) per year.

Why do children work?

Child labour in the Federal Republic of Germany needs to be considered in the context of a continuing process of individualisation. With this we see an associated de-structuring of childhood, youth and the adult phase of the life-course, alongside an extension of the transitional phase of youth. Youth, with all its associated forms of social differentiation, represents a transitional phase which leads, or at least should lead, to young people separating themselves from the parental home and generating their own independent forms of social existence. The activity of earning money while still in full-time schooling should be regarded as an aspect of this phase of separation, even if this is not regarded as the primary motivation among young people themselves.

The de-structuring of youth and the possibility of a very long phase of transition from an essentially youthful existence to an adult role demands special forms of finance which in this phase of youth can come from a number of different sources. This financing is so defined that neither funds from parents, the family nor the state are either exclusively or predominantly available to support youths fully in undergoing their transitions. It is in this context that school students take part of the responsibility for financing their upkeep through work. These young people need to earn supplementary amounts of money in order to be able to satisfy their changing consumer needs and aspirations. For both female and male school students, getting a job can be regarded as the starting point for the financing of this increasingly prolonged phase of youthful transition, even if the individual pathways that these school students follow vary. Taking on permanent, short-term or occasional part-time employment while still in full-time schooling has become the main form of finance for young people.

Money as the key to consumption

Thus the dominant motivation for working is the wage, or at least what these children can buy with it. For about two-thirds of children money is regarded as the single most important reason for working (Ingenhorst *et al.* 1994). Money earned from working is regarded by children as a key to the consumer world of adults; it opens up to them the possibility of purchasing such things as brand name clothing, televisions, computers, mountain bikes and other desirable items. Only through working can these children buy these more expensive types of status symbols, the sorts of goods that are 'in' with their peer groups and friends, without having to worry about potentially disruptive and conflicting arguments with parents.

Recognition in the adult world

'Fun at work' emerges as the second most important reason why these children work, with around a fifth seeing work as a source of fun and amusement. The children place considerable importance on the communicative aspect of working: the contact with others at work, the breaks and pauses in working, and its value as a source of recognition in the adult world. Both female and male school students are largely indifferent to the content of work itself. Of prime importance is the value of work as a source of experience and the opportunity it brings to move outside the family as an individual, the possibility of acquiring a greater degree of social recognition, and the way in which work conveys a change in social roles from the dependency of the child to the independence of adulthood.

It is in this context that the results of the 'scales of self-conception' prove interesting. These scales measure sensitivity, mood, self-respect and degree of irritability, and were produced by the children interviewed in Hessen (Ingenhorst *et al.* 1994). They show that, among both male and female school students in work, there is generally speaking a greater feeling of independence and self-confidence than is apparent in comparable groups of children who are not working. These particular dispositions may either be a requirement for becoming a successful school age worker or the effect of being in work.

Relieving the family budget

There was hardly any evidence of compulsion or of direct economic crises in the family as a motivating factor in the decision to take up work. In the first investigations we carried out, only a few children reported family poverty or the need to work. This does not exclude the fact however, that the individual incomes these children generated through working went some way towards relieving the strain on parents and household, through directing their considerable spending towards the status symbols of commercial youth culture; and that an independent income could help reduce the possibilities for domestic conflict concerning expenditure on what the children identify as 'necessary' and 'justified' expenses. In the study made by Senatsverwaltung für Soziales (1994) there are, however, indications that, with an expanding labour market and growing economy, an increasing number of children transfer all or part of their wages from school age working directly to their parents and the household budget. Nevertheless, the over-riding majority spend the money they earn from work on themselves.

Children's autonomous income is the material aspect of their separation from parents and the basis upon which the moulding of their individual consumer tastes and styles, and the development of their own cultural world, takes place. Commercialised as this culture is, it is also part of the symbolic politics of youth, through which they can express their autonomy and independence, and initiate a break or departure from the modes of conduct of previous generations.

Self-determination, fun and money

The children surveyed believe that work has to be undertaken on the basis of free will, that the rewards have to be acceptable and that work must in the main be fun. This in turn relates to concepts that are important to many young people in the Federal Republic of Germany today. The strong emphasis on independence, self-determination and fun casts a more positive light on the strong orientation towards money and consumption (an orientation frequently complained about by parents). Children's reasons for working do not simply reflect a consumer-oriented drive on their part. The value, enjoyment and seriousness with which they approach their work also point to the communicative aspects of working. Work facilitates the search for recognition in a sphere separate from parents, family and household, and away from the formal modes of measuring performance that characterise their schooling. Work can also be a source of fun that may be absent from school.

The work that these children do can also be somewhat playful and experimental. Provided that it meets the criteria mentioned earlier, employment while still at school is regarded by working children and their non-working friends as something that has many positive things to offer.

The consequences of child labour

Work for these children is, however, not just related to the positive outcomes of earning money and having fun. Work also brings about a loss of free time, and children often find themselves exposed to a whole host of other negative consequences, including exposure to various pressures, risks and dangers while at work.

A sixty-hour week is not uncommon

The survey findings demonstrate that children in employment work an average of about four hours per day. The average number of days worked per year is around forty, resulting in an average annual working time of 160 hours. Many children work fewer hours per year (under eighty) but for around 10 per cent of the children the hours worked amount to a heavy 500 or more per year. The children that work these long hours represent the 'hard core' of child labourers in the Federal Republic of Germany (Ingenhorst *et al.* 1994). These children are, however, not only burdened by their work. When examining the total pressures, we need to take into account the fact that these children are also attending school for around thirty hours per week, with additional homework responsibilities as well. On top of this, many children also have responsibilities around the household in the form of domestic chores for parents. Thus the work burdens placed on these children can in some instances be very time-consuming, since school and work together could add up to about sixty hours per week. The cost of this is obvious, since additional time spent in paid employment is time not available for children's relaxation and recuperation, the pursuit of hobbies and other free time activities. Performance at school can also suffer from the additional pressures of paid work, although this is something that few of the children complain about.

Competition within the labour market

Children get to know about the market for child labour through their social life. Knowledge of job opportunities is found mainly through informal networks such as those of friends and relatives. There are a limited number of ways to look for work, and only a limited number of workplaces, so not everyone who wants a job can find one. This is despite the fact that jobs for children and youths are not restricted to areas typically regarded as 'children's work', such as baby-sitting and paper rounds although, as we note later, opportunities for employment in the service sector are still relatively small.

Child labour takes place outside the household primarily in three different areas (Ingenhorst *et al.* 1994): a different household (about 20 per cent); the family business (about 10 per cent); and in someone else's business (around 70 per cent). More than half of working children find employment in small enterprises with between two and ten employees. However, a quarter of working children do find jobs in enterprises with between 11 and 100 employees, although work in larger enterprises with over 100 employees is rare (only about 3 per cent). Where children do work for such large enterprises, their employment is normally restricted to a holiday job. Many of these jobs reproduce aspects of the typical work situations and challenges which employees in general face.

A new study would be needed in order to clarify questions of whether the current crisis in the labour market of the German Federal Republic is having an effect on the scale and structure of child labour. In recent years, farming and harvesting have come under pressure from the increasing prominence of large scale agri-business and the intensification of traditional methods of agricultural production. Work opportunities for harvesting asparagus, fruit and vegetables are now mainly taken by itinerant adult workers, for example Polish travellers, and asylum seekers. In addition, job centres have become much keener to place the unemployed in such seasonal and casual forms of work, although success in this has been only moderate. Similar developments can be observed in the construction industry.

More and more marginal groups of workers, such as immigrants, asylum seekers and the unemployed, are therefore appearing in work places that would perhaps have previously been the preserve of children. Newspaper deliveries and the distribution of flyers is another important example. Whether the loss of potential job opportunities for school age children in areas like these is balanced out by new possibilities for work in other areas of the private sector is difficult to judge, given the absence of reliable information.

In which industries do children work?

From the detailed accounts documented in the questionnaires of those children interviewed in the various research projects (Ingenhorst and Wienold 1988, 1991; Ingenhorst *et al.* 1994), it is possible to establish general categories of economic activity (see Figure 10.1). About 30 per cent of children with jobs work for private employers, usually for other households in such tasks as baby-sitting, housework and gardening. About another 25 per cent hold jobs delivering newspapers. Another 15 per cent can be found working in the service sector, where their work generally includes employment as cleaners, helping out at petrol stations, care work, other forms of delivery work, painting and other forms of paid employment done outside the home. Of more importance are opportunities for work in the business sector, usually in the form of temporary work in supermarkets, shops and other retail outlets, undertaken by around 10 per cent of working children. Opportunities for employment in the industrial sector are rare. The evidence suggests that only around 2 per cent of working children find jobs in industry.

In some areas, the number of children employed illegally is disproportionately high: on average around 50 per cent of all children working in these areas. This scale of forbidden or illegal child labour clearly suggests that the

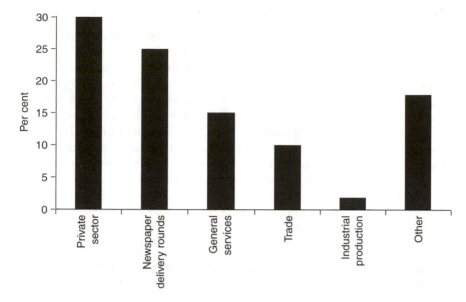

Figure 10.1 Child labour by sector

youth employment laws designed to ensure the protection of children are being extensively ignored. This is the case in bars and public houses, in business, in the distribution of flyers and other advertising material and in construction work. The majority of opportunities for child labour in the Federal Republic of Germany are not found in the countryside or inner city areas but in the suburbs. In these areas there is a labour market structure favourable to children as there are many jobs available that can be found by relatively informal methods.

The informal nature of the market for child labour is also characterised by the fact that only a tenth of children in work have a formal scheme of payment (the German *Steuerkarte*); the great majority are paid informally, even among those children who put in long hours at work. It is only in exceptional cases that children's working conditions are formalised and protected by a contract of employment and work insurance.

As the survey results show, the structure of child labour in the Federal Republic is extremely difficult to define. It may be casual work restricted to a few days or hours each year, or intensive temporary work for a few weeks, including jobs undertaken in school vacations. The employment of children may have a regular character, for example each week-day in the case of newspaper delivery rounds. In between these casual typical forms, we can also identify more transient and diverse combinations. Child labour represents a broad range of activities, intensities and forms, which is very difficult to put into clearly defined categories. In this context there are no 'normal' working conditions for school age children but an area of activity characterised by diversity.

Does child labour differ between boys and girls?

The evidence suggests that boys work somewhat more frequently than girls. For the boys, entry into the labour market appears to be a more profitable activity, since female school age workers earn around one to two German Marks per hour less than the males in all areas of work. Not only do girls find employment in poorer paid jobs, when they work in the same types of employment they still receive lower hourly rates of pay (Ingenhorst 1994). Girls tend to work in other households as baby-sitters, in public houses, in offices, in doctors' surgeries and in providing extra school work tuition for other pupils. Boys mainly obtain employment doing newspaper delivery rounds, manual labouring and working within the agriculture and farming industries. Thus, while boys often find employment outside the family context, girls are more likely to work in the types of jobs that women have traditionally been restricted to.

Does child labour involve preparation for the adult 'world of work'?

Work during a child's time at school provides a direct insight into the 'world of work' for only a few young people. Much of the work taken on is purely physical in character and therefore does not provide much in the way of experience for subsequent training or entry into a career. Only a few children are offered training during their school time employment, and it is even rarer for a job to lead to a training contract when the child leaves school. Furthermore, the notion that such work may have educational value for children appears to be far removed from the reality of working life. Neither schools nor parents take much interest in what happens outside school hours or immediate family life. Many teachers simply ignore the fact that their pupils work, even if the demands of paid employment have a noticeable impact on a child's educational performance.

Thus the value of child labour as preparation or practice for entry into the subsequent world of work is extremely limited. Children do not regard it as a particularly meaningful form of labour, nor as something that is important to their social development. Work for most children is seen as a burden to be tolerated in order to gain money, not as something that offers potential social advantages for their future (Ingenhorst and Wienold 1992).

A work ethic acquired through practice

Holding a part-time job is also characterised by a lack of emphasis upon such factors as quality, context, durability, security and the ability to exercise self-determination. In the main, the 'work ethic' among working children is primarily orientated towards such features as the the chance of a job providing money relatively quickly. Traditional work values such as endurance, punctuality, industriousness and self-organisation are not really at issue here. Only in the areas of gaining some form of work experience, including exposure to the vicissitudes and risk of working, do children place much value on their employment while still at school.

Pressures on working children are greatly underestimated

Approximately a fifth of working children find their job psychologically stressful, while a third find their employment physically demanding. In the main, the stresses and strains are regarded as of slight to medium intensity. Nearly half of all the children report that they suffer from aches and pains as a consequence of work, and that they experience 'unpleasant feelings' while at work. The most frequent consequences of school age working are tiredness and exhaustion, sweating, backaches, anger and irritability, nervous tension, colds and headaches. Most of the children put these symptoms down to the fact that work is stressful both mentally and physically. For children, as for most people new to it, entry into work is of primary significance as a trigger for increased levels of stress.

If we examine the working conditions and dangers experienced by children at work, other questions concerning their safety arise. For the vast majority of working children, the dangers and risks to their health are minor. Only in a few cases do children experience serious injury or health-related problems at work. Nevertheless, there is an absence among both parents and employers of any systematic regard for the potential risks to health from school age working. Given the extensive illegality of child employment in the German Federal Republic, recognition of the injustices and risks of working are low. Indeed, the main *limits to the spread of child labour* (Ingenhorst and Wienold 1992) are set by parental authority over their children, not by the laws regulating children's employment. The main barriers to more extensive forms of child employment are to be found in lack of opportunity, inability to find work, lack of motivation among children themselves and the absence of imperatives for working. This is particularly important given that the evidence suggests that children view work positively (Figure 10.2) and that more children would work given the opportunity.

Conclusion

Child labour in the Federal Republic of Germany presents itself to us as an extremely heterogeneous and ambiguous phenomenon, which cannot be understood if discussion of it is trivialised as it has been by parents and politicians. Equally, however, over-dramatising the issues will not overcome the problems that the employment of children entails. We should also bear in mind that more restrictive regulation of children's employment might deny children a sense of social worth and value which entry to paid employment is seen to offer.

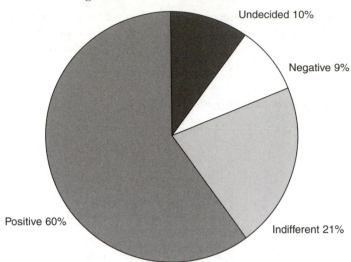

Figure 10.2 Attitudes to child labour

It is therefore crucial to understand and support those groups of children who feel highly pressurised by working. These children also need protection against exploitation at work, and this implies full acknowledgement amongst the public at large of the significance of employment to children's lives. In addition, future debate needs to recognise the potential for working to meet children's communicative and expressive needs, which school age children feel they can fulfil by earning money.

11 Child labour in Russia

Valery Mansurov

Child labour remains a serious problem in the world today. According to revised estimates by the International Labour Organisation's Bureau of Statistics, the number of working children between the age of 5 and 14 is at least 120 million. As may be expected given the prevailing economic conditions, the overwhelming majority of these are in developing countries in Africa, Asia and Latin America, but pockets of child labour also exist in many industrialised countries. Numerous children work in occupations and industries which are plainly dangerous and hazardous. Child labour is a serious violation of children's rights, and may well represent the single most common form of child abuse and neglect in the world today. In the late 1980s and early 1990s, as the issue of child labour began to receive public attention, it became increasingly evident that there was an urgent need, first, to better understand the critical and complex issues inherent to child labour and, second, to develop and implement creative new strategies to address the diverse problems related to this area.

Many governments have embarked on a review and updating of national legislation on child labour and have adopted practical policies and programmes towards it (these include Brazil, India, Indonesia, Kenya, Nepal, Pakistan, Philippines, United Republic of Tanzania, Thailand, Zimbabwe). The ILO's International Programme on the Elimination of Child Labour (IPEC) is now operational in more than twenty-five countries.

Within the last year, a number of television and news accounts have drawn attention to the growing child labour problem in Russia, portraying it as one indicator of the economic stress which families are experiencing during this period of transition. Beyond such anecdotal observations, virtually nothing is known about this new phenomenon.

This chapter describes research commissioned by the International Labour Office, which looks below the surface to examine the dynamics of child labour in Russia today and to determine the reasons behind its recent upsurge. It describes the current nature and extent of child work, the way in which it is viewed by various sectors of Russian society, and what future trends are likely to be.

The research was undertaken by the Institute of Sociology of the Russian Academy of Sciences. Four different population groups were sampled in the

Russian population (through a subset of questions on the all-Russia socio-demographic survey), as well as schoolchildren, parents and teachers in Moscow. The samples were stratified to ensure adequate representation by age, sex, and geographical area. The Moscow studies covered suburbs as well as urban core areas; the all-Russia survey sampled all regions of the country, both rural and urban. The total number of respondents from these combined sources was a little over 2,500. To elucidate the findings of the surveys further, a more open-ended survey was conducted of thirty-eight policymakers and professionals from national child welfare institutions, law enforcement bodies, ministries of labour and education, and leaders of opinion recognised as knowledgeable in the subject. In addition, pertinent data from an in-depth sociological study of teenagers conducted in Kirov (a medium-sized city) were also used.

Another study was conducted by senior figures from the Institute of Comparative Labour Relations Studies (ISITO) in Samara *oblast*, the Regional Scientific and Research Center in Ulyanovsk *oblast*, the ISITO in Kemerovo *oblast* and the Russian Sociologist Society in Moscow. This study was conducted under the World Campaign Against Child Labour which was launched by the International Confederation of Free Trade Unions (ICFTU). Its objective was to further investigate the scale and nature of the use of child labour in both formal and informal sectors of the Russian economy, as well as the exploitation of children's labour by adults engaged in criminal activity. The major objective of the preliminary phase of the study was to identify the main sectors and occupations where child labour is to be found. The principal areas of investigation were

- the forms of labour activity of children aged 6–16
- the reasons for early commencement of labour activity
- the reasons for the use of child labour by employers and persons in charge of training and educational activity
- the influence of labour activity on socialisation
- institutional mechanisms for regulation of child labour activity (role of organisations in charge of management, protection and control functions in the sphere).

The task of identifying the scale and spread of child labour was to be implemented in the second phase of the research. Three major forms of child labour were studied. The first comprised the forms of child labour which are organised under the education system. These include the professional training schools and vocational classes in extra-mural education institutions. The second was work for a wage, which takes two distinct forms: on the one hand is the official placement of young people in full-time job placements including those made via the Committee for Youth at commercial enterprises and organisations; on the other there is informal work for a wage, including jobs at small businesses, as individual sellers, in family enterprises and as news vendors. The third type that was studied was self-employment, which is characterised for example by work at filling stations and car wash stations.

The regions selected allowed comparison of child labour in a large city (Moscow), in a depressed region (Kemerovo region), in a region where market reforms are advanced (Samara), and in a traditional region where implementation of market reforms is being hampered by communists and their supporters dominating local authorities (Ulianovsk).

The scale and nature of the problem

The extent of child labour in Russia

It is impossible at this point to obtain accurate statistical information on the number of working children, given the rapid and spontaneous growth of this phenomenon. Nevertheless, indirect evidence gives some indication of the scale. Over half of the respondents in the all-Russia survey, for example, reported that they were personally acquainted with working children, and almost a fifth acknowledged that their own children were engaged in paid work. The Moscow surveys yield similar findings (51 per cent of teachers knew students who were working, 15 per cent of parents acknowledged that their own children worked, and 10 per cent of the students admitted that they were working). Although not all of the responses to the survey may refer to illegal employment – that is, work by children under the age of 16, for long hours, or in proscribed occupations – nevertheless, these reports do indicate that child work is widespread.

Drawing upon the views of policymakers and practitioners, we can distinguish several types of organisation and use of child and teenage labour which differ by methods of job placement and character of employment and which demonstrate different patterns of development in modern Russia.

Work as educational training

The first of these types is the organisation of job placements for children within the educational system. Work placement of older secondary school pupils during the summer was traditional in the Soviet era. State Employment Services generally employed children in the production sphere and city communal services. Commercial Employment Services placed children more with commercial firms and private businessmen, and employed children in small scale retail outlets or as individual sellers, news vendors, cooks and so on.

Labour and recreation camps have gradually ceased to exist and have lost their initial aim: labour practice or work experience. The main purpose of the remaining camps is to organise and occupy teenagers during the long summer break from school. Children mostly relax there; the ostensible purpose of carrying out work in agriculture or in workshops occupies considerably less of their time, and the work is not obligatory.

In the current straitened financial climate some school administrations increasingly use their students' labour in the vegetable gardens which supply food for the school. This is not paid work and can consist of fairly specialised and demanding agricultural labour – adult work. The agricultural activities of schools are on a wide scale: they grow seedlings, use tractors, harvesters, cars and trucks, organise the production process from beginning to end. The activities are essentially self-provisioning in character in that all food products grown in school vegetable gardens are used in school canteens. Such food production is presented as 'training'. However, there is no formal procedure for hiring; therefore, working conditions are not agreed, and employers (that is, school administrations) assume few obligations to the unpaid students. State agencies which would normally oversee such 'training' do not, in this instance, control the character of the work or the extent to which children's labour is extracted or exploited.

Work under contract

The official practice of placing teenagers directly in enterprises was well-developed in the pre-*perestroika* period and was controlled by state agencies. A system of professional training of young employees at workplaces (apprenticeships) was based mainly on large industrial enterprises of the region. This practice has all but disappeared as a result of the current economic circumstances of such large-scale urban and regional enterprises. The number of under-age employees officially hired in permanent jobs in the regional economy is insignificant and has been decreasing over the last few years (a trend connected both with the general downsizing of industrial production and the difficulties posed by hiring under-age employees).

Another system of official job placement is organised by the Committee for Youth, which arranges both temporary and permanent jobs. The Committee places teenagers over 14 years old in close co-operation with the Commission for Under-age Children. However, finance for this type of job placement for teenagers is gradually decreasing. At the same time, it has been officially decreed that priority should be given to delinquent and pre-delinquent teenagers sent by the Department for the Prevention of Youth Delinquency. The number of teenagers wanting to earn money is growing, but it is getting more difficult for teenagers who have not been identified as delinquent to find a legitimate job. Policymakers and practitioners fear that children and teenagers who cannot obtain official job placements might turn to criminal activities.

As State Employment Services became associated with the placement of those 14–15 year old children registered at the Commission for Child Crime, broader state programmes of job placements for children aged 14–15 and older have withered due to the lack of funds to pay wages. Similarly, wage arrears for adult employees have increased. The absence of funds results in the mutual writing-off of debts (between the Employment Service and enterprises which should transfer a fixed amount of funds to the Employment Fund as recompense for the placement of children there). As a result, with no funds to pay wages, the Employment Service attempts to place children in provisional jobs at enterprises which are indebted to it so that it can recoup its losses. Those children who are thus employed receive a minimal official wage for their work, but problems over payment were evident in these placements via the Employment Service. Furthermore, child employees receive lower wages than adults for the same work; even when placed in jobs via state services (e. g. the Committee for Youth), they received only half as much as adults, and in some cases only a sixth (Samara *oblast*). In addition, the study showed that delays in payment of wages and non-payment are usually due to the absence of funds at the Employment Fund, which are in any case paid only once or twice per month. A private employer, on the other hand, pays child employees either each day or per task. The more frequent payment associated with the informal sector acts as a stimulus for children to seek jobs without applying to official employment agencies.

Children placed in the informal sector

Informal employment is characterised by illegality and a low level of remuneration. However, children from families with low and high incomes alike are to be found in this sector. Unsurprisingly, the children to be found in the informal sector come from a wider age range than those in official placements (from 9 years old). Standards and conditions of labour are not regulated by legislation, being set by the employer. Very often under the condition of informal hiring children work an unregulated working day, and their working regime is more intensive. Children and teenagers in this sector mainly work under verbal agreements. Most seem to like the work they are doing, some of them continuing in the same job for several years. In the accounts given later by children in this sphere, some represent themselves as experiencing a degree of self-realisation. The experts surveyed predicted that child employment in this sphere will increase.

Self-employment

Children as young as 7 years old may be found in forms of self-employment. Arguably, these children and teenagers are demonstrating economic agency, as they actively search for work rather than being placed into employment. They organise their own labour and utilise the resultant income for their own wants and needs. Some will try to match work to their interests. Clearly, satisfying their financial requirements is the main motivation. Child labour in this sphere has a semi-legal character; for example, a licence and a patent are needed to engage in private trading. Some forms of self-employment are reportedly accompanied by the opportunity for criminal activities (for example, some of those who work at filling stations are found to be stealing). Self-employment occupies an intermediate position between the more organised spheres of formal or informal job placement and what may be thought of as organised criminal activities in which children and young people are involved by adults. Again, policymakers and practitioners predict that the number of self-employed children and teenagers will increase.

The employment of children and teenagers by adults engaged in organised crime

Inevitably, the involvement of children in organised criminal activities such as prostitution, begging and stealing is a closed sphere. Gaining access and gathering reliable information are problematic. Clearly, child labour in this sphere is not controlled by state agencies. Teenagers involved in obviously criminal activities are often controlled by criminal organisations, who are believed to view the young people that they recruit almost as apprentices. In the majority of cases the activities are deleterious to both physical and moral health. Children involved in this sphere are mainly recruited from orphanages and boarding schools and from 'at-risk' families. They use paid criminal activities to support themselves and in some cases their family. For some children prostitution, begging and stealing are not just a way of getting money; for some they become a life style and for others a means of survival.

Age differences can be identified within the known forms of delinquent employment. For example, drug dealers rarely hire children under 14. As far as under-age prostitution is concerned, in Samara it exists in 'non-institutionalised' forms in that the organised 'centres' steer clear of involvement with girls younger than 18 years old to avoid prosecution. According to experts and teenagers themselves, the children involved in criminal activity perceive it to be a life style. An activity such as begging is carried out by children from 6 to 15 years old, more commonly in the town where there is less danger of apprehension and more potential for profit. Again the prediction is that the number of children involved in this sphere will increase as, against a background of general impoverishment of the population, children and teenagers can not only make 'quick and easy' money but many perceive their choice of begging or criminal activity as a life style issue and do not regard such activities as work.

Themes from interviews with teenagers

Group interviews were carried out with all working teenagers to gather general impressions from the youngsters about their work. At the end of this interview, two or three of the most interesting youngsters were selected for individual interviews. The criteria for choice were varied; they included wide work experience, the attitude of the family to the teenager's employment, motives for seeking work and so on. In these individual interviews the particular conditions and type of work, together with the material and social status of the young workers' families, were investigated. In some cases, the consent of the parents was needed to carry out the interview. Analysis revealed the following themes:

- the specific characteristics of the various forms of teenage employment
- motives for work
- channels for finding work
- attitude of parents to the child's earnings
- work conditions
- work regime and wages.

The characteristics of the various forms of teenage employment

Urban teenagers

Teenagers working in the city are largely involved in the informal labour market. Their work is distinguished by low pay, the absence of promotion prospects, instability and high fluidity. The youngsters are mainly engaged in newspaper distribution, car washing and small-time market trading. The most 'prestigious' of these jobs is considered to be newspaper selling. Car washing is considered 'dirty labour': 'it's too much trouble and the pay is poor . . . but there's more freedom selling papers in the centre and the money is better' was the comparison made between the two occupations by 15 year old Sergei, who has been selling newspapers for four years. Work in the market, on the one hand, attracts teenagers because it is possible 'to earn a lot'. On the other hand, they understand that this job is not really suitable for their age. For example, Zhenya is 15 years old. His mother works in the market and, from time to time, Zhenya takes her place. 'At first, I wanted to work on the market all summer. Then I understood that to stand from morning to night was not good for my body, you can not sing or do anything normal.'

Urban teenagers can be provisionally divided into two groups: active and passive. The first group seek work on their own initiative and are distinguished by a serious, responsible attitude to their job. Such teenagers realistically weigh up the opportunities and know what they can expect from the different jobs available. It is they who want to work, not their parents or teachers who push them to do so. These youngsters want their own money. This economic independence allows them to overcome the lack of rights typically felt by teenagers of their age. It lets them feel on the same level not only as their contemporaries from well-off families, but as adults. 'On average, we earn more than an adult' boasted some 14 year old newspaper sellers.

The passive teenagers do not try to find work, even if they need money just as much. They prefer to 'roam the streets or visit girlfriends'. A vivid example is the passive attitude to work of the school students at a summer work camp who perceived work as pointless. In essence, they are not interested and do not need it. 'It's a drag', reported most teenagers at this summer work camp.

For the youngsters from the active group money is a symbol of success in life. 'Now everything depends on money. It depends how much you can spend', reported 14 year old Alyesha, a newspaper distributor. Youngsters

working in the petrol stations think the same way. 'In my life, it is important
to be secure', said 12 year old Andrei. In this context, there were interesting
answers to the question 'What would you most like for yourselves?' Teenagers
in the active group wanted most of all to have 'a wad of money', 'to earn a
million or two' and so on. Youngsters in the passive group were not interested
in money. They wanted to 'get the work over with', 'have a good holiday' or
'to get into college'. Success for teenagers from the passive group consists of
'doing well in school so that I can go on to study further'. They recognised
that there had never been a moment in their life when they realistically did
not have enough money.

Youngsters in the active and passive groups had different attitudes to ways
of earning money. The actives preferred having 'their own business': selling
newspapers, petrol pump attendance, car washing or market trading. They
were sceptical about working in a factory. They were inclined to criminal
methods of gaining money. Teenagers from the passive group assumed, that
if necessary, they would seek work in factories. Newspaper and car washing was not acceptable work for them. 'It's harmful, hard work. . . . They
chase us off.'

A close connection can be seen between the attitude of the teenager to
work and the material status of his family. A family in need, as a rule, pushes
youngsters into work. Practically all teenagers in the active group were from
poor or unsuccessful families. By the time they reach 13 or 15 years old, they
often have two to three years of work experience. For example, Dima, 13,
has been selling newspapers in the market since he was 12. His mother works
in the 'Mechanical factory, which says it all. They hardly ever pay wages . . .
My stepfather lives at our expense, just think, he just lives. He doesn't do a
damn, only drinks.' Dulnara, a 16 year old, has similar difficulties with her
family. Since the age of 14, she has been selling in the market together with
her older sister. She says of her family: 'Our mother drinks, so our sister has
taken us and our brothers away. Our dad died in 1995 but he hasn't lived
with our mother since I was small.' Dulnara started work at 12, at first going
into the country to collect onions, apples and potatoes, and was then taken
on by a farm. Both Dima and Dulnara think that if there had been money
in the house, they wouldn't have had to work. Teenagers in the passive group
described their family's standard of living as average. Their families have, not
always large, but stable sources of income. Respondents typically state parents
'can certainly not allow me to buy everything I want, but not so badly that
I need to go out to work myself'.

An important distinguishing feature of the youngsters from the active group
is their understanding of adulthood. They, in contrast to those of the passive
group, no longer consider themselves children. They have already passed the
stage of school. 'Study is not interesting, you only sit on your backside all day.
It's better to work' was how Nikolai, a 14 year old newspaper seller, expressed
a common opinion. The youngsters do not see the need for any vocational
training, assuming that 'I can always find something good'. 'I've got no aims in

life', says 13 year old Dima. 'As long as there are newspapers, I'll sell them. It's easy money'.

An evident differentiation of teenagers' attitudes to work is taking place in the city, with a growing group of teenagers actively looking work. Such teenagers are a qualitatively new element in the labour market. They find their own work and the money that they earn is largely theirs to dispose of. Their work occupies an intermediate 'niche' between legal and illegal methods of earning money.

Rural teenagers

Opportunities for teenagers to find work in the villages are very limited, mainly because of the terrible state of the rural economy. On one state farm, Yacashno-Tashlinskii, 80 per cent of the fields were untilled and productivity had fallen significantly to no more than 600–800 kilogrammes a hectare. Engineering facilities had not been updated for a long while and repairs to machinery were made using hand-made parts. The farm was due to be closed down and there were few jobs to be found there. Adults were taken on for what was at one time 'child's work': weeding, work in the fields and so on. The state farm pays both adults and teenagers only in produce: grain, fodder, fire-wood etc. The only way of getting hard cash is to work on the combine harvester. Teenagers can win these 'prestigious jobs' only if they agree to work a complete working day from 6 in the morning until 9 at night.

Rural youngsters commented on the sharp reduction in the number of jobs available to them in the past two years. Before that, the state farm accepted sixty rural and urban teenagers during the summer vacations but now employed only six youngsters. Rural teenagers saw no opportunities to organise their own businesses, since car washing or newspaper selling were practical only in the city. The state farm was the only source of employment. Teenagers from the countryside are distinguished, first of all, by their labour passivity. None aspired to vocational training, believing that it 'is not necessary in the country-side. They'll take us on to work whether we have an education or not', thinks 16 year old Andrei from the Yasashno-Tashlinskii state farm.

Teenagers, in their own opinion, have no prospects. For them today's work-place 'on a combine [harvester]' is work for a lifetime. They, as a rule, do not connect their life to work in the city: 'There's nowhere to go from here. To set yourself up in the city you need money. Look how much the bus ticket costs. And then you need to eat and pay for your flat.' The only way of escaping from the country in the youngster's opinion is to join the army. 'I am now 16', says Andrei. 'I have two years in the army and in two years nothing will remain of the state farm . . . I want to stay in the army.'

Job opportunities for rural teenagers are determined mainly by the state of the agricultural economy. The absence of a market infrastructure leaves no opportunity for the development of various forms of self-employment. In today's situation, the creation of new jobs for teenagers depends on the speed of re-organisation of the whole agricultural complex in rural areas such as the Ulyanovsk region.

Gendered characteristics of work

Boys have more chance of finding work than girls. Out of forty-six working teenagers who have taken part in this research, only fifteen were girls. It is easier for boys to find work because, first, enterprises offer 14–15 year old teenagers only low qualified auxiliary work. Most vacancies are for trainee turners and metal workers, and only boys are taken on for such work. Second, the boys can earn extra money at petrol pumps and selling newspapers while girls consider this business dangerous: 'anyone can turn nasty!' Girls commented that 'the only way to work normally' is at the market or in show-business. It is interesting to note that the girls from the market and models viewed each other with contempt; each belittling the other's work.

Rural girls find it particularly hard to get work. We were told of instances where village girls of 13 or 14 years of age will live with well-off single men in return for economic support. 'Here, some Armenians have been moved in', says 16 year old Andrei from Yasashno-Tashlinskii. 'They basically have 14 year old girls living with them. . . . They are rich, they have money, and that's all the girls need.' Special attention needs to be paid to the creation of new jobs just for teenage girls. Employment programmes aimed at minors should include reserved vacancies for 14–15 year old girls. The service sector has the most potential from the point of view of job creation for girls. Vocational training for girls should be redirected into those service sector specialities that are in demand on the labour market.

Children and teenagers up to 14 years of age

Children of up to 14 years of age usually help their parents in the market or distribute newspapers. It is difficult for this age group to get work. For example petrol stations are controlled by local gangs who have established an informal minimum age of 13–14 years. The study discovered cases of children under 14 gaining official job placements with the use of false documents. As birth-certificates in Russia have no photographs of children, it is difficult to know whether the actual holder of a birth-certificate is employed, or it has been used to employ another child of younger age.

'We used to go down with the larger lads but they didn't let us wash because we were too small', one 'experienced' car washer told us. Newspaper distribution is practically the only work which younger children can find independently. For example, brothers Timur, 11, and Vadim, 12, sought summer work to save up for a moped. 'We accidentally met up with Irik and Marat, who have been selling papers for five years. . . . It was through them that we ended up here.' The brothers like selling papers and appreciate the independence.

All the working children that we interviewed could be seen as belonging to the active group, which we defined above. However there are costs associated with the early start to their working life. The youngsters miss out on important stages in their social development, in particular part of their education. Their life tends to develop in a simplified way, arguably one which jumps straight from childhood to adulthood. For example, 11 year old Timur believes, that 'one should start work at ten years of age; school is only a waste of time'. 12 year old Sasha, who sells cardboard boxes in the market, also considers himself a fully adult person. 'This is the future. There's no point in learning. Nobody gets wages or their salary paid anyway. At least here, you can do something.' Children who have started to work early are channelled into unskilled work. They are convinced, that the earnings they get today are the best they could get. 'Newspapers are the limit of my dreams. It's good money. I am used to it', says 13 year old Dima after a year of selling papers.

This early beginning of labour activity leads to the 'suspension' of children and teenagers at the level of low-skilled, routine work. Working children are less well equipped to aspire to and plan towards a future career at a higher level. The transition from less qualified work to more complex, creative work is a difficult one, particularly where children have opted out of education. This strengthens the case that some children, those who cannot or do not want to learn, need vocational training.

The motivation to work

The motivations of 12 to 15 year old teenagers to work are elaborated in the rest of the chapter. It will consider, first, their internal motives, when it is clearly the teenagers themselves who intend to find work. The second kind of motive is external, in which the impulse to find work comes not from the teenager, but from parents, teachers, police or administrative bodies. The distinctive feature of external motivation is the lack of interest by the young person in the work. An extreme case of external motivation is that poverty and privation within the family can compel children to work. At the opposite end of the spectrum, some parents who are relatively affluent by current standards in some regions of Russia rely upon children's input to family businesses. However, the outcomes of external motivation are not always entirely negative; for example, many teenagers selling in the market were recruited by parents to help set up displays, look after stalls and so on. Having worked for a time the youngsters then trade independently; internal motivation has developed.

Internal motivation

Internal motives are varied, the main ones being:

- the desire to earn
- sociability and peer pressure

- work as a lifestyle
- the wish to increase self-esteem and enhance personal development.

Economic motivation

While lack of money is clearly something over which children have no control, and might therefore be considered as an external motivating factor, it is still the case that children have differing responses to situations of economic need and so something of the child's internal motivation comes into play. First, and most fundamental, the desire to earn money derives from low family income; for the child, the absence of pocket money. Interviews with teenagers confirmed a common focus on money. 'To work means to make money', says Marat, 12, a newspaper seller. 'They sometimes call as speculators, because we earn money. We buy, resell, buy, sell again a bit dearer – that's speculating', says Nikolai, 14, another newspaper seller. Nevertheless, there are different degrees of financial need; some teenagers support not only themselves, but their families. 'I dress myself; I buy myself and younger brother shoes and clothes; I give my Mother some money too', says 13 year old Alekcei. Teenagers frequently referred to their parent's wages as 'peanuts' but their own wages as 'above average'. However, the majority of teenagers, as a rule, do not aim to support themselves; they are earning to buy something specific: a football, bicycle, boots, toys or clothes.

Sociability and peer pressure

Teenagers usually begin to work with friends because working as an individual is 'risky and dangerous' and could disrupt their social life. For example, Ruslan worked for three months at a filling station, dispensing petrol. 'Then I chucked it in as I was losing friends. They didn't come to see me often.' Working in groups protects the youngsters from the racketeers. 'If I go with someone or am near my friends, it is possible to overcome anyone. But if you go alone, and one of the thugs comes up, you have to do what he says. No-one will help you.'

Working with friends or peers was important to the youngsters. Unfortunately, this fact was not taken into account by the organisers of the summer work camps when deciding where the teenagers should work, splitting friends into different brigades so that they hardly see each other. Work also created opportunities for expanding peer groups. Girls from the model agency commented that before arriving at the agency they had few friends, and gained friends through work.

Work as a lifestyle

While earning money is by far the most important motivation, an early start to working life leads to the position where having earnings and being a worker can become a lifestyle. For example, 14 year old Olecya has worked in the market since she was 10. At first, she and her brother sold packets and seeds. Now she has her own business looking after weighing scales. 'You had to pay out with the packets and you had no guarantee you would sell. Here there's nothing to pay out.' Olecya works all day, having left school two years ago. The only things that she thinks are important are what is going on on her 'patch', that a competitor has appeared or that the administration 'are clearing people out'.

Trouble in the family can also promote the transformation of work into a lifestyle particularly where a child or young person is the only wage earner. 'This is why I arranged work', said a 14 year old paper seller. 'I'm the only one left in the family. My mother doesn't work, father's in hospital.' Such teenagers are not in a position to be demanding about wages and conditions. Two features distinguish these young people. First, they have no clear idea what they are going to do when they grow up. They cannot envisage life without their current work. Second, they have no free time and have become used to a life without leisure, even saying that they 'have no time for it'.

To increase self-esteem and enhance personal development

A very few young people had gained prestigious, 'elite' occupations, for example in the Terminal model agency. In this sort of work the meagre 10 to 15 roubles per show for two or three catwalk shows a year was not the primary motivation. On the contrary, according to the girls, their expenses exceed their fees. They need to pay for their own footwear, stockings, aerobic classes and modelling lessons. What attracts them is the opportunity to acquire professional skills, and the prospect of future work. The girls get to know employers from the elite model agencies of Moscow, St Petersburg and Europe. They have the chance to enter the selection process for these agencies and apply for work abroad. The model agency is a stepping stone to further work. In contrast to most workers in other occupations they enjoy their work, the charge of energy, the attention and the applause. Working in the agency has helped them to gain confidence and find new friends.

Those who are motivated by money quickly leave the model agency. 'They think that after the first show, they'll get half a million. One girl was really disappointed when they told her she would get 10 to 15 roubles. After this, basically everyone leaves' are the impressions of 16 year old Kristina, who has worked in Terminal for four years. Interestingly, Kristina earns her pocket money by selling Max Factor cosmetics with her mother. Few of the girls viewed modelling as a long-term career choice, planning instead to enter higher education in one of the currently prestigious specialties – law or medicine – and to stop modelling at that point. The internal motivations of teenagers can include both socio-economic motives (earnings), and psychological motivation (self-expression). This research has shown, that it is precisely such strong internal motives that are so crudely exploited by adults through the criminal gangs.

External motivation

Employers' motivation

Although employers are not the focus of this chapter it is worth exploring in brief the situation from their side of the economic exchange between child and adult, as this helps to explain the growing problem of children's recruitment into organised crime. Employers are, by and large, not interested in employing 14 and 15 year old teenagers, for two reasons. First, it is not profitable to grant children the benefits due to them under labour law: a reduced working day and higher holiday allocation. Private businessmen and small and medium sized firms do not employ teenagers because they cannot carry the financial liability. Second, teenagers lack even the initial qualifications required in many businesses. The state of the Russian labour market is such that 'cheap labour' is provided not by children but by adults who accept work at low wages, in difficult working conditions and for long hours.

Reluctant employers: the dwindling supply of sanctioned jobs for teenagers

One firm reported their recent problems with teenage labour, even though the management had agreed a shorter working day from 8 till 12 am: 'well, they worked for us for two or three days before one got a bad back, another a bad leg. A third was just too lazy to get up. Children will be children', the personnel manager concluded. Another company employed ten girls as ice-cream saleswomen, paying 500 roubles with a bonus at the end of the first month. 'One of them just spent the time chewing sunflower seeds', said the representative of the Youth Employment Service. 'Another just looked around. By the end of the week, one had a shortfall of 1,500, another of 1,000. They will not take any responsibility and their parents do not want to pay.' Employers believe that school students are the most irresponsible workers, and take only those who have reached 16 years of age. Similarly collective farms take 14 and 15 year olds only as a last resort when faced with severe shortages of labour, and then only for temporary, low-skilled work: sorting grain, collecting grass, preparing forage, weeding and so on.

The supply of jobs for rural teenagers depends directly on the economic condition of agriculture. Collective and state farms, which are in decline, cannot take on students from training colleges and technical schools. In such cases, as a rule, connections with schools are broken. The Ulyanovsk Regional Labour Inspectorate has noted an increasing tendency to infringe the law on teenage working hours, especially in agricultural enterprises. The Deputy Chief of the Labour Inspectorate has highlighted the following infringements: teenagers working a full eight-hour day, working on days off and working overtime. Employers initiate these infringements; it is not profitable to leave jobs unfilled for half the day. As a rule, they do not inform teenagers of the reduced work entitlement. 'He's still young and the work is not that hard' is the attitude of the personnel manager of the Yasashno-Tashlinskii state farm. For their part, teenagers themselves want the increased working day and wages.

Conclusion

Despite the changing pattern of employment prospects – a broad shift in where working children are to be found, and the migration of child employment from the formal to the informal and criminal sectors – child labour was found in all areas covered by the study.

The survey did not reveal mass use of child labour or child employment as a major sector of the general economy. However, according to IUF data, the use of child labour is an integral part of the economy of many agricultural areas, especially in south Russia during the labour-intensive seasons of spring and autumn. Surveys conducted in 1998 upon request by journalists of the 'Solidamost' newspaper in the Vologda and Stavropol regions, revealed mass employment at harvest time of school students (who broke off their studies to take on the work). However, while agriculture has traditionally been the sector where child labour has been used on a mass scale, there is as yet too little research to determine its full extent today.

It is too early to claim that child labour is a major economic factor in Russia. At the same time, experts stress that it is on the increase. Our expert interviews revealed a consensus that there has been a rise in the number of child employees during recent years; and that new businesses which involve children have appeared. The organised use of children in criminal activities such as begging has proliferated during the last five or six years. Organised child prostitution has not spread as widely due to the risk of prosecution for employing children for sex. At the same time, drug distribution is viewed as the most rapidly growing field of criminal activity. According to experts, employment of children at private businesses in general has increased compared to that at state enterprises and organisations (where jobs are often reserved for delinquent youth).

Children involved in labour activity are usually less oriented towards education. According to experts and child employees, the majority commence work in the summer vacation, ceasing work when school begins again. A moderate number of children are employed all year round. Some begin to pay much less attention to their studies and others are reported to cease attending school when they start work. The most disengaged see education as worthless. Their early socialisation and independent earning of money make them think of school as a waste of time. As a rule, children who begin work early and earn some money begin to think of themselves as adults and to take the initiative in improving their working conditions by changing jobs until they find the one they like.

Most children employed in private businesses and agricultural enterprises have no contract to regulate labour relations but work on the basis of oral agreements. In some cases child employees have to work ten and more hours a day. Such cases are particularly common in agriculture, work in cafes and trade markets.

This study has uncovered the exertion of moral and physical influence by parents over children to make them work. Usually children who are forced to work come from low income families, particularly those where a parent misuses alcohol or where there is only one parent. As a rule, when parents force children to work, public opinion remains silent because parents are expected to have authority over their children. In some cases parents force children to assist them in their own work. Few parents pay their children or give reasonable pocket money. This situation is a matter of great concern as, quite apart from the problem of child labour, it raises a larger problem of the recognition of children's civil and moral rights within families.

A pattern emerged that associated the age of employees with the form of their engagement in labour activity. In particular, begging involves children above 7 years old; self-employment, children 8 and above (e.g. car washing); drug distribution, children aged 10 to 14 (up to 80 per cent of professional drug dealers use child labour because children under 14 years old cannot be held criminally responsible for drug distribution); few children under 12 are engaged in the private sector (employers do not want to hire younger children who cannot cope with physical labour); and children above 14 are more likely to have access to official job placements at state enterprises.

Two social groups provide the largest number of child employees in the commercial sphere. The first includes children from low income and socially vulnerable families, or families where at least one parent suffers from wage arrears of a few months or more. The second comprises children from more affluent families whose parents are involved in commercial activity. For the first group, the prime motivation for labour is the need to provide money for the family budget, while parents from the second group largely consider their children's commercial activity to be a means of socialisation and adaptation to the new market economy. Some children are essentially being forced to work, sometimes treated violently in order to make them comply, and some are being used by criminal gangs. To summarise, the reasons that children commence labour activity include the following.

1   Children may start work because of family impoverishment and the lack of money for food in the most financially vulnerable families. In more affluent professional families (who are also vulnerable to long delays in payment of wages) children may have too little pocket money.
2   Children may be forced to work by parents or employers on whom they are financially dependent.
3   Russian society is increasingly stratified; the families of pupils in the same school may have huge income differentials. Children try to keep up with

peers from more affluent families and try to earn money to buy fashionable clothes and other goods.

4 The transfer of children's camps from enterprises to municipalities made summer vacations at these camps impossible for many families; such camps were practically free before market reforms (up to 80 per cent or even 100 per cent of the cost was paid by the enterprise trade union). At present, the cost would have to be completely paid by families, and might be higher than their monthly income. Consequently, many parents cannot send children to summer camps. Children thus have too much spare time and nothing to do. Policymakers reported that in these circumstances, parents often apply to the Committee for Youth to have their children placed in jobs.

Public opinion does not currently oppose child labour. Russian society suffers from an ongoing economic crisis and now faces a dilemma. Taking into account the decrease in social benefits and wage guarantees, the worsening of family conditions and the early economic socialisation of children, society has to choose between, on the one hand, the establishment of a broad system of officially controlled job placements for children or, on the other, the involvement of children in criminal activity, in the context of the liquidation of opportunities for official work for wages.

The inability of the Russian state to support poor families is the key factor. Members of impoverished families, including children, will inevitably seek extra income. In such a situation, state action against child labour may only diminish the opportunities for children to take legitimate work, leaving them more vulnerable to recruitment by criminal gangs. In today's situation of economic crisis and widespread poverty among families, it is unrealistic to hope to ban children and teenagers from paid work.

Serious constraints on education funding have weakened the influence of schools on children, for many of whom school has ceased to be credible as the cultural and educational centre of childhood. The moral value of education in Russian society has decreased. To an extent Russian society has become accustomed to the absence of a system of officially guaranteed schooling. Children themselves cannot protect their right to education; many see it as having no relevance to their lives. As a result, the erstwhile dilemma of 'to study or not to study' may in practice mean the choice between child labour and child crime. The economic imperatives upon many children leave them with little choice of remaining in education amid diminishing provision of state funding for schools. Public opinion in Russia faces a choice between child labour and child crime, and the former seems the less damaging option. Child labour is tolerated at present because it is viewed as a more positive option than the increasing involvement of children in criminal activity. In short, Russian society is willing to tolerate illegal child labour as the lesser of two evils.

Executive authorities are still largely guided by Soviet stereotypes of child labour as an education for adult life. The re-orientation of society towards a market economy has not changed anything in the public approach to child labour. Official agencies still organise labour education via the implementation of summer labour and leisure programmes, while the growth of private business has produced increases in unsanctioned child employment. The definition of child labour as a problem has not yet been realised by Russian authorities in the way it is understood by most European countries. Therefore, we may conclude that child labour in Russia is beyond the control of authorities.

Note

The study was financed by the Federation of Trade Unions of Norway (LO Norway).

Bibliography

Alanen, L. (1988) 'Rethinking Childhood', *Acta Sociologica* 31: 53–67.

Aldridge, J. and Becker, S. (1993a) *Children Who Care: Inside the World of Young Carers*, Loughborough: Young Carers Research Group, Loughborough University.

—— (1993b) 'Punishing Children for Caring: The Hidden Cost of Young Carers', *Children and Society* 7, 4: 277–88.

—— (1994) *My Child, My Carer: The Parents' Perspective*, Loughborough: Young Carers Research Group, Loughborough University.

—— (1998) *The National Handbook of Young Carers Projects*, London: Carers National Association.

Alex, L. and Stoos, F. (1996) *Berufsreport. Daten, Fakten, Prognosen zu allen wichtigen Berufen. Der Arbeitsmarkt in Deutschland: das aktuelle Handbuch*, Berlin: Argon Verlag.

Alvarez, L. (1995) 'Interpreting New Worlds for Parents', *New York Times*, 1 October, Metro Report: L29 and L36.

Ariès, P. (1962) *Centuries of Childhood: A Social History of Family Life*, New York: Vintage.

—— (1972) *Centuries of Childhood*, London: Peregrine.

Aronson, P. J., Mortimer, J. T., Zierman, C. and Hacker, M. (1996) 'Generational Differences in Early Work Experiences and Evaluations', in J. T. Mortimer and M. D. Finch (eds) *Adolescents, Work, and Family: An Intergenerational Developmental Analysis*, Thousand Oaks, Calif.: Sage.

Atkinson, P. (1990) *The Ethnographic Imagination: Textual Constructions of Reality*, London: Routledge.

Auernheimer, G. (1990) 'How "Black" are the German Turks?' in L. Chisholm, P. Buchner, H-H. Kruger and P. Brown (eds) *Childhood, Youth, and Social Change*, Basingstoke: Falmer.

Bachman, J. G. and Schulenberg, J. (1993) 'How Part-Time Work Intensity Relates to Drug Use, Problem Behaviour, Time Use, and Satisfaction Among High School Seniors: Are These Consequences Or Merely Correlates?' *Developmental Psychology* 29, 2: 220–35.

Baker, F. and Green, G. M. (1991) 'Work Health and Productivity: Overview', in G. M. Green and F Baker (eds) *Work, Health, and Productivity*, New York: Oxford University Press.

Baldwin, S. and Twigg, J. (1991) 'Women and Community Care: Reflections on a Debate', in I. Maclean and D. Groves (eds) *Women's Issues in Social Policy*, London: Routledge.

Barling, J., Rogers, K. A. and Kelloway, E. K. (1995) 'Some Effects of Teenagers' Part-Time Employment: The Quantity and Quality of Employment Make the Difference', *Journal of Organizational Behavior* 16: 143–54.

Baxter, S. (1988) 'A Political Economy of the Ethnic Chinese Catering Industry', unpublished Ph.D. dissertation, University of Aston.

Baxter, S. and Raw, G. (1988) 'Fast Food, Fettered Work: Chinese Women in the Ethnic Catering Industry', in S. Westwood and P. Bhachu (eds) *Enterprising Women,* London: Routledge.

Bechofer, F. and Elliott, B. (1981) 'Petty Property: The Survival of a Moral Economy', in F. Bechofer and B. Elliott (eds) *Comparative Study of an Uneasy Stratum,* London: Macmillan.

Bechofer, F., Elliott, B., Rushforth, M. and Bland, R. (1974) 'The Petit-Bourgeois in the Class Structure: The Case of Small Shopkeepers', in F. Parkin (ed.) *The Social Analysis of Class Structure,* London: Tavistock.

Becker, S. (1997) 'Carers', *Research Matters* international edition, August: 25–30.

—— (1999) 'Carers', *Research Matters* international edition, August: 19–22.

—— (2000) 'Young Carers', in M. Davies (ed.) *The Blackwell Encyclopaedia of Social Work,* Oxford: Blackwell.

—— (2001) 'Social Services', in L. Polnay (ed.) *Community Paediatrics,* London: Harcourt Brace.

Becker, S., Aldridge, J. and Dearden, C. (1998) *Young Carers and Their Families,* Oxford: Blackwell Science.

Becker, S. and Silburn, R. (1999) *We're In This Together: Conversations with Families in Caring Relationships,* London: Carers National Association.

Bequele, A. and Myers, W. (1995) *First Things First in Child Labour: Eliminating Work Detrimental to Children,* Geneva: ILO.

Bertaux, D. and Bertaux-Wiame, I. (1981) 'Artisanal Bakery in France: How it Lives and Why it Survives', in F. Bechofer and B. Elliott (eds) *The Petite Bourgeoisie: Comparative Study of an Uneasy Stratum,* London: Macmillan.

Bilsborrow, S. (1992) *'You Grow Up Fast As Well . . .' Young Carers on Merseyside,* Liverpool: Carers National Association, Personal Services Society and Barnardo's.

Blossfeld, H. P. (1987) 'Entry Into the Labour Market and Occupational Career in the Federal Republic: A Comparison with American Studies', *International Journal of Sociology* 17: 86–115.

Borman, K. M., Cookson, P. W. Jr., Sadovnik, A. R. and Spad, J. Z. (1996) *Implementing Educational Reform: Sociological Perspectives on Educational Policy,* Norwood, N.J.: Ablex.

Boyden, J. (1994) 'The Relationship between Education and Child Work', Innocenti Occasional Papers, Child Rights Series, no.9, Florence: UNICEF.

Boyden, J., Ling, B. and Myers, W. (1998), *What Works for Working Children,* Stockholm: Rädda Barnen and UNICEF.

Bradshaw, J. (1990) 'Child Poverty and Deprivation in the United Kingdom', Innocenti Occasional Papers, Economic Policy Series, no. 8, Florence: UNICEF.

Brah, A. (1992) 'Women of South Asian Origin in Britain', in P. Braham, A. Rattansi and R. Skellington (eds) *Racism and Antiracism,* London: Sage.

Brannen, J. (1995) 'Young People and Their Contributions to Household Work', *Sociology* 29, 2: 317–38.

BUS (Bremer Uni-Schlüssel) (1999) Presse aktuell der Universität Bremen, H. 4.

Bronfenbrenner, U. (1979) *The Ecology of Human Development: Experiments by Nature and Design,* Cambridge, Mass.: Harvard University Press.

Brunner, O. (1978) 'Vom "ganzen Haus" zur "Familie" im 17. Jahrhundert', in H. Rosenbaum (ed.) *Seminar: Familie und Gesellschaftsstruktur.* Suhrkamp: Franfurt am Main: 83–92.

Bryson, A., Ford, R. and White, M. (1997) *Making Work Pay: Lone Mothers, Employment and Well-Being*, York: Joseph Rowntree Foundation.

Bundesministerium für Familie und Senioren (1994) *Familie und Familienpolitik im geeinten Deutschland: Zukunft des Humanvermögens. Fünfter Familienbericht.* Bonn.

Bundesministerium für Bildung, Forschung und Technologi (Federal Ministry for Education and Science) (1995) *Das soziale Bild der Studentenschaft in der Bundesrepublik Deutschland* (14). Bonn: BMBF: Sozialerhebung des Deutschen Studentenwerks.

Cain, M. (1977) 'The Economic Activities of Children in a Village in Bangladesh', *Population and Development Review* 3, 3: 201–28.

Caldwell, J. C. (1982) *Theory of Fertility Decline,* London: Academic Press.

Carr, R., Wright, J. and Brody, J. (1996) 'Effects of High School Work Experience a Decade Later: Evidence from the National Longitudinal Survey', *Sociology of Education* 69 (January): 66–81.

Chan, Y. M. and Chan, C. (1997) 'The Chinese in Britain', *New Community* 23, 1: 123–31.

Cheal, D. (1983) 'Intergenerational Family Transfers', *Journal of Marriage and the Family* 45: 805–13.

—— (1991) *Family and the State of Theory,* Hemel Hempstead: Harvester Wheatsheaf.

Cheng, Y. (1994) *Education and Class: Chinese in Britain and the US,* Aldershot: Avebury.

Children's Rights Development Unit (1994) *UK Agenda for Children,* London: CRDU.

Chisholm, L., Buchner, P., Kruger, H-H., Brown, P. (eds) (1990) *Childhood, Youth and Social Change,* Basingstoke: Falmer.

Christensen, P. and James, A. (eds) (2000) *Research with Children: Perspectives and Practices,* Brighton: Falmer.

Chung, Y. K. (1990) 'At the Palace: Researching Gender and Ethnicity in a Chinese Restaurant', in L. Stanley (ed.) *Feminist Praxis,* London: Routledge.

Clifford J. and Marcus G. (eds) (1986) *Writing Culture: The Poetics and Politics of Ethnography,* Berkeley: University of California Press.

Clough, R. (2000) 'Poor Relations', *Guardian*, Society, 15 March: 71.

Coleman, J. S. (1993) 'The Rational Reconstruction of Society', *American Sociological Review* 58, 1: 1–15.

Committee on the Health and Safety Implications of Child Labour, NRC (1998) *Protecting Youth at Work: Health, Safety and Development of Working Children and Adolescents in the United States,* Washington, D.C.: National Academy Press.

Cornwell, D., Graham, K. and Hobbs, S. (1999) 'Honoured in the Breach: Child Employment Law in Britain', in M. Lavalette (ed.) *A Thing of the Past?*, Liverpool: Liverpool University Press.

Corsaro, W. A. (1997) *The Sociology of Childhood,* Thousand Oaks, Calif.: Pine Forge.

Crabtree, H. and Warner, L. (1999) *Too Much to Take On: A Report on Young Carers and Bullying,* London: Princess Royal Trust for Carers.

Cunningham, S. (1999) 'The Problem that Doesn't Exist: Child Labour in Britain 1918–1970', in M. Lavalette (ed.) *A Thing of the Past?*, Liverpool: Liverpool University Press.

Dalton, G. (1957) 'Introduction' to K. Polanyi, *Primitive, Archaic, and Modern Economies: Essays by Karl Polanyi*, ed. G. Dalton, Boston, Mass.: Beacon.

Darling, A. (1999a) 'Welfare Reform Bill Heralds Radical Changes to Benefits Culture', London: Central Office of Information.

—— (1999b) 'Fight Against Poverty Returns to Centre Stage of Politics', London, 18 February: Central Office of Information.

Davies, E. (1972a) 'Part-Time Employment of School Children: Report of Enquiry Carried out for the Department of Health and Social Security'.

—— (1972b) 'Work out of School', *Education*, November, i–iv.

Davis, K. (1937) 'Reproductive Institutions and the Pressure for Population', *Sociological Review* 29, 3: 289–306.

Dearden, C. and Becker, S. (1995) *Young Carers: The Facts*, Sutton: Reed.

—— (1998) *Young Carers in the United Kingdom: A Profile*, London: Carers National Association.

—— (2000) *Growing up Caring: Vulnerability and Transition to Adulthood – Young Carers' Experiences*, York: Joseph Rowntree Foundation.

de Coninck-Smith, N. (1997) 'The Struggle for the Child's Time – At All Times: School and Children's Work in Town and Country in Denmark from 1900 to the 1960s', in N. de Coninck-Smith, B. Sandin and E. Schrumpf (eds) *Industrious Children: Work and Childhood in the Nordic Countries 1850–1990*, Odense: Odense University Press.

Delphy, C. and Leonard, D. (1992) *Familiar Exploitation*, Cambridge: Polity.

DfEE (Department for Education and Employment) (1999) *Statistical First Release: Participation in Education and Training by 16–18 Year Olds in England: 1988 to 1998*, July, London: Stationery Office.

DoH (Department of Health) (1989) *Caring for People: Community Care in the Next Decade and Beyond*, London: HMSO.

—— (1996a) *Young Carers: Making a Start*, London: Department of Health.

—— (1996b) *Young Carers: Something to Think About*, London: Department of Health.

—— (1996c) *Carers (Recognition and Services) Act 1995: Policy Guidance and Practice Guide*, London: Department of Health.

—— (1999) *Caring About Carers: A National Strategy for Carers*, London: Department of Health.

—— (2000a) *Framework for the Assessment of Children in Need and their Families*, London: Stationery Office.

—— (2000b) *The Child's World: Assessing Children in Need*, London: Department of Health, NSPCC and University of Sheffield.

Department of Social Security (1997) *Households Below Average Income*, London: Stationery Office.

Dietz, G-U., Mariak, V., Matt, E., Seus, L. and Schumann, K. F. (1997) *Lehre tut Viel*, Münster: Votum.

Drury, B. (1991) 'Sikh Girls and the Maintenance of an Ethnic Culture', *New Community* 17, 3: 387–401.

Dustman, C., Micklewright, J., Rajah, N. and Smith, S. (1996) 'Earning and Learning: Educational Policy and the Growth of Part-Time Work by Full-Time Pupils', *Fiscal Studies* 17: 79–103.

Easey, W. (1979) *Child Labour in Hong Kong*, London: Anti-Slavery Society.

Eccles, J., Hansen, D. M., Krüger, H., Mortimer, J. T., Saraswathi, T. S. and Shanahan, M. J. (2000) *Preparation for Work in the Twenty-First Century: A Report of Work in Progress*, report presented at the Biennial Meeting for the Society for Research on Adolescence.

Elliott, A. (1992) *Hidden Children: A Study of Ex-Young Carers of Parents with Mental Health Problems in Leeds*, Leeds: City Council Mental Health Development Section.

Elliot, L. (2000) '£40 a Week to Stay at School', *Guardian*, 20 March.

Ennew, J. (1982) 'Family Structure, Unemployment and Child Labour in Jamaica', *Development and Change* 13: 551–63.

Entwisle, D. R., Alexander, K. L. and Olson, L. S. (1998) *The Beginning of the Work*

Transtition: Urban Youth, paper presented at the Annual Meeting of the American Sociological Association, San Francisco.

Erikson, E. H. (1968) *Identity, Youth, and Crisis*, New York: Norton.

Family Rights Group (1991) *The Children Act 1989: Working in Partnership with Families*, London: HMSO.

Fels, G. (1989) 'Beruf und Arbeitswelt im EG-Binnenmark', in G. Fels (ed.) *Beiträge zur Gesellschafts- und Bildungspolitik 147*, Cologne.

Fernandez-Kelly, P. and Schauffler, R. (1994) 'Divided Fates: Immigrant Children in a Restructured US Economy', *International Migration Review* 28, 4: 662–89.

Ferree, M. M. (1985) 'Between Two Worlds: German Feminist Approaches to Working-Class Women and Work', *Signs* 10, 3: 517–36.

Fewster, C. (1990) 'The Great Wall of Silence', *Social Work Today*, February 15: 14–15.

Finch, J. (1983) *Married to the Job*, London: Unwin Hyman.

—— (1989) *Family Obligations and Social Change*, Cambridge: Polity.

Finch, J. and Groves, D. (eds) (1983) *A Labour of Love: Women, Work and Caring*, London: Routledge and Kegan Paul.

Finch, M. D., Mortimer, J. T. and Ryu, S. (1997) 'Transition into Part-Time Work: Health Risks and Opportunites', in J. Schulenberg, J. Maggs and K. Hurrelmann (eds) *Health Risks and Developmental Transitions during Adolescence*, New York: Cambridge University Press.

Foundation, W. T. G. (1988) *The Forgotten Half: Pathways to Success for America's Youth and Young Families*, Washington, D.C.: William T. Grant.

Fox, A. (1974) *Beyond Contract*, London: Faber and Faber.

Frank, J., Tatum, C. and Tucker, S. (1999) *On Small Shoulders: Learning from the Experiences of Former Young Carers*, London: Children's Society.

Frone, M. R. (1999) 'Developmental Consequences of Youth Employment', in J. Barling and E. K. Kelloway (eds) *Young Workers: Varieties of Experience*, Washington: American Psychological Association.

Fyfe, A. (1989) *Child Labour*, Cambridge: Polity.

Gabriel, Y. (1988) *Working Lives in Catering*, London: Routledge.

Glendinning, C. (1992) *The Costs of Informal Care: Looking Inside the Household*, London: HMSO.

Gold, S. (1992) *Refugee Communities*, Newbury Park: Sage.

Green, D. L. (1990) 'High School Student Employment in Social Context: Adolescents' Perceptions of the Role of Part-Time Work', *Adolescence* 25: 425–34.

Greenberger, E. (1983) 'A Researcher in the Policy Arena: The Case of Child Labour', *American Psychologist* 38: 104–10.

Greenberger, E. and Steinberg, L. D. (1986) *When Teenagers Work: The Psychological and Social Costs of Adolescent Employment*, New York: Basic.

Griesbach, H. and Leszczensky (1993) *Studentische Zeitbudgets: empirische Ergebnisse zur Diskussion ueber Aspekte des Teilzeitstudiums* (vol. Hochschul-Informations-System), Hanover: HIS.

Griffiths, Sir R. (1988) *Community Care: Agenda for Action*, London: HMSO.

Grimshaw, R. (1991) *Children of Parents with Parkinson's Disease: Research Report for the Parkinson's Disease Society*, London: National Children's Bureau.

Hamilton, S. F. (1990) *Apprenticeship for Adulthood: Preparing Youth for the Future*, New York: Free Press.

Hamilton, S. F. and Hurrelman, K. (1994) 'The School-to-Career Transition in Germany and the United States', *Teachers College Record* 96, 2: 329–44.

Hanson, D. M. and Jarvis, P. A. (2000) 'Adolescent Employment and Psychosocial Out-comes: A Comparison of Two Employment Contexts', *Youth and Society* 31, 4: 417–36.

Hartmann, H. (1981) 'The Unhappy Marriage of Marxism and Feminism', in L. Sargent (ed.) *Women and Revolution*. Boston, Mass.: South End.

Heinz, W. (1996) 'Youth Transitions in Cross-Cultural Perspectives: School-to-Work in Germany', in B. Gallaway and J. Hudson (eds) *Youth in Transition: Perspectives on Research and Policy,* Toronto: Thompson Educational.

Hessisches Ministerium für Frauen, Arbeit und Sozialordnung (1994) *Kinderarbeit in Hessen,* ed. H. Ingenhorst *et al.*, Wiesbaden.

Hibbett, A. and Beatson, M. (1995) 'Young People at Work', *Employment Gazette* 103: 169–77.

Hills, J. (1995) *Inquiry into Income and Wealth,* York: Joseph Rowntree Foundation.

HM Government (1989) *Children Act,* London: HMSO.

Hobbs, S., Lavalette, M. and McKechnie, J. (1992) 'The Emerging Problem of Child Labour', *Critical Social Policy* 12, 1: 93–105.

Hobbs, S., Lindsay, S. and McKechnie, J. (1993) *Children at Work: Part-Time Employment in North Tyneside,* Paisley: University of Paisley.

—— (1996) 'The Extent of Child Employment in Britain', *British Journal of Education and Work* 9, 1: 5–18.

Hobbs, S. and McKechnie, J. (1997) *Child Employment in Britain,* London: Stationery Office.

—— (1998) 'Children and Work in the UK: The Evidence', in B. Pettitt (ed.) *Children and Work in the UK: Reassessing the Issue,* London: Child Poverty Action Group.

Hotz, V. J., Xu, L., Tienda, M. and Ahituv, A. (1989) 'Are There Returns to the Wages of Young Men from Working While in School?' unpublished paper, Department of Economics, University of California, Los Angeles.

Imrie, J. and Coombes, Y. (1995) *No Time to Waste: The Scale and Dimensions of the Problem of Children Affected by HIV/AIDS in the United Kingdom,* Ilford: Barnardo's.

Income Data Services (1999) 'Students in Employment, Report 776', London: Income Data Services.

Ingenhorst, H. and Wienold, H. (ed.) (1988) Ausschuß für Jugendarbeitsschutz beim Staatlichen Gewerbeaufsichtsamt Münster, *Kinderarbeit: Eine Untersuchung in der Region Münsterland*, Münster.

—— (1991) 'Soziologische Aspekte der Kinderarbeit in Deutschland – heute; Einige Forschungsergebnisse und Forschungsfragen', in *Diskurs – Studien zu Kindheit, Jugend, Familie und Gesellschaft*, Heft 2/91, Munich.

—— (1992) 'Wie und wofür arbeiten Kinder? – Kinder und Jugendliche als Lohnarbeiter', in C. Büttner, D. Elschenbroich and A. Ende (eds) *Kinderkulturen – Neue Freizeit und alte Muster,* Jahrbuch der Kindheit Bd. 9, Weinheim and Basel.

ILO (International Labour Organisation) (1996) *Child Labour: Targeting the Intolerable,* Geneva: ILO.

Jackson, B. and Garvey, A. (1974) 'The Chinese Children of Britain', *New Society* 30 (3 October): 9–12.

——(1975) *Chinese Children,* National Education Research and Development Trust.

James, A., Jenks, C. and Prout, A. (1998) *Theorising Childhood,* Cambridge: Polity.

James, A. and Prout, A. (eds) (1990) *Constructing and Reconstructing Childhood,* London: Falmer.

—— (1996) 'Strategies and Structures: Towards a New Perspective on Children's Experiences of Family Life', in J. Brannen and M. O'Brien (eds) *Children in Families,* London: Falmer.

Jenks, C. (1996) 'The Postmodern Child', in J. Brannen and M. O'Brien (eds) *Children and Families: Research and Policy*, London: Falmer.

Jones, T. (1993) *Britain's Ethnic Minorities*, London: Policy Studies Institute.

Kanitz, O. F. (1970) *Das proletarische Kind in der bürgerlichen Gesellschaft*, Frankfurt am Main: März Verlag.

Kaufmann, F-X. (1996) *Modernisierungsschübe, Familie und Sozialstaat*, Munich: R. Oldenbourg Verlag.

Keith, L. and Morris, J. (1995) 'Easy Targets: A Disability Rights Perspective on the "Children as Carers" Debate', *Critical Social Policy* 44/45: 36–57.

Kempson, E. (1996) *Life on a Low Income*, York: Joseph Rowntree Foundation.

Kerckhoff, A. C. (1990) 'Educational Pathways to Early Career Mobility in Great Britain', *Research in Social Stratification and Mobility* 9: 131–57.

—— (1996) 'Building Conceptual and Empirical Bridges between Studies of Educational and Labour Force Careers', in A. C. Kerckhoff (ed.) *Generating Social Stratification: Toward a New Research Agenda*, Boulder, Colo.: Crestview.

Kerschensteiner, G. (1901) *Staatsbürgerliche Erziehung der deutschen Jugend, gekrönte Preisschrift*: Erfurt.

Kibria, N. (1994) 'Household Structure and Family Ideologies: The Dynamics of Immigrant Economic Adaptation among Vietnamese Refugees', *Social Problems* 41: 81–96.

Kim, K. C. and Hurh, W. M. (1988) 'The Burden of Double Roles: Korean Wives in the USA', *Ethnic and Racial Studies* 11, 2: 151–67.

Klein, D. (1982) 'The Problem of Multiple Perception in Family Research', in L. Larson and J. White (eds) *Interpersonal Perception in Families*.

Kleinau, E. and Mayer, C. (1996) *Erziehung und Bildung des weiblichen Geschlechts. Eine kommentierte Quellensammlung zur Bildungs- und Berufsbildungsgeschichte von Mädchen und Frauen*, Weinheim: Deutscher Studien Verlag.

Kohn, M. and Schooler, C. (1983) *Work and Personality: An Inquiry Into the Impact of Social Stratification*, Norwood, N.J.: Ablex.

Krahn, H. (1991) 'The School-to-Work Transition in Canada: New Risks and Uncertainties', in W. R. Heinz (ed.) *The Life Course and Social Change: Comparative Perspectives*, Weinheim: Deutscher Studien Verlag.

Krueger, H. (1999) 'Gender and Skills: Distributive Ramifications of the German Skill System', in P. D. Culpepper and D. Finegold (eds) *The German Skills Machine: Comparative Institutional Advantage?*, New York: Berghahn.

Lai, A-E. (1982) 'The Little Workers: A Study of Child Labour in the Small-Scale Industries of Penang', *Development and Change* 13: 565–85.

Landells, S. and Pritlove, J. (1994) *Young Carers of a Parent with Schizophrenia: A Leeds Survey*, Leeds: City Council, Department of Social Services.

Lasch, C. (1977) *Haven in a Heartless World: The Family Besieged*, New York: Basic.

Lavalette, M. (1994) *Child Employment in the Capitalist Labour Market*, Avebury: Aldershot.

—— (1998) 'Child Labour: Historical, Legislative and Policy Context', in B. Pettitt (ed.) *Children and Work in the UK: Reassessing the Issue*, London: Child Poverty Action Group.

Lavalette, M., Hobbs, S., Lindsay, S. and McKechnie, J. (1995) 'Child Employment in Britain: Policy, Myth and Reality', *Youth and Policy* 47: 1–15.

Leidner, R. (1993) *Fast Food, Fast Talk: Service Work and Routinization of Everyday Life*, Berkeley: University of California Press.

Leonard, M. (1998) 'Children's Contribution to Household Income: A Case Study from Northern Ireland', in B. Pettitt (ed.) *Children and Work in the UK: Reassessing the Issue*, London: Child Poverty Action Group.

—— (1999a) 'Child Work in the UK 1970–1998', in M. Lavalette (ed.) *A Thing of the Past?*, Liverpool: Liverpool University Press.

—— (1999b) *Play Fair With Working Children: A Report on Working Children in Belfast*, Belfast: Save the Children.

Light, I. (1972) *Ethnic Enterprise in America: Business and Welfare Among Chinese, Japanese, and Blacks*, Berkeley: University of California Press.

Light, I. and Bonacich, E. (1988) *Immigrant Entrepreneurs: Koreans in L.A., 1965–1982*, Berkeley: University of California Press.

Liljestrøm, R. (1979), *Opvækst til hvad? Samspillet mellom voksne og børn i et samfund under forandrin*, Copenhagen: Fremad.

Lindsay, S. (1997) 'The Gender Divide: Evidence of the Sexual Division of Labour in School Students' Paid Employment', unpublished M.Phil. thesis, University of Paisley.

Linge, P. and Wille, H. P.(1981), *Barn i arbeid, lek og læring*, Oslo: Aschehoug.

Lucas, R. (1997) 'Youth, Gender and Part-Time Work: Students in the Labour Process', *Work, Employment and Society* 11, 4: 595–614.

Lucas, R. and Lamont, N. (1998) 'Combining Work and Study: An Empirical Study of Full-Time Students in School, College and University', *Journal of Education and Work* 11: 41–56.

Luhmann, N. (1991) 'Das Kind als Medium der Erziehung', *Zeitschrift für Pädagogik* 37: 19–40.

Maclennan, E., Fitz, J. and Sullivan, J. (1985) *Working Children*, London: Low Pay Unit Pamphlet no. 34.

McKechnie, J. and Hobbs, S. (1995) *Child Labour in Britain: A Report to the International Working Group on Child Labour*, Paisley: University of Paisley.

—— (1998a) 'Work by the Young: The Economic Activity of School Aged Children', paper presented at the Johann Jacobs Foundation Conference on 'Youth in Cities: Successful Mediators of Normative Development', 22 to 25 October.

—— (1998b) *Child Labour: Reconsidering the Debates*, Amsterdam: Defence for Children International and International Society for the Prevention of Child Abuse and Neglect.

—— (2000) 'Child Employment: Filling the Research Gaps', *Youth and Policy* 66: 19–33.

McKechnie, J., Hobbs, S. and Lindsay, S. (1997) 'Bringing Child Labour Centre Stage', in S. McCloskey (ed.) *No Time To Play*, Belfast: One World Centre.

McKechnie, J., Lindsay, S. and Hobbs, S. (1993) *Child Employment in Cumbria: A Report for Cumbria County Council*, Paisley: University of Paisley.

—— (1996) 'Child Employment: A Neglected Topic', *Psychologist* 9, 5: 219–22.

—— (1998) 'Work and the Older School Student', in B. Pettitt (ed.) *Children and Work in the UK: Reassessing the Issues*, London: Child Poverty Action Group.

McKechnie, J., Lindsay, S., Hobbs, S. and Lavalette, M. (1996) 'Adolescents' Perceptions of the Role of Part-Time Work', *Adolescence* 31: 193–204.

McKechnie, J., Stack, N., Lindsay, S. and Hobbs, S. (1999) *Child Employment in Glasgow: A Preliminary Study*, Paisley: University of Paisley.

McMorris, B. and Uggen, C. (forthcoming) 'Alcohol and Employment in the Transition to Adulthood', *Journal of Health and Social Behavior*.

Manning, W. D. (1990) 'Parenting Employed Teenagers', *Youth and Society* 22: 184–200.

Markel, K. S. and Frone, M. R. (1998) 'Job Characteristics, Work–School Conflict and Academic Outcomes: Testing a Structural Model', *Journal of Applied Psychology* 83: 277–87.

Marsden, R. (1995) *Young Carers and Education*, London: Borough of Enfield Education Department.

Marsden, D. and Ryan, P. (1991) 'Initial Training, Labour Market Structure and public Policy: Intermediate Skills In British and German Industry', in P. Ryan (ed.) *International Comparisons of Vocational Education and Training for Intermediate Skills*, London: Falmer.

Marsh, H. W. (1991) 'Employment During High School: Character Building or a Subversion of Academic Goals?' *Sociology of Education* 64: 172–89.

Middleton, S., Ashworth, K. and Braithwaite, I. (1997) *Small Fortunes: Spending on Children, Childhood Poverty and Parental Sacrifice*, York: Joseph Rowntree Foundation.

Middleton, S. and Shropshire, J. (1998) 'Earning Your Keep? Children's Work and Contributions to Family Budgets', in B. Petit (ed.) *Children and Work in the UK*, London: CPAG.

Min, P. G. (1996) *Caught in the Middle*, Berkeley: University of California Press.

—— (1998) *Changes and Conflicts*, Boston, Mass.: Allyn and Bacon.

Ministerium für Arbeit, Gesundheit und Soziales NRW (1991) *Kinderarbeit. Untersuchung zur Kinderarbeit in den Aufsichtsbezirken der Gewerbeaufsichtsämter Köln, Recklinghausen und Münster*, ed. H. Ingenhorst and H. Wienold, Düsseldorf.

Mizen, P. (1992) 'Learning the Hard Way: The Extent and Significance of Child Working in Britain', *British Journal of Education and Work* 5: 5–17.

Mizen, P., Bolton, A. and Pole, C. (1999) 'School Age Workers in Britain: The Paid Employment of Children in Britain', *Work, Employment and Society* 13, 3: 423–38.

Mizen, P., Pole, C. and Bolton, A. (1999) *Work Labour and Economic Life in Late Childhood*, Final Report, award no. L 129251035, Coventry: University of Warwick.

Mo, T. (1982) *Sour Sweet*, London: Vintage.

Modood, T., Beishon, S. and Virdee, S. (1994) *Changing Ethnic Identities*, London: Policy Studies Insitute.

Modood, T., Berthoud, R. and Lakey, J. (1997) *Ethnic Minorities in Britain,* London: Policy Studies Institute.

Morrow, V. (1992) 'A Sociological Study of the Economic Roles of Children, with Particular Reference to Birmingham and Cambridgeshire', unpublished Ph.D. thesis, University of Cambridge.

—— (1994), 'Responsible Children? Aspects of Children's Work and Employment Outside School in Contemporary UK', in B. Mayall (ed.) *Children's Childhoods: Observed and Experienced*, London: Falmer.

—— (1996) 'Rethinking Childhood Dependency: Children's Contributions to the Domestic Economy', *Sociological Review* 44, 1: 58–76.

Mortimer, J. T. (1974) 'Patterns of Intergenerational Occupational Movements: A Smallest-Space Analysis', *American Journal of Sociology* 79: 1278–99.

Mortimer, J. T. and Finch, M. D. (1986) 'The Effects of Part-Time Work on Adolescent Self-Concept and Achievement', in K. M. Borman and J. Reisman (eds) *Becoming a Worker*, Norwood, N.J.: Ablex.

Mortimer, J. T. and Finch, M. D. (1996) *Adolescents Work and Family: An Intergenerational Developmental Perspective*, Thousand Oaks, Calif.: Sage.

Mortimer, J. T., Finch, M. D., Dennehy, K., Lee, C. and Beebe, T. (1994) 'Work Experience in Adolescence', *Journal of Vocational Education Research* 19, 1: 39–70.

Mortimer, J. T., Finch, M. D., Ryu, S. and Shanahan, M. J. (1996) 'The Effects of Work Intensity on Adolescent Mental Health, Achievement, and Behavioral Adjustment: New Evidence from a Prospective Study', *Child Development* 67, 3: 1243–61.

Mortimer, J. T., Harley, C. and Aronson, P. (1999) 'How do Prior Experiences in the Workplace Set the Stage for Transitions to Adulthood?' in A. C. Booth and M. J. Shanahan (eds) *Transitions to Adulthood in a Changing Economy: No Work, No Family, No Future?*, Westport, Conn.: Praeger.

Mortimer, J. T., Harley, C. and Johnson, M. K. (1998) *Adolescent Work Quality and the Transition to Adulthood*, paper presented at the Seventh Biennial Meeting of the Society for Research on Adolescence San Diego, Calif.

Mortimer, J. T. and Johnston, M. K. (1998a) 'Adolescent Part-Time Work and Educational Achievement', in K. Borman and B. Schneider (eds) *The Adolescent Years: Social Influences and Educational Challenges*, Chicago: University of Chicago Press.

—— (1998b) 'New Perspectives on Adolescent Work and the Transition to Adulthood', in R. Jessor (ed.) *New Perspectives on Adolescent Risk Behaviour*, Cambridge: Cambridge University Press.

—— (1999) 'Adolescent Part-Time Work and Post-Secondary Transition Pathways in the United States', in W. Heinz (ed.) *From Education to Work: Cross-National Perspectives*, Cambridge: Cambridge University Press.

Mortimer, J. T. and Krüger, H. (2000) 'Transitions from School to Work in the United States and Germany: Formal Pathways Matter', in M. Hallinan (ed.) *Handbook of the Sociology of Education*, New York: Plenum.

Mortimer, J. T. and Kumka, D. S. (1982) 'A Further Examination of the "Occupational Linkage Hypothesis"', *Sociological Quarterly* 23: 3–16.

Mortimer, J. T. and Lorence, J. (1995) 'The Social Psychology of Work', in K. S. Cook, G. A. Fine and J. S. House (eds) *Sociological Perspectives on Social Psychology*, Boston, Mass.: Ally and Bacon.

Mortimer, J. T., Lorence, J. and Kumka, D. (1986) *Work, Family, and Personality: Transition to Adulthood*, Norwood, N.J.: Ablex.

Mortimer, J. T., Pimentel, E. E., Ryu, S., Nash, K. and Lee, C. (1996) 'Part-Time Work and Occupational Value Formation in Adolescence', *Social Forces* 74, 4: 1405–18.

Murray, J. (1991) 'The Working Children Project', in M. Lavalette, J. McKechnie and S. Hobbs (eds) *The Forgotten Workforce: Scottish Children at Work, 76–95*, Glasgow: Low Pay Unit.

National Research Council/Institute of Medicine (1998) *Protecting Youth at Work*, Washington: National Academy Press.

NOS B 378 (1983) *Tidsnyttingsundersøkelsene 1980–81 (The Time Budget Survey 1980–81)*, Oslo: Statistisk setnralbyrå.

NOS C 10 (1992) *Tidsnyttingsundersøkelsene 1970–90 (The Time Budget Surveys 1970–90)*, Oslo: Statistisk sentralbyrå.

O'Donnell, C. and White, L. (1998) *Invisible Hands: Child Employment in North Tyneside*, London: Low Pay Unit.

Office for National Statistics (1998) *Informal Carers: Results of an Independent Study Carried Out on Behalf of the Department of Health as Part of the 1995 General Household Survey*, London: Stationery Office.

OPCS (Office of Population Censuses and Surveys) (1992) *General Household Survey: Carers in 1990*, OPCS Monitor, London: HMSO.

Oldham, G. R. (1996) 'Job Design', *International Review of Industrial and Organizational Psychology* 11: 33–60.

Oldham, G. R. and Gordon, B. I. (1999) 'Job Complexity and Employee Substance Use: The Moderating Effects of Cognitive Ability', *Journal of Health and Social Behavior* 40, 3: 290–306.

Olk, T. and Mierendorff, J. (1998a) 'Existenzsicherung für Kinder: Zur sozialpolitischen Regulierung von Kindheit im bundesdeutschen Sozialstaat', in *Zeitschrift für Soziologie der Erziehung und Sozialisation*, 18 Jahrgang, Heft 1: 38–52.

—— (1998b) 'Kinderarmut und Sozialpolitik. Zur sozialpolitischen Regulierung von Kindheit im modernen Wohlfahrtsstaat', in J. Mansel and G. Neubauer (eds) *Armut und Soziale Ungleichtheit bei Kindern*, Opladen: Leske+Budrich: 230–57.

O'Neill, A. (1988) *Young Carers: The Tameside Research*, Tameside: Metropolitan Borough Council.

OECD (1996) 'Growing Into Work: Youth and the Labour Market Over the 1980s and 1990s', Economic Outlook, Paris: Organisation for Economic Co-operation and Development.

Owen, D. (1993) 'Ethnic Minorities in Great Britain: Age and Gender Structure', National Ethnic Minority Data Archive 1991 Census Statistical Paper no. 2, Centre for Research in Ethnic Relations, University of Warwick.

Page, R. (1988) *Report on the Initial Survey Investigating the Number of Young Carers in Sandwell Secondary Schools*, Sandwell: Metropolitan Borough Council.

Pang, M. (1993) 'Catering to Employment Needs: The Occupations of Young Chinese Adults in Britain', unpublished Ph.D. thesis, University of Warwick.

Park, K. (1997) *The Korean American Dream*, Ithaca: Cornell University Press.

Park, L. (1999) 'Between Adulthood and Childhood: The Boundary Work of Immigrant Entrepreneurial Children', paper given at the American Sociological Association conference, Chicago, 6 to 10 August.

Parker, D. (1995) *Through Different Eyes: The Cultural Identities of Young Chinese People in Britain*, Aldershot: Avebury.

Parker, G. and Olsen, R. (1995) 'A Sideways Glance at Young Carers', in *Department of Health Young Carers: Something to Think About*, papers presented at Four SSI Workshops May to July 1995, London: Department of Health.

Parliament (1985) House of Commons, Home Affairs Committee Report, 'Chinese Community in Britain', London: HMSO.

Pettitt, B. (ed.) (1998) *Children and Work in the UK: Reassessing the Issues*, London: Child Poverty Action Group.

Phillips, S. and Sandstrom, K. L. (1990) 'Parental Attitudes Toward Youth Work', *Youth and Society* 22, 2: 160–83.

Phizacklea, A. (1988) 'Entrepreneurship, Ethnicity, and Gender', in S. Westwood and P. Bhachu (eds) *Enterprising Women*, London: Routledge.

Pistrang, N. (1990) 'Leaping the Culture Gap', *Social Work Today*, February 15: 16–17.

Platt, A. (1977) *The Child Savers: The Invention of Delinquency*, Chicago: University of Chicago Press.

Polanyi, K. (1957) *Primitive, Archaic, and Modern Economies: Essays by Karl Polanyi*, ed. G. Dalton, Boston, Mass.: Beacon.

Pole, C., Mizen, P. and Bolton, A. (1999a) '"You Need to Get a Job": Motivation and Family Context – An Illustrated Ethnography of Child Workers', paper presented at the 'Hidden Hands' conference, University of Warwick.

—— (1999b) 'Realising Children's Agency in Research: Partners and Participants?'

International Journal of Social Research Methodology, Theory and Practice 2, 1: 33–54.

Pond, C. and Searle, A. (1991) *The Hidden Army: Children at Work in the 1990s*, London: Birmingham City Council Education Department and the Low Pay Unit.

Preston, S. H. (1984) 'Children and the Elderly: Divergent Paths for America's Dependents', *Demography* 21, 4: 435–57.

Prout, A. and James, A. (1990) 'A New Paradigm for the Sociology of Childhood?' in A. James and A. Prout (eds) *Constructing and Reconstructing Childhood*, London: Falmer.

Prout, A. and James, A. (1997) 'Introduction', in A. James and A. Prout (eds) *Constructing and Reconstructing Childhood*, London: Falmer.

Qvortrup, J. (1985) 'Placing Children in the Division of Labour', in P. Close and R. Collins (eds) *Family and Economy in Modern Society*, Basingstoke: Macmillan.

—— (1995) 'From Useful to Useful: The Historical Continuity of Children's Constructive Participation', in A-M. Ambert (ed.) *Sociological Studies of Children* 7: 49–76.

—— (1997) 'Childhood and Social Macrostructures', chapter presented to ESRC Seminar, *Conceptualising Childhood: Perspectives on Research*. ESRC Children 5–16: Growing Into the 21st Century Programme, University of Keele, United Kingdom.

Rainwater, L. and Smeeding, T. M. (1995) *Doing Poorly: The Real Income of American Children in a Comparative Perspective*, Luxembourg: Income Study, Working Paper no. 127.

Rapp, R., Ross, E. and Bridenthal, R. (1979) 'Examining Family History', *Feminist Studies* 5, 1: 174–200.

Revell, P. (2000) 'A Taste of Real Life', *Guardian*, 4 April 2000.

Ringen, S. (1997) *Citizens, Families, and Reform*, Oxford: Clarendon.

Roche, J. (1996) 'The Politics of Children's Rights', in J. Brannen and M. O'Brien (eds) *Children in Families*, London: Falmer.

Rogoff, B. and Lave, J. (1984) *Everyday Cognition: Its Development in Social Context*, Cambridge, Mass.: Harvard University Press.

Rosenbaum, J. E., Kariya, T., Settersten, R. and Maier, T. (1990) 'Market and Network Theories of the Transition from High School to Work: Their Application to Industrial Societies', *Annual Review of Sociology* 16: 263–99.

Rossi, A. and Rossi, P. (1990) *Of Human Bonding: Parent–Child Relations Across the Life Course*, New York: Aldine De Gruyter.

Ruhm, C. J. (1995) 'The Extent and Consequences of High School Employment', *Journal of Labour Research* 16: 293–303.

Ryu, S. and Mortimer, J. T. (1996) 'The "Occupational Linkage Hypothesis" Applied to Occupational Value Formation in Adolescence', in J. T. Mortimer (ed.) *Adolescents, Work, and Family: An Intergenerational Developmental Analysis. Understanding Families*, Thousand Oaks, Calif.: Sage.

Sanders, J. and Nee, V. (1996) 'Immigrant Self-Employment: The Family as Social Capital and the Value of Human Capital', *American Sociological Review* 61: 231–49.

Save the Children (1998) 'Children's Perspectives on Work', in B. Pettitt (ed.) *Children and Work in the United Kingdom*, London: Child Poverty Action Group.

Saxe, G. (1988) 'The Mathematics of Child Street Vendors', *Child Development* 59: 1415–25.

Scase, R. and Goffee, R. (1980) *The Real World of the Small Business Owner*, London: Croom Helm.

Scheuch, E. (1969) 'Methodische Probleme gesamtgesellschaftlicher Analysen', in T. W. Adorno (ed.) *Spätkapitalismus oder Industriegesellschaft?*, Stuttgart: Ferd Enke.

Schildkrout, E. (1980) 'Children's Work Reconsidered', *International Science Journal* 32, 3: 479–89.

Schneider, B. and Stevenson, D. (1999) *The Ambitious Generation: America's Teenagers, Motivated but Directionless*, New Haven: Yale University Press.

Schoenhalls, M., Tienda, M. and Schneider, B. (1998) 'The Educational and Personal Consequences of Adolescent Employment', *Social Forces* 77: 723–62.

Segal, J. and Simkins, J. (1993) *My Mum Needs Me: Helping Children with Ill or Disabled Parents*, Harmondsworth: Penguin.

Senatsverwaltung für Soziales Berlin (ed.) (1994) *Kinderarbeit in Berlin –1994–*, Berlin.

Sgritta, G. B. (2000) 'Inconsistencies: Childhood on the Economic and Political Agenda', in F. Mouritsen and J. Qvortrup (eds) *Childhood and Children's Culture*, Odense: Odense University Press.

Shanahan, M. J., Elder, G. H., Jr., Burchinal, M. and Conger, R. D. (1996) 'Adolescent Earnings and Relationships with Parents', in J. T. Mortimer and M. D. Finch (eds) *Adolescents, Work, and Family: An Intergenerational Developmental Analysis*, Thousand Oaks, Calif.: Sage.

Shanahan, M. J., Finch, M. D., Mortimer, J. T. and Ryu, S. (1991) 'Adolescent Work Experience and Depressive Affect', *Social Psychology Quarterly* 54, 4: 299–317.

Shanahan, M. J. and Flaherty, B. (forthcoming) 'Dynamic Patterns of Time Use Strategies In Adolescence', *Child Development*.

Shaw, A. (1994) 'The Pakistani Community in Oxford', in R. Ballard and. D. Pardesh (eds) *The South Asian Presence in Britain*, London: Hurst.

Shropshire, J. and Middleton, S. (1999) *Small Expectations: Learning to be Poor*, York: Joseph Rowntree Foundation.

Simpson, M. M. (1987) *Children of the Dragon*, Bradford: Bradford and Ilkley Community College.

Social Services Inspectorate (1995) Letter to all Directors of Social Services, 28 April.

Solberg, A. (1990) 'Negotiating Childhood: Changing Constructions of Age for Norwegian Children', in A. James and A. Prout (eds) *Constructing and Reconstructing Childhood*, London: Falmer.

—— (1994) 'Negotiating Childhood: Empirical Investigations and Textual Representations of Children's Work and Everyday Life', unpublished dissertation, Stockholm: Nordic Institute for Studies in Urban and Regional Planning.

—— (1996) 'The Challenge in Child Research: From "Being" to "Doing"', in J. Brannen and M. O'Brien (eds) *Children in Families: Research and Policy*, London: Falmer.

—— (1997) 'Seeing Children's Work', in N. Coninck-Smith, B. Sandin and E. Schrumph (eds) *Industrious Children: Work and Childhood in the Nordic Countries 1850–1990*, Odense: Odense University Press.

Solberg, A. and Vestby, G. M. (1987) *Barns arbeidsliv (The Working Life of Children)*, Oslo: NIBR (NIBR-report 1987: 3).

Song, M. (1995) 'Between "the Front" and "the Back": Chinese Women's Work in Family Businesses', *Women's Studies International Forum* 18, 3: 285–98.

—— (1997) '"You're Becoming More and More English Every Day": Investigating Chinese Siblings' Cultural Identities', *New Community* 23, 3: 343–62.

—— (1999) *Helping Out: Children's Labour in Ethnic Businesses*, Philadelphia: Temple University Press.

Standard Occupational Classification (1995) vol. 2, HMSO: London.

Statistisches Bundesamt (1997) *Statistisches Jahrbuch*.

Steel, L. (1991) 'Early Work Experience Among White and Non-White Youths: Implications for Subsequent Enrolment and Employment', *Youth and Society* 22: 419–47.

Steinberg, L. (1983) 'The Varieties and Effects of Work During Adolescence', *Advances in Developmental Psychology* 3: 1–37.

Steinberg, L. and Dornbusch, S. M. (1991) 'Negative Correlates of Part-Time Employment During Adolescence: Replication and Elaboration', *Developmental Psychology* 27, 2: 304–13.

Steinberg, L., Fegley, S. and Dornbusch, S. M. (1993) 'Negative Impact Of Part-Time Work on Adolescent Adjustment: Evidence from a Longitudinal Study', *Developmental Psychology* 29, 2: 171–80.

Steinberg, L. and Avenevoli, S. (1998) 'Disengagement from School and Problem Behaviour in Adolescence: A Developmental-Contextual Analysis of the Influences of Family and Part-Time Work', in R. Jessor (ed.) *New Perspectives on Adolescent Risk Behaviour*, Cambridge: Cambridge University Press.

Steinberg, L. and Cauffman, E. (1995) 'The Impact of Employment on Adolescent Development', *Annals of Child Development* 11, 131–66.

Stern, D. and Nakata, Y. (1989) 'Characteristics of High School Student's Paid Jobs and Employment Experiences after Graduation', in D. Stern and D. Eichorn (eds) *Adolescence and Work: Influences of Social Structure, Labour Markets, and Culture*, Hillsdale, N.J.: Lawrence Erlbaum.

Stone, J. R. I., Stern, D., Hopkins, C. and McMillion, M. (1990) 'Adolescents' Perceptions of Their Work: School Supervised and Non-School Supervised', *Journal of Vocational Education Research* 15, 2: 31–49.

Stooß, F. (1997) 'Reformbedarf in der beruflichen Bildung: Expertise im Auftrag des Ministeriums für Arbeit, Gesundheit und Soziales des Landes Nordrhein-Westfalen', in *Reformbedarf der beruflichen Bildung: Reihe: pro Ausbildung*, Ausbildungskonsens NRW, hrsg. vom Ministerium für Wirtschaft, und Mittelstand, Technologie und Verkehr, Düsseldorf, S. 47–111.

Stopes-Roe, M. and Cochrane, R. (1990) *Citizens of this Country*, Clevedon: Multilingual Matters.

Thorne, B. (1987) 'Re-visioning Women and Social Change: Where are the Children?' *Gender and Society* 1: 85–109.

Treasury (1999) *The Modernisation of Britain's Tax and Benefit System: Tackling Poverty and Extending Opportunity, no. 4*, London: HM Treasury.

Tymms, P. B. and Fitz-Gibbon, C. T. (1992) 'The Relationship between Part-Time Employment and A-level Results', *Educational Research* 34: 193–99.

UNICEF (2000) *Child Poverty in Rich Nations*, Florence: UNICEF International Centre for Child Development.

Wadel, C. (1979) 'The Hidden Work of Everyday Life', in S. Wallman (ed.) *Social Anthropology and Work*, London: Academic Press.

Waksler, F. (1986) 'Studying Children: Phenomenological Insights', *Human Studies* 9: 71–82.

Waldinger, R., Aldrich, H. and Ward, R. (1990) *Ethnic Entrepreneurs: Immigrant Business in Industrial Societies*, Newbury Park: Sage.

Walker, A. (1996) *Young Carers and their Families*, London: Stationery Office.

Walker, K. and Woods, M. (1976) *Time Use: A Measure of Household Production of Family Goods and Services*, Washington, D.C.: Center for the Family of the American Home Economics Association.

Ward, R. (1985) 'Minority Settlement and the Local Economy', in B. Roberts, R. Finnegan and D. Gallie (eds) *New Approaches to Economic Life*, Manchester: Manchester University Press.

Ward, R. and Jenkins, R. (eds) (1984) *Ethnic Communities in Business: Strategies For Economic Survival*, Cambridge: Cambridge University Press.

Watson, J. (1977) 'The Chinese: Hong Kong Villagers in the British Catering Trade', in J. Watson (ed.) *Between Two Cultures: Migrants and Minorities in Britain*, Oxford: Blackwell.

Weiner, M. (1991) *The Child and the State in India: Child Labour and Education Policy in Comparative Perspective*, Delhi: Oxford University Press.

Werbner, P. (1987) 'Enclave Economies and Family Firms: Pakistani Traders in a British City', in J. Eades (ed.) *Migrants, Workers, and the Social Order*, Association of Social Anthropologists Monographs 2b.

Westwood, S. and Bhachu, P. (eds) (1988) *Enterprising Women*, London: Routledge.

White, B. (1996) 'Globalisation and the Child Labour Problem', *Journal of International Development* 8, 6: 829–39.

White, L. and Brinkerhoff, D. (1981) 'Children's Work in the Family: Its Significance and Meaning', *Journal of Marriage and the Family* 43: 789–98.

Zelizer, V. A. (1985) *Pricing the Priceless Child: The Changing Social Value of Children*, Princeton, N.J.: Princeton University Press.

Zhou, M. (1992) *Chinatown*, Philadelphia: Temple University Press.

Index

Carr, R. 121, 131
casual work 40
Cauffman, E. 19, 20
Cheal, D. 55
child labour: battle against 9; compulsory 65, 97, 99, 104, 114, 159, 164; or crime 165; defined 139; expropriated by state 93, 99, 102; essential to families 4; less stigmatised than previously 21; nature of work 13, 109–10, 112, 113; pre-modern 101; residual/anachronistic 93; seen as foreign to developed world 1, 10, 139; widespread nature of 1; *see also* child/youth employment, employment types, laws
Child Protection Register 76
child/youth employment: children's experience of 20, 26–31, 34, 35, 142; changing legal framework of 10; common experience xv, 12, 21, 37, 46, 52, 121, 140 (numbers 12, 27, 29, 140, 149, 151); competition for jobs 111, 112, 143–4, 147, 157, 158, 161; diverse outcomes 123–8; and graduation delays 134; health risks 123, 143, 147, 149, 154; historical continuity 94–6, 97; and personal/skills development 10, 18, 110, 122, 123–5, 127, 128–9, 132, 134, 135, 136, 146–7 (scarcity of such experience 39, 52); positive view of 9–10, 21, 103, 110, 123 (in Germany 134, 136, 142) (in US 37, 122, 124, 128, 135, 136); and socialisation 2, 37, 122, 123, 125, 127–8, 150, 164; as preparation for career 5, 10, 14–15, 19, 34, 110, 111, 122, 130, 131–3, 146–7 (limited value of 146); as rational response to circumstances 2; as role model 33–5; and school performance *see* school performance; stress 126, 132, 147; valued by child workers 103, 109, 110, 114, 147, 153; variety of forms of 11–12, 52 (*see also* employment types); *see also* child labour, jobs, motivation for working
childhood xv, xvi, 2, 3, 52–3; adult-centred perception of 117; defined as play and socialisation 108; idealised 55; impact of education on 102; invention of 97, 98; loss of 61; new sociology of 52; and young carers 83
child-rearing, costs of 91–2, 96, 98, 102
children: as consumers 2, 6, 31–3, 46, 50,

98, 100, 130, 141, 160, 165; Convention on 11; dependent/protected view of 5, 55, 56, 57, 59, 68, 71, 92, 98, 100–1, 102, 141; in ethnic family businesses 56, 57, 65, 69, 159 (*see also* Chinese take-away businesses); experience of work 3, 4, 43, 59, 63–5; labour expropriated by state 93, 102; lack of research on 56, 57, 68; in need, definition of 81; overlooked in household research 114–15; as producers 2, 3, 100, 101, 114, 117, 119; rights of 13, 55, 86, 103, 149; segregated from adulthood 110; view of work 2; as workers 22
Children Act 55, 76, 81–4 *passim*
Children's Rights Development Unit 76
'children's voices perspective' 11, 13, 19, 37, 53, 57, 61; ignored in legislation 14; research methodology 38
Chinese community: British Born Chinese (BBCs) 67; employment trajectory 59, 62; life histories and expectations 67; marginalisation 58; negative depiction of 58; numbers of 58; school performance 58; *see also* Chinese take-away businesses 57–9
Chinese take-away businesses 57–9; and cultural identity 63–5; incorporation of children into 59–61; hours worked 58, 60; interdependence 62–3, 65, 68; negotiation of labour 65–8 (use of guilt 65–6); types of work 60; unspoken contract 60, 61–5
Christensen, P. 120n1
Chung, Y. K. 57
Clifford J. 117
Clough, R. 72
Cochrane, R. 65
cod-tongues 109–10, 111, 118, 119
Coleman, J. S. 96, 106n7, 107n9
communism 137; Soviet view of child labour 165–6
community care 70; Act 82; charges for services 80; staffing 71–2; authorities seen as intrusive 78, 84
Conger, R. D. 129
consumption 14, 31–3, 50, 126, 129–30, 141, 160, 165; pocket money v. earned money 45; *see also* youth culture
contracts 113–14, 152–3; family work (FWC) 61–3, 64, 66, 67, 68; generational 92, 98, 103; lack of 145, 146,